Reading Aesthetics and Philosophy of Art

Selected Texts with Interactive Commentary

Christopher Janaway

Blackwell
Publishing

BLACKWELL PUBLISHING
350 Main Street, Malden, MA 02148-5020, USA
9600 Garsington Road, Oxford OX4 2DQ, UK
550 Swanston Street, Carlton, Victoria 3053, Australia

First published 2006 by Blackwell Publishing Ltd

1   2006

Library of Congress Cataloging-in-Publication Data

Reading aesthetics and philosophy of art: selected texts with interactive commentary / Christopher Janaway.
p. cm.
Includes bibliographical references (p.) and index.
ISBN 1–4051–1807–5 (alk. paper)—ISBN 1–4051–1808–3 (pbk.: alk. paper)
1. Aesthetics. 2. Art—Philosophy. I. Janaway, Christopher.

BH39.R343 2005
111′.85—dc22

2005041121

ISBN-13: 978-1-4051-1807-1 (alk.paper)—ISBN-10: 978-1-4051-1808-8 (pbk.:alk.paper)

A catalogue record for this title is available from the British Library.

Set in 10.5/12.5 pt Sabon
by SPI Publisher Services, Pondicherry, India
Printed and bound in India
by Replika Press, Pvt Ltd

For further information on
Blackwell Publishing, visit our website:
www.blackwellpublishing.com

Contents

Sources and Acknowledgements

The author and publisher gratefully acknowledge the permission granted to reproduce the copyright material in this book:

Plato, pp. 265–79 from *Republic*, Book 10, ed. G. M. A. Grube, revised C. D. C. Reeve (Indianapolis: Hackett Publishing, 1992). Copyright © 1992 by Hackett Publishing. Reprinted by permission of Hackett Publishing Co., Inc. All rights reserved.

Friedrich Nietzsche, pp. 33–42, 46, 54–64, 73–4, 81–6, 89–92 from *The Birth of Tragedy*, ed. Walter Kaufmann (New York: Vintage Books, 1967). Copyright © 1967 by Walter Kaufmann. Reprinted by permission of Random House, Inc.

Noël Carroll, 'Art and Interaction', pp. 57–68 from *The Journal of Aesthetics and Art Criticism* XLV: 1 (Oxford: Blackwell Publishing, 1986). Copyright © 1986 by *The Journal of Aesthetics and Art Criticism*. Reprinted by permission of Blackwell Publishing.

R. W. Hepburn, 'Contemporary Aesthetics and the Neglect of Natural Beauty', pp. 9–26 from *'Wonder' and Other Essays: Eight Studies in Aesthetics and Neighbouring Fields* (Edinburgh: Edinburgh University Press, 1984; first published in 1966). Copyright © 1984 by Edinburgh University Press Ltd. Reprinted by permission of Edinburgh University Press, www.eup.ed.ac.uk.

David Hume, 'Of the Standard of Taste', pp. 226–49 from Eugene F. Miller (ed.), *Essays Moral, Political and Literary* (Indianapolis: Liberty Classics, 1987). Copyright © 1987 by Liberty Classics.

Immanuel Kant, pp. 162–71 from *Critique of the Power of Judgement*, ed. Paul Guyer and Eric Matthews (Cambridge: Cambridge University Press, 2000). Copyright © 2000 by Cambridge University Press. Reprinted by permission of Cambridge University Press and the editors.

R. G. Collingwood, pp. 105, 107–17, 121–3, 128–9, 131–2, 134–5, 139–41 from *The Principles of Art* (Oxford: Oxford University Press, 1938). Copyright © 1938 by Oxford University Press. Reprinted by permission of Oxford University Press.

George Dickie, pp. 82–93 from *Introduction to Aesthetics: An Analytic Approach* (Oxford: Oxford University Press, 1997). Copyright © 1997 by Oxford University Press. Reprinted by permission of Oxford University Press, Inc.

Roland Barthes, 'The Death of the Author', pp. 142–8 from *Image Music Text*, ed. Stephen Heath (London: Fontana, 1997). Copyright © 1977 by Stephen Heath. Reprinted by permission of Hill and Wang, a division of Farrar, Straus and Giroux, LLC and Editions Sevil.

Arthur C. Danto, pp. 115–25, 142–8, 172–5 from *The Transfiguration of the Commonplace* (Cambridge, MA: Harvard University Press, 1981). Copyright © 1981 by Arthur C. Danto. Reprinted by permission of Harvard University Press and Georges Borchardt, Inc., for the author.

Nelson Goodman, pp. 3–9, 21–6, 31–9 from *Languages of Art* (Indianapolis: Hackett Publishing, 1976). Copyright © 1976 by Hackett Publishing Company. Reprinted by permission of Hackett Publishing Co., Inc. All rights reserved.

Richard Wollheim, pp. 46–8, 50–4, 56, 58–62, 64–5, 67, 69–73, 75–7 from *Painting as an Art* (London: Thames & Hudson, 1987). Copyright © 1987 by Trustees of the National Gallery; 1990 paperback edition. Reprinted by permission of Princeton University Press.

Every effort has been made to trace copyright holders and to obtain their permission for the use of copyright material. The publisher apologizes for any errors or omissions in the above list and would be grateful if notified of any corrections that should be incorporated in future reprints or editions of this book.

Introduction

'Aesthetics' and 'Philosophy of Art' can seem to be competing names for the same field of enquiry. But if that were the case in any simple way, there would be little point in conjoining the two terms as in the title of this book. The real situation is more complex. The philosophy of art has a history stretching back to Plato and Aristotle – or may be said to have such a history if one is prepared to overlook the fact that our concept *art* emerged in recognizable form only in the eighteenth century. Questions that philosophers have asked about art are many and varied. One may be concerned with defining or giving an essence for art, or indeed questioning whether there is any such essence. One may ask what kind of entity an art work is: is it a physical thing, a mental state or event, a universal, or something with a characterization more complex and elusive than any of these, such as an institutional entity, which relies for its existence on a set of conventions and practices? One may ask what the value of art is, or what its most characteristic values are if, as is likely, it has more than one: does art entertain, does it give us knowledge and insight, does it offer consolation and confirmation of our feelings, does it help us by mirroring reality or help us by creating illusions? Does art have autonomous value, unrelated to questions of ethics or social utility or knowledge, is it a supreme form of play or freedom that expresses the true potential of human beings? How does art relate most characteristically to the human mind: is it that it arouses our emotions, that it brings us pleasure, or that it expresses emotions, embodies imagination, or allows us to confront pain in a palatable way? How do we interpret and respond to the particular art forms, and why are they of value or interest to us? Why do we value the apparently negative experiences of tragedy and horror? What makes something a picture as opposed to another kind of symbol or representation? What makes some writing literary and other writing not, one piece of music expressive and another not?

You would find all of these philosophical questions about art – some ancient, others recent in provenance – within the scope of a course or textbook entitled 'Aesthetics'. So what distinguishes aesthetics from philosophy of art? For much of its history, art became entangled with the concept of the aesthetic, which came into use in the eighteenth century, its inauguration usually credited to the German philosopher Alexander Baumgarten. The Greek word from which 'aesthetic' derives applies to sensation, feeling, or perception. The thought is that there are certain ways of responding to our experience of objects in which we have feelings of pleasure or liking, and that these felt responses lead us to regard objects as beautiful, or as having other qualities such as elegance or sublimity, or in general (as we would now put it) aesthetic value. The idea of this kind of response and its link with the notion of aesthetic judgement was important in establishing aesthetics as a distinct branch within philosophy.

But what has become increasingly unclear in recent aesthetics is whether aesthetic response is distinctive of encounters with works of art. For one thing, aesthetic responses would seem to occur in encounters with other kinds of thing, for example ordinary kinds of human artefact that we do not classify as art, and more importantly natural objects. Since aesthetic value is attributed to many more things in the world than just art works, we might seek a more general account of aesthetic value (as Kant appears to be doing in his seminal *Critique of Judgement*). However, such generality brings the risk of submerging what is really distinctive of art, and a complementary worry that, in taking art works as our paradigm of things with aesthetic value, we may ignore or falsify the aesthetic value that nature has for human beings.

A more fundamental doubt about this approach is whether 'aesthetic response' is even central to the existence and use of most art works. For art is often political, didactic, critical, knowledge-forming and attitude-changing; it is discordant, shocking, exploratory of the ugly, the repressed, the inchoate. Art is polyvalent and diverse, apparently always changing and challenging its own assumptions. Our reactions to art are both playful and serious, pleasurable, emotional, ethical, cognitive, and interpretive, so the idea that the value of art can be captured by investigating something called 'aesthetic response', something that we also feel when appreciating natural beauty or an ordinary wallpaper design, begins to seem at best too narrow, and at worst an irrelevance. Some recent writers have accordingly objected to the term 'aesthetics' and wish their subject to be referred to as the philosophy of art.

On the other hand, unless we deny that there is any such practice as attributing aesthetic value to things, we have to face questions about the nature of that value, of the kinds of judgement in which it is attributed and the kinds of experience on which such judgements might be founded. There is, or should be, therefore, a philosophy of the aesthetic, even if we reserve judgement about the extent to which art is accounted for when we think about the aesthetic. And under the concept of beauty there has arguably been a philosophy of the aesthetic for almost as long as there has been philosophy. Once again Plato's writings contain foundational passages on the subject of beauty, which remained a topic for philosophers right through the ancient and medieval periods. Secondly, much art has been produced under the assumption that beauty or aesthetic value is an important dimension of achievement for artists, and if we theorize the aesthetic out of our conception of art altogether (perhaps influenced by some dominant trends among artists of the late twentieth century), we may lose sight of the breadth of what constitutes art. Thirdly, there are still theorists today who would want a comprehensive definition of art that makes essential reference to the intention to bring about aesthetic experience, however that is defined. In other words, the aesthetic remains a topic for philosophy, and the place of the aesthetic within the philosophy of art is still a matter for debate.

The twelve pieces selected in this book are deliberately varied, ranging from Plato's famous critique of art in the *Republic* to eighteenth- and nineteenth-century classics of the subject (Hume, Kant, Nietzsche), through to twentieth-century pieces, the most recent of which was published in 1997. R. G. Collingwood wrote in the first half of the twentieth century, and his theory of expression, still much discussed, might be said to have some affinities with both romanticism and modernism. Roland Barthes's short piece is also a classic in that it states a founding premiss of the movement in art theory that has been called postmodernism. The remaining twentieth-century pieces belong within the tradition of analytical philosophy, though the specific techniques and interests of that school of thought have probably penetrated less into aesthetics than other areas. In the issues they raise concerning interpretation, the institutional nature of art, the aesthetic, the nature of pictorial representation, and the aesthetics of nature, the pieces by Noël Carroll, Arthur C. Danto, George Dickie, Nelson Goodman, R. W. Hepburn, and Richard Wollheim challenge many traditional assumptions about art and the aesthetic.

One aim of the book is to show that there are dialogues that unite the pieces chosen, despite their disparate origins. This applies not only within a chapter, where pieces have been chosen to complement or oppose one another quite explicitly, but across different chapters as well. Notions of aesthetic experience that one may find underlying the pieces from Hume and Kant, for example, are applied and criticized in the more recent selections on art and nature that form chapter 2. Carroll's central notion of interpretive play in that chapter is taken up to some extent by the pieces on interpretation in chapter 5. Danto's claim that an artworld provides the interpretive framework that art requires in order to exist is paralleled by Dickie's definition of art in terms of institutional practices. The concern with the arousal of the emotions by artistic representations shown in different ways in the passages from Plato, Nietzsche, and

Hepburn is counter-balanced by the emphasis on expression of emotion in the piece by Collingwood, and the phenomenon of depiction that figures in Plato's notion of mimesis is given a modern analysis in the pieces by Goodman and Wollheim.

This book will serve the reader as an introduction to aesthetics. Its aim is to guide the reader into the kinds of questioning and reading that may be required in order to do the subject well. The method adopted in the interactive commentaries is designed to provoke active reading.[1] By following the boxed questions addressed to the reader and pursuing the trail of marginal markers that accompany each text, the reader will be assisted in developing an approach that looks for the structure of the argument in each extract and also reflects on the processes involved in reading texts in a variety of styles representative of aesthetics as it is currently studied. So the book is neither merely an anthology of texts nor a collection of essays expressing views about those texts: it is a direct induction into the practice of philosophizing about art and the aesthetic.

---

[1] The method first developed in Samuel Guttenplan, Jennifer Hornsby, and Christopher Janaway, *Reading Philosophy: Selected Texts with a Method for Beginners* (Oxford: Blackwell, 2003).

1

Art, Value, and Philosophy

Introduction to the Issues

This chapter comprises two historical classics in the philosophy of art, written centuries apart in quite different styles and with quite different aims. They are united in that the later piece of writing by Friedrich Nietzsche looks back to the culture of ancient Greece in which the first piece was written, and both concern what Plato in that piece calls an 'ancient quarrel between poetry and philosophy'. As philosophy became established as a discipline that could pose questions concerning truth and value in its own right – one of Plato's dominant concerns – it could ask about the value of other activities that traditionally had a central place in the culture out of which it was born. What is the value of poetry, drama, or artistic representation more generally? Plato's writings are regarded as containing the first serious philosophy of art in the Western tradition because he refuses to accept the evaluation of the arts given by artists themselves. He argues that knowledge of truths is not required in order to create fine, pleasure-giving representations in art, that pleasure is not a proper criterion of value, that the typical psychological effects of poetry are deleterious to the human soul, and that it brings no ethical benefits. The negativity of Plato's philosophical account of poetry has been a spur to many thinkers in different eras to come to the defence of poetry and the arts.

Out of the range of responses or alternative accounts that address the questions Plato raises, the position adopted by Nietzsche is fairly radical. He argues that the art Plato objects to – in particular the tragic dramas of his age – was superseded and destroyed precisely by the kind of philosophy that Plato instigated; that philosophy as Plato wanted it to be – an enquiry by rational argument into truths about universal values that would help us to live better as individuals and in communities – must find tragedy a potent counter-force that was not amenable to its own methods and vision of reality. Philosophy supplanted tragedy as the dominant force in Greek culture, and was inevitably blind to the positive value of that which it ousted. Hence a proper realization of the value ancient tragedy had for its own culture (and by extension the value art could come to have again in the future) can be gained only by seeing philosophy itself as the problem. The conjunction of Plato and Nietzsche therefore throws up profound issues not just about the nature and value of art, but about the nature of philosophy and the viability of a philosophy of art.

On some matters our protagonists agree, though at first sight this may not be apparent. Both raise questions about the nature of artistic representation: is it a way of transmitting truth? Does the artist require knowledge of the world in order to make representations? Is art concerned only with image and illusion at the expense of truth and knowledge? Both place art on the side of mere image-making, though for different reasons. Both raise questions about the emotional effects of tragedy and agree that it by-passes rationality and has a thrilling effect because it touches a more primitive irrational layer of the psyche. For Plato this irrational appeal is so powerful as to undermine the capacity to retain a properly rational and ethically ordered personality. For Nietzsche, by contrast, the elemental power of tragedy's address to the psyche was itself undermined by the move towards the valorization of rational understanding and control that Plato instigated. Plato feared that tragic art would overwhelm and exclude philosophy; Nietzsche diagnosed that philosophy had killed what was truly artistic about tragedy. Nietzsche is thus important among modern thinkers as one who keeps alive the ancient quarrel that Plato mentions.

Introduction to Plato

Plato is widely known as one of the greatest philosophers of the ancient Greek world, and of all time. He lived from 427 to 347 BC and wrote around thirty works, predominantly in dialogue form, in which all of the major areas of philosophy are subjected to original and searching treatment. Plato is recognized as what the modern world would call a supremely 'literary' writer. There is a tradition that he wrote tragedies before turning to philosophy, and in his philosophical works he uses dramatic characters, a range of linguistic forms from conversational idiom, poetic diction, and elaborate invented myths to attract the reader into debate and into valuing the philosophical life. However, Plato's attitude to the established poetry and drama of his own culture is often highly critical. The Homeric epic poems the *Iliad* and the *Odyssey* were conventionally regarded not only as supreme poetic achievements, but as sources for education in a great range of matters. Plato challenges this orthodoxy, asking whether a 'good poet' is really someone whose words carry knowledge of ethical values.

The following extract from the final book of Plato's *Republic* contains his most focused attack on the arts, and on poetry in particular. The *Republic* has presented a highly specific set of proposals as to how the ideal human community (city or city-state) and the ideal human individual should be conceived. Plato's ideal city is authoritarian and subject to strict regulation of the roles of individuals. He argues that it will be a just city if and only if its diverse classes (commercial, military, and governing) fulfil their own roles properly without encroaching on those of the others. But a parallel with the just individual runs throughout the argument: the just, and psychologically healthy, individual is the one in whom the rational part of the soul governs, with the spirited emotions in alliance with it, regulating the part of us which has bodily appetites. When Plato suggests excluding poetry from the city, he is just as much concerned that the individual should overcome his or her attachment to poetry and not let it dwell within the soul. Plato has also set out an original and ambitious account of truth and knowledge, centred on his notion of timeless universal Forms, such as the Beautiful, the Just, and the Good. Only by being a philosopher and working towards knowledge of these absolutes in pure thought can one have genuine knowledge; and only if the city is governed by philosophers with such knowledge can it succeed in being genuinely just.

Against this background, there are two main objections to poetry: that it deals only in images and is far removed from truth and knowledge, and that it undermines the rule of reason in the individual by promoting the kind of pleasures that foster the emotional and appetitive sides of our nature.

Plato, *Republic*, Book 10 (extract)

Indeed, I said, our city has many features that assure me that we were entirely right in founding it as we did, and, when I say this, I'm especially thinking of poetry.

What about it in particular? Glaucon said.

[a] →   That we didn't admit any that is imitative. Now that we have distinguished the separate parts of the soul, it is even clearer, I think, that such poetry should be altogether excluded.

What do you mean?

[b] →   Between ourselves – for *you* won't denounce me to the tragic poets or any of the other imitative ones – all such poetry is likely to distort the thought of anyone who hears it, unless he has the knowledge of what it is really like, as a drug to counteract it.

What exactly do you have in mind in saying this?

I'll tell you, even though the love and respect I've had for Homer since I was a child make me hesitate to speak, for he seems to have been the first teacher and leader of all these fine tragedians. All the same, no one is to be honored or valued more than the truth. So, as I say, it must be told.

That's right.

Listen then, or, rather, answer.

Ask and I will.

Could you tell me what imitation in general is? I don't entirely understand what sort of thing imitations are trying to be.

Is it likely, then, that *I'll* understand?

That wouldn't be so strange, for people with bad eyesight often see things before those whose eyesight is keener.

That's so, but even if something occurred to me, I wouldn't be eager to talk about it in front of you. So I'd rather that you did the looking.

Do you want us to begin our examination, then, by adopting our usual procedure? As you know, we customarily hypothesize a single form in connection with each of the many things to which we apply the same name. Or don't you understand?

I do.

Then let's now take any of the manys you like. For example, there are many beds and tables.

Of course.

But there are only two forms of such furniture, one of the bed and one of the table.

Yes.

And don't we also customarily say that their makers look towards the appropriate form in making the beds or tables we use, and similarly in the other cases? Surely no craftsman makes the form itself. How could he?

There's no way he could.

Well, then, see what you'd call *this* craftsman?

Which one?

The one who makes all the things that all the other kinds of craftsmen severally make.

That's a clever and wonderful fellow you're talking about.

Wait a minute, and you'll have even more reason to say that, for this same craftsman is able to make, not only all kinds of furniture, but all plants that grow from the earth, all animals (including himself), the earth itself, the heavens, the gods, all the things in the heavens and in Hades beneath the earth.

He'd be amazingly clever!

You don't believe me? Tell me, do you think that there's no way any craftsman could make all these things, or that in one way he could and in another he couldn't? Don't you see that there is a way in which you yourself could make all of them?

What way is that?

It isn't hard: You could do it quickly and in lots of places, especially if you were willing to carry a mirror with you, for that's the quickest way of all. With it you can quickly make the sun, the things in the heavens, the earth, yourself, the other animals, manufactured items, plants, and everything else mentioned just now.

Yes, I could make them appear, but I couldn't make the things themselves as they truly are.

Well put! You've extracted the point that's crucial to the argument. I suppose that the painter too belongs to this class of makers,[1] doesn't he?

Of course.

But I suppose you'll say that he doesn't truly make the things he makes. Yet, in a certain way, the painter does make a bed, doesn't he?

Yes, he makes the appearance of one.

What about the carpenter? Didn't you just say that he doesn't make the form – which is our term for the being of a bed – but only *a* bed?

Yes, I did say that.

Now, if he doesn't make the being of a bed, he isn't making that which is, but something which is like that which is, but is not it. So, if someone were to say that the work of a carpenter or any other craftsman is completely that which is, wouldn't he risk saying what isn't true?

That, at least, would be the opinion of those who busy themselves with arguments of this sort.

Then let's not be surprised if the carpenter's bed, too, turns out to be a somewhat dark affair in comparison to the true one.

All right.

Then, do you want us to try to discover what an imitator is by reference to these same examples?

I do, if you do.

We get, then, these three kinds of beds. The first is in nature a bed, and I suppose we'd say that a god makes it, or does someone else make it?

No one else, I suppose.

---

[1]   Throughout the following passage, Plato takes advantage of the fact that the Greek word *poiein* means both "to make" generally and also "to compose poetry." Indeed, the word *poiētēs* means both "poet" and "maker" so that to class the poet (and the painter) as "makers" is much more natural in Greek than it is in English.

The second is the work of a carpenter.

Yes.

And the third is the one the painter makes. Isn't that so?

It is.

Then the painter, carpenter, and god correspond to three kinds of bed?

Yes, three.

Now, the god, either because he didn't want to or because it was necessary for him not to do so, didn't make more than one bed in nature, but only one, the very one that is the being of a bed. Two or more of these have not been made by the god and never will be.

Why is that?

Because, if he made only two, then again one would come to light whose form they in turn would both possess, and *that* would be the one that is the being of a bed and not the other two.

That's right.

The god knew this, I think, and wishing to be the real maker of the truly real bed and not just *a* maker of *a* bed, he made it to be one in nature.

Probably so.

Do you want us to call him its natural maker or something like that?

It would be right to do so, at any rate, since he is by nature the maker of this and everything else.

What about a carpenter? Isn't he the maker of a bed?

Yes.

And is a painter also a craftsman and maker of such things?

Not at all.

Then what do you think he does do to a bed?

He imitates it. He is an imitator of what the others make. That, in my view, is the most reasonable thing to call him.

All right. Then wouldn't you call someone whose product is third from the natural one an imitator?

I most certainly would.

Then this will also be true of a tragedian, if indeed he is an imitator. He is by nature third from the king and the truth, as are all other imitators.

It looks that way.

We're agreed about imitators, then. Now, tell me this about a painter. Do you think he tries in each case to imitate the thing itself in nature or the works of craftsmen?

The works of craftsmen.

As they are or as they appear? You must be clear about that.

How do you mean?

Like this. If you look at a bed from the side or the front or from anywhere else is it a different bed each time? Or does it only appear different, without being at all different? And is that also the case with other things?

That's the way it is – it appears different without being so.

Then consider this very point: What does painting do in each case? Does it imitate that which is as it is, or does it imitate that which appears as it appears? Is it an imitation of appearances or of truth?

Of appearances.

Then imitation is far removed from the truth, for it touches only a small part of each thing and a part that is itself only an image. And that, it seems, is why it can produce everything. For example, we say that a painter can paint a cobbler, a carpenter, or any other craftsman, even though he knows nothing about these crafts. Nevertheless, if he is a good painter and displays his painting of a carpenter at a distance, he can deceive children and foolish people into thinking that it is truly a carpenter.

Of course.

Then this, I suppose, is what we must bear in mind in all these cases. Hence, whenever someone tells us that he has met a person who knows all the crafts as well as all the other things that anyone else knows and that his knowledge of any subject is more exact than any of theirs is, we must assume that we're talking to a simple-minded fellow who has apparently encountered some sort of magician or imitator and been deceived into thinking him omniscient and that the reason he has been deceived is that he himself can't distinguish between knowledge, ignorance, and imitation.

That's absolutely true.

Then, we must consider tragedy and its leader, Homer. The reason is this: We hear some people say that poets know all crafts, all human affairs concerned with virtue and vice, and all about the gods as well. They say that if a good poet produces fine poetry, he must have knowledge of the things he writes about, or else he wouldn't be able to produce it at all. Hence, we have to look to see whether those who tell us this have encountered these imitators and have been so deceived by them that they don't realize that their works are at the third remove from that which is and are easily produced without knowledge of the truth (since they are only images, not things that are), or whether there is something in what these people say, and good poets really do have knowledge of the things most people think they write so well about.

We certainly must look into it.

Do you think that someone who could make both the thing imitated and its image would allow himself to be serious about making images and put this at the forefront of his life as the best thing to do?

No, I don't.

I suppose that, if he truly had knowledge of the things he imitates, he'd be much more serious about actions than about imitations of them, would try to leave behind many fine deeds as memorials to himself, and would be more eager to be the subject of a eulogy than the author of one.

I suppose so, for these things certainly aren't equally valuable or equally beneficial either.

Then let's not demand an account of any of these professions from Homer or the other poets. Let's not ask whether any of them is a doctor rather than an imitator of what doctors say, or whether any poet of the old or new school has made anyone healthy as Asclepius did, or whether he has left any students of medicine behind as Asclepius did his sons. And let's not ask them about the other crafts either. Let's pass over all that. But about the most important and most beautiful things of which Homer undertakes to speak – warfare, generalship, city government, and people's education – about these it *is* fair to question him, asking him this: "Homer, if you're not third from the truth about virtue, the sort of craftsman of images that we defined an imitator to be, but if you're even second and capable of knowing what ways of life make people better in private or in public, then tell us which cities are better governed because of you, as Sparta is because of Lycurgus, and as many others – big and small – are because of many other men? What city gives you credit for being a good lawgiver who benefited it, as Italy and Sicily do to Charondas,[2] and as we do to Solon? Who gives such credit to you?" Will he be able to name one?

I suppose not, for not even the Homeridae[3] make that claim for him.

Well, then, is any war in Homer's time remembered that was won because of his generalship and advice?

None.

[2] Charondas probably lived in the sixth century BC and gave laws to Catane and other cities in Italy and Sicily.

[3] The Homeridae were the rhapsodes and poets who recited and expounded Homer throughout the Greek world.

Or, as befits a wise man, are many inventions and useful devices in the crafts or sciences attributed to Homer, as they are to Thales of Miletus and Anacharsis the Scythian?[4]

There's nothing of that kind at all.

Then, if there's nothing of a public nature, are we told that, when Homer was alive, he was a leader in the education of certain people who took pleasure in associating with him in private and that he passed on a Homeric way of life to those who came after him, just as Pythagoras did? Pythagoras is particularly loved for this, and even today his followers are conspicuous for what they call the Pythagorean way of life.

Again, we're told nothing of this kind about Homer. If the stories about him are true, Socrates, his companion, Creophylus,[5] seems to have been an even more ridiculous example of education than his name suggests, for they tell us that while Homer was alive, Creophylus completely neglected him.

They do tell us that. But, Glaucon, if Homer had really been able to educate people and make them better, if he'd known about these things and not merely about how to imitate them, wouldn't he have had many companions and been loved and honored by them? Protagoras of Abdera, Prodicus of Ceos,[6] and a great many others are able to convince anyone who associates with them in private that he wouldn't be able to manage his household or city unless they themselves supervize his education, and they are so intensely loved because of this wisdom of theirs that their disciples do everything but carry them around on their shoulders. So do you suppose that, if Homer had been able to benefit people and make them more virtuous, his companions would have allowed either him or Hesiod to wander around as rhapsodes? Instead, wouldn't they have clung tighter to them than to gold and compelled them to live with them in their homes, or, if they failed to persuade them to do so, wouldn't they have followed them wherever they went until they had received sufficient education?

---

[4] Thales of Miletus, on the Ionian coast of Asia Minor, is the first philosopher we know of in ancient Greece. He seems to have regarded water as the fundamental principle of all things and is said to have predicted the solar eclipse of 585 BC. Anacharsis, who lived around 600 BC and is often included among the Seven Sages, is credited with beginning Greek geometry and with being able to calculate the distance of ships at sea.

[5] Creophylus is said to have been an epic poet from Chios. His name comes from two words, *kreas*, meaning "meat," and *phylon*, meaning "race" or "kind." A modern equivalent, with parallel comic overtones, would be "meathead."

[6] Protagoras and Prodicus were two of the most famous fifth-century sophists.

It seems to me, Socrates, that what you say is entirely true.

[h]→ Then shall we conclude that all poetic imitators, beginning with Homer, imitate images of virtue and all the other things they write about and have no grasp of the truth? As we were saying just now, a painter, though he knows nothing about cobblery, can make what seems to be a cobbler to those who know as little about it as he does and who judge things by their colors and shapes.

That's right.

And in the same way, I suppose we'll say that a poetic imitator uses words and phrases to paint colored pictures of each of the crafts. He himself knows nothing about them, but he imitates them in such a way that others, as ignorant as he, who judge by words, will think he speaks extremely well about cobblery or generalship or anything else whatever, provided – so great is the natural charm of these things – that he speaks with meter, rhythm, and harmony, for if you strip a poet's works of their musical colorings and take them by themselves, I think you know what they look like. You've surely seen them.

I certainly have.

Don't they resemble the faces of young boys who are neither fine nor beautiful after the bloom of youth has left them?

Absolutely.

[i]→ Now, consider this. We say that a maker of an image – an imitator – knows nothing about that which is but only about its appearance. Isn't that so?

Yes.

Then let's not leave the discussion of this point halfway, but examine it fully.

Go ahead.

Don't we say that a painter paints reins and a mouth-bit?

Yes.

And that a cobbler and a metal-worker makes them?

Of course.

Then, does a painter know how the reins and mouth-bit have to be? Or is it the case that even a cobbler and metal-worker who make them don't know this, but only someone who knows how to use them, namely, a horseman?

That's absolutely true.

And won't we say that the same holds for everything?

What?

That for each thing there are these three crafts, one that uses it, one that makes it, and one that imitates it?

Yes.

Then aren't the virtue or excellence, the beauty and correctness of each manufactured item, living creature, and action related to nothing but the use for which each is made or naturally adapted?

They are.

It's wholly necessary, therefore, that a user of each thing has most experience of it and that he tell a maker which of his products performs well or badly in actual use. A flute-player, for example, tells a flute-maker about the flutes that respond well in actual playing and prescribes what kind of flutes he is to make, while the maker follows his instructions.

Of course.

Then doesn't the one who knows give instructions about good and bad flutes, and doesn't the other rely on him in making them?

Yes.

Therefore, a maker – through associating with and having to listen to the one who knows – has right opinion about whether something he makes is fine or bad, but the one who knows is the user.

That's right.

Does an imitator have knowledge of whether the things he makes are fine or right through having made use of them, or does he have right opinion about them through having to consort with the one who knows and being told how he is to paint them?

Neither.

Therefore an imitator has neither knowledge nor right opinion about whether the things he makes are fine or bad.

Apparently not.

Then a poetic imitator is an accomplished fellow when it comes to wisdom about the subjects of his poetry!

Hardly.

Nonetheless, he'll go on imitating, even though he doesn't know the good or bad qualities of anything, but what he'll imitate, it seems, is what appears fine or beautiful to the majority of people who know nothing.

Of course.

It seems, then, that we're fairly well agreed that an imitator has no worthwhile knowledge of the things he imitates, that imitation is a kind of game and not something to be taken seriously, and that all the tragic poets, whether they write in iambics or hexameters, are as imitative as they could possibly be.

That's right.

Then is this kind of imitation concerned with something that is third from the truth, or what?

Yes, it is.

k ⟼ And on which of a person's parts does it exert its power?

What do you mean?

This: Something looked at from close at hand doesn't seem to be the same size as it does when it is looked at from a distance.

No, it doesn't.

And something looks crooked when seen in water and straight when seen out of it, while something else looks both concave and convex because our eyes are deceived by its colors, and every other similar sort of confusion is clearly present in our soul. And it is because they exploit this weakness in our nature that *trompe l'oeil* painting, conjuring, and other forms of trickery have powers that are little short of magical.

That's true.

And don't measuring, counting, and weighing give us most welcome assistance in these cases, so that we aren't ruled by something's looking bigger, smaller, more numerous, or heavier, but by calculation, measurement, or weighing?

Of course.

And calculating, measuring, and weighing are the work of the rational part of the soul.

They are.

But when this part has measured and has indicated that some things are larger or smaller or the same size as others, the opposite appears to it at the same time.

Yes.

And didn't we say that it is impossible for the same thing to believe opposites about the same thing at the same time?

We did, and we were right to say it.

Then the part of the soul that forms a belief contrary to the measurements couldn't be the same as the part that believes in accord with them.

No, it couldn't.

Now, the part that puts its trust in measurement and calculation is the best part of the soul.

Of course.

Therefore, the part that opposes it is one of the inferior parts in us.

Necessarily.

This, then, is what I wanted to get agreement about when I said that painting and imitation as a whole produce work that is far from the truth, namely, that imitation really consorts with a part of us that is far from reason, and the result of their being friends and companions is neither sound nor true.

That's absolutely right.

Then imitation is an inferior thing that consorts with another inferior thing to produce an inferior offspring.

So it seems.

Does this apply only to the imitations we see, or does it also apply to the ones we hear – the ones we call poetry?

It probably applies to poetry as well.

1→ However, we mustn't rely solely on a mere probability based on the analogy with painting; instead, we must go directly to the part of our thought with which poetic imitations consort and see whether it is inferior or something to be taken seriously.

Yes, we must.

m→ Then let's set about it as follows. We say that imitative poetry imitates human beings acting voluntarily or under compulsion, who believe that, as a result of these actions, they are doing either well or badly and who experience either pleasure or pain in all this. Does it imitate anything apart from this?

Nothing.

Then is a person of one mind in all these circumstances? Or, just as he was at war with himself in matters of sight and held opposite beliefs about the same thing at the same time, does he also fight with himself and engage in civil war with himself in matters of action? But there is really no need for us to reach agreement on this question now, for I remember that we already came to an adequate conclusion about all these things in our earlier arguments, when we said that our soul is full of a myriad of such oppositions at the same time.

And rightly so.

It *was* right, but I think we omitted some things then that we must now discuss.

What are they?

We also mentioned somewhere before that, if a decent man happens to lose his son or some other prized possession, he'll bear it more easily than the other sorts of people.

Certainly.

But now let's consider this. Will he not grieve at all, or, if that's impossible, will he be somehow measured in his response to pain?

The latter is closer to the truth.

Now, tell me this about him: Will he fight his pain and put up more resistance to it when his equals can see him or when he's alone by himself in solitude?

He'll fight it far more when he's being seen.

But when he's alone I suppose he'll venture to say and do lots of things that he'd be ashamed to be heard saying or seen doing.

That's right.

And isn't it reason and law that tells him to resist his pain, while his experience of it tells him to give in?

True.

And when there are two opposite inclinations in a person in relation to the same thing at the same time, we say that he must also have two parts.

Of course.

Isn't one part ready to obey the law wherever it leads him?

How so?

The law says, doesn't it, that it is best to keep as quiet as possible in misfortunes and not get excited about them? First, it isn't clear whether such things will turn out to be good or bad in the end; second, it doesn't make the future any better to take them hard; third, human affairs aren't worth taking very seriously; and, finally, grief prevents the very thing we most need in such circumstances from coming into play as quickly as possible.

What are you referring to?

Deliberation. We must accept what has happened as we would the fall of the dice, and then arrange our affairs in whatever way reason determines to be best. We mustn't hug the hurt part and spend our time weeping and wailing like children when they trip. Instead, we should always accustom our souls to turn as quickly as possible to healing the disease and putting the disaster right, replacing lamentation with cure.

That would be the best way to deal with misfortune, at any rate.

Accordingly, we say that it is the best part of us that is willing to follow this rational calculation.

Clearly.

Then won't we also say that the part that leads us to dwell on our misfortunes and to lamentation, and that can never get enough of these things, is irrational, idle, and a friend of cowardice?

We certainly will.

Now, this excitable character admits of many multicolored imitations. But a rational and quiet character, which always remains pretty well the same, is neither easy to imitate nor easy to understand when imitated, especially not by a crowd consisting of all sorts of people gathered together at a theater festival, for the experience being imitated is alien to them.

Absolutely.

Clearly, then, an imitative poet isn't by nature related to the part of the soul that rules in such a character, and, if he's to attain a good reputation with the majority of people, his cleverness isn't directed to pleasing it. Instead, he's related to the excitable and multicolored character, since it is easy to imitate.

Clearly.

Therefore, we'd be right to take him and put him beside a painter as his counterpart. Like a painter, he produces work that is inferior with respect to truth and that appeals to a part of the soul that is similarly inferior rather than to the best part. So we were right not to admit him into a city that is to be well-governed, for he arouses, nourishes, and strengthens this part of the soul and so destroys the rational one, in just the way that someone destroys the better sort of citizens when he strengthens the vicious ones and surrenders the city to them. Similarly, we'll say that an imitative poet puts a bad constitution in the soul of each individual by making images that are far removed from the truth and by gratifying the irrational part, which cannot distinguish the large and the small but believes that the same things are large at one time and small at another.

That's right.

However, we haven't yet brought the most serious charge against imitation, namely, that with a few rare exceptions it is able to corrupt even decent people, for that's surely an altogether terrible thing.

It certainly is, if indeed it can do that.

Listen, then, and consider whether it can or not. When even the best of us hear Homer or some other tragedian imitating one of the heroes sorrowing and making a long lamenting speech or singing and beating his breast, you know that we enjoy it, give ourselves up to following it, sympathize with the hero, take his sufferings seriously, and praise as a good poet the one who affects us most in this way.

Of course we do.

But when one of us suffers a private loss, you realize that the opposite happens. We pride ourselves if we are able to keep quiet and master our grief, for we think that this is the manly thing to do and that the behavior we praised before is womanish.

I do realize that.

Then are we right to praise it? Is it right to look at someone behaving in a way that we would consider unworthy and shameful and to enjoy and praise it rather than being disgusted by it?

No, by god, that doesn't seem reasonable.

No, at least not if you look at it in the following way.

How?

If you reflect, first, that the part of the soul that is forcibly controlled in our private misfortunes and that hungers for the satisfaction of weeping and wailing, because it desires these things by nature, is the very part that receives satisfaction and enjoyment from poets, and, second, that the part of ourselves that is best by nature, since it hasn't been adequately educated either by reason or habit, relaxes its guard over the lamenting part when it is watching the sufferings of some-body else. The reason it does so is this: It thinks that there is no shame involved for it in praising and pitying another man who, in spite of his claim to goodness, grieves excessively. Indeed, it thinks that there is a definite gain involved in doing so, namely, pleasure. And it wouldn't want to be deprived of that by despising the whole poem. I suppose that only a few are able to figure out that enjoyment of other people's sufferings is necessarily transferred to our own and that the pitying part, if it is nourished and strengthened on the sufferings of others, won't be easily held in check when we ourselves suffer.

That's very true.

And doesn't the same argument apply to what provokes laughter? If there are any jokes that you yourself would be ashamed to tell but that you very much enjoy hearing and don't detest as something evil in comic plays or in private, aren't you doing the same thing as in the case of what provokes pity? The part of you that wanted to tell the jokes and that was held back by your reason, for fear of being thought a buffoon, you then release, not realizing that, by making it strong in this way, you will be led into becoming a figure of fun where your own affairs are concerned.

Yes, indeed.

And in the case of sex, anger, and all the desires, pleasures, and pains that we say accompany all our actions, poetic imitation has the very same effect on us. It nurtures and waters them and establishes them as rulers in us when they ought to wither and be ruled, for that way we'll become better and happier rather than worse and more wretched.

I can't disagree with you.

And so, Glaucon, when you happen to meet those who praise Homer and say that he's the poet who educated Greece, that it's worth taking up his works in order to learn how to manage and educate people, and that one should arrange one's whole life in accordance with his teachings, you should welcome these people and treat them as friends, since they're as good as they're capable of being, and you should agree that Homer is the most poetic of the tragedians and the first among them. But you should also know that hymns to the gods and eulogies to good people are the only poetry we can admit into our city. If you admit the pleasure-giving Muse, whether in lyric or epic poetry, pleasure and pain will be kings in your city instead of law or the thing that everyone has always believed to be best, namely, reason.

That's absolutely true.

Then let this be our defense – now that we've returned to the topic of poetry – that, in view of its nature, we had reason to banish it from the city earlier, for our argument compelled us to do so. But in case we are charged with a certain harshness and lack of sophistication, let's also tell poetry that there is an ancient quarrel between it and philosophy, which is evidenced by such expressions as "the dog yelping and shrieking at its master," "great in the empty eloquence of fools," "the mob of wise men that has mastered Zeus," and "the subtle thinkers, beggars all." Nonetheless, if the poetry that aims at pleasure and imitation has any argument to bring forward that proves it ought to have a place in a well-governed city, we at least would be glad to admit it, for we are well aware of the charm it exercises. But, be that as it may, to betray what one believes to be the truth is impious. What about you, Glaucon, don't you feel the charm of the pleasure-giving Muse, especially when you study her through the eyes of Homer?

Very much so.

Therefore, isn't it just that such poetry should return from exile when it has successfully defended itself, whether in lyric or any other meter?

Certainly.

 Then we'll allow its defenders, who aren't poets themselves but lovers of poetry, to speak in prose on its behalf and to show that it not only gives pleasure but is beneficial both to constitutions and to human life. Indeed, we'll listen to them graciously, for we'd certainly profit if poetry were shown to be not only pleasant but also beneficial.

How could we fail to profit?

 However, if such a defense isn't made, we'll behave like people who have fallen in love with someone but who force themselves to stay away from him, because they realize that their passion isn't beneficial. In the same way, because the love of this sort of poetry has been implanted in us by the upbringing we have received under our fine constitutions, we are well disposed to any proof that it is the best and truest thing. But if it isn't able to produce such a defense, then, whenever we listen to it, we'll repeat the argument we have just now put forward like an incantation so as to preserve ourselves from slipping back into that childish passion for poetry which the majority of people have. And we'll go on chanting that such poetry is not to be taken seriously or treated as a serious undertaking with some kind of hold on the truth, but that anyone who is anxious about the constitution within him must be careful when he hears it and must continue to believe what we have said about it.

I completely agree.

Yes, for the struggle to be good rather than bad is important, Glaucon, much more important than people think. Therefore, we mustn't be tempted by honor, money, rule, or even poetry into neglecting justice and the rest of virtue.

After what we've said, I agree with you, and so, I think, would anyone else.

Commentary on Plato

One of the chief tasks of interpretation is to try to discover what is meant by the terms 'imitation' and 'imitative' in this passage ('mimetic' and 'mimesis' are alternatives closer to the original Greek). On a first read through, concentrating on Plato's opening and closing statements, one might try to decide how much of poetry is included as 'imitative' and what qualifies it as such.

> Pay attention to the opening statements at $\boxed{a}\mapsto$ and $\boxed{b}\mapsto$ and then read the concluding part from $\boxed{o}\mapsto$ to the end of the selection. Does Plato defend the exclusion of all poetry from his ideal city, or only some that is 'imitative'? Does Plato think that all poetry is 'imitative'?

There is no easy way to resolve these questions. At times Plato implies that some poetry is not imitative and would survive his critique, at other times that all poetry is implicated and must be 'banished'. In the paragraph starting at $\boxed{o}\mapsto$ he favours some hymns and eulogies that he calls a kind of poetry, but is against another kind of poetry that he calls 'pleasure-giving'. In the following paragraph he groups together 'poetry that aims at pleasure and imitation'. But the overall tone of this passage is to oppose and exclude simply 'poetry'.

It is clear from these opening and closing words that the Homeric poems and tragedy are specifically in Plato's sights. (Passages at $\boxed{h}\mapsto$, $\boxed{i}\mapsto$, and $\boxed{m}\mapsto$ arguably support this emphasis too.) Given the prominence of these poetic works in Greek culture (and indeed their paradigmatic claim to inclusion under the modern concept of art), one approach to this whole passage is to concentrate on features of these works that make them problematic for Plato, and initially worry less about the general questions 'What counts as poetry?' and 'What counts as imitative?'

At $\boxed{b}\mapsto$Plato puts the negative evaluation of imitative poetry as a charge that it tends to distort the thought of anyone who hears it, unless they have knowledge of its nature. Plato sets out to provide us with that knowledge, so that we can use it as a drug to protect ourselves. He uses a similar idea in the paragraph after $\boxed{q}\mapsto$ where he talks of his own arguments as an incantation to break poetry's hold over the listener.

So what, according to Plato, is the nature of imitative poetry? One plausible way of dividing up the main body of Plato's text is as follows.

1.   **Imitation and its relation to truth and knowledge** ([c]→ to [k]→)
     (i)   Imitation in general: removed from truth ([c]→ to [e]→)
     (ii) Claims commonly made about poets having knowledge (at [f]→)
     (iii) Arguments against poets having knowledge ([g]→ to [k]→).

2.   **Imitation's power over the soul** ([k]→ to [o]→)
     (i)   Parts of the soul adopt conflicting attitudes to illusions ([k]→ to [l]→)
     (ii) The appeal of imitative poetry to a lower part of the soul ([l]→ to [n]→)
     (iii) The 'most serious charge': poetry corrupts the soul of the best individuals ([n]→ to [o]→)

The remainder of the commentary will be organized around this structuring of Plato's argument.

Imitation and its relation to truth and knowledge ([c]→ to [k]→)

(i)   The passage from [c]→ to [e]→ tries to explain the nature of imitation in general.

At [c]→ Plato poses the question: 'Could you tell me what imitation in general is?' On the basis of the passage from here until [e]→, state as succinctly as possible what answer he gives to his own question.

Given the extensiveness of the argument here, the answer can seem surprisingly simple. Imitation occurs when someone makes an image of the way some kind of thing appears, rather than making a real thing. A painting of a bed is an imitation in that it is not a real bed, but an image of a bed, and one that attempts to show a way in which a bed might happen to appear.

Plato attempts to locate this rather simple view about artistic representation within his metaphysical theory usually referred to as the theory of Forms. Forms are unique, unchanging, real entities, of which particular things are the instances or copies. This theory is introduced at [d]→, though many features of this passage sit oddly with what he says about Forms elsewhere, especially in Books 6–7 of the *Republic* itself. For example, Forms are usually considered to exist eternally, not to have been created, as here; they are often thought to be paradigms existing in nature, which perhaps makes it puzzling how there could be Forms of man-made objects such as a bed (as opposed to the Forms of justice, beauty, largeness, equality and such like mentioned in other passages); finally, the role of the Forms in the main body of the *Republic* is to be the objects of knowledge for philosophers, which appears to be a different role from that of providing patterns from which craftsmen can construct objects like beds. For someone seeking a coherent interpretation of Plato's philosophy, this passage from Book 10 may raise more puzzles than its solves.

The comparison between painting and the images in a mirror raises a conceptual issue concerning representation that Plato does not explicitly address. While every mirror-image is the copy of some definite existing object, and in a sense a mere replication of that object, not all representation in an artistic medium is like this. Some paintings of beds are fictional, in that they make no reference to any particular actual bed, let alone being a mere replica of some actual bed.

> In this passage, does Plato hold that all artistic representation is a mere replication of existing originals?

Plato has been read this way, and accredited with a derogatory and implausible conception of representation as a result. But it is simply not clear that this is his view. It would seem implausible that he did not realize there were fictional representations that were literally replicas of nothing. And of these paintings it is plausible to say, as he does, that they are images of a bed, and that the bed in the painting shows the viewer how a bed might appear.

(ii)   At $\boxed{f}\!\mapsto$ we see for the first time why it matters to Plato whether artistic image-making is 'removed from truth': because there are those who make grandiose claims to knowledge of truths on the poet's behalf. But if the poet is another example of a mere image-maker, then we should be suspicious of those claims.

> At $\boxed{f}\!\mapsto$ what grounds do 'some people' have for attributing profound knowledge to poets? Are they good grounds?

The grounds look a little thin. It is conceded that Homer, for example, produces 'fine' poetry. But then it is assumed that for poetry to be fine it must be well made in every sense, or at least made with full knowledge of the subject-matter it portrays. Plato's resistance to this assumption opens up many questions: What are the criteria for something being a fine poem? Do we judge a poem's quality on the basis of truths that it conveys? Can a work of art succeed in presenting a convincing, pleasing image of human life with its goods and ills without its producer having any special or distinctive knowledge?

Between $\boxed{e}\!\mapsto$ and $\boxed{f}\!\mapsto$ Plato makes a new analogy between poets and a kind of painter.

> What new point, if any, does this analogy with a 'painter of craftsmen' contribute to Plato's argument?

This is clearly a specially concocted example, since painters do not normally paint a succession of craftsmen with the intention of deceiving anyone, let alone 'foolish people'. The culmination at $\boxed{h} \!\!\rightarrow$ offers some clarification of the point of this example: that poets can portray a panoply of characters in image without having the knowledge that real people of the kinds portrayed would have.

(iii)   There follow (from $\boxed{g} \!\!\rightarrow$ to $\boxed{k} \!\!\rightarrow$), some arguments against poets having knowledge.

> What are Plato's grounds here for denying knowledge to the poets? How strong are they?

These seem the weakest stretches of argument in the whole extract. To argue that nobody would want to write poetry, or be allowed to write poetry, if they also had genuine expertise in a useful field of knowledge, assumes that everyone agrees writing poetry to be an activity of low value, hence begging the question. The ensuing division (from $\boxed{i} \!\!\rightarrow$) between maker, user and imitator, takes knowledge away from the maker and re-assigns it to the user of an object. This is confusing, but does nothing to change the position of the artistic 'imitator', who in all cases is said to lack knowledge. Despite the unconvincing nature of these last passages, the questions raised by (ii) are still very much alive, and it is hard to sustain the assumption that fine poetry must proceed from some special kind or degree of knowledge on the part of the poet.

Imitation's power over the soul ($\boxed{k} \!\!\rightarrow$ to $\boxed{o} \!\!\rightarrow$)

Plato now moves to a different set of considerations: What characteristic effects does the experience of poetic imitation, say in the poetry of Homer and the tragedians, have upon its audience?

(i)   Parts of the soul adopt conflicting attitudes to illusions ($\boxed{k} \!\!\rightarrow$ to $\boxed{l} \!\!\rightarrow$). Plato here reverts to an analogy with the visual: the mind is deceived on one level by illusions of depth in *trompe-l'oeil* painting or by a stick in water seeming to be bent. But at the same time we can measure and calculate that we are dealing with a flat surface or a straight object. Plato argues that this opposition of attitude – the stick seems bent but we rationally believe it is straight – could not happen unless distinct parts of us, or of the soul, were involved.

(ii)   But what has this to do with poetry, or indeed with 'imitation' in general? Painting that uses illusionistic techniques can count as 'imitation', not by virtue of the illusion it engenders, arguably, but simply by virtue of its being representational and producing recognizable images rather than real things. But what light do these cases of visual illusion throw on poetry's power over the soul? At ⒤→ Plato sensibly decides not to rely 'solely on a mere probability based on the analogy with painting', and turns to examine the effects of poetry on the soul directly.

> Reading from ⒤→ to ⒩→, in what way is the appeal of poetry to the soul analogous to the case of visual illusions?

The point is that we can be 'at war with ourselves' in both instances. In the case of ethical attitudes, we can be powerfully drawn towards extreme, expressive lamentation and at the same time wish to register events with calm rational thought for what is best. So, Plato argues, because of the conflict of attitudes, two parts of the soul are at work here; and the question about imitative poetry is: which part does it appeal to?

Plato's answer is that there is part of our souls that revels in thrilling images of emotionally driven, often violent action, and that this brings us an irresistible pleasure that occurs independently of any rational judgement we may make. A moment's reflection on the products of our contemporary popular culture may suggest that Plato is right. And imitative poetry, which can produce pleasing images of human action and suffering, plays to this part of the soul. Again, Plato seems to have a good point. But why does this matter?

> Why is poetry's appeal to a part of the soul other than the rational part an objection to poetry? How might we reply to this objection?

Plato loads the question by designating the non-rational part of the soul 'inferior' to the rational part. Various modern theories of art since the time of Romanticism (early nineteenth century) would be in broad agreement with Plato that poetry communicates with and stimulates a part of us that does not operate fully rationally: that poetry awakens profound understanding through its expessiveness, its emotional quality, its use of symbols and images to enable insights that cannot adequately be discharged into rational thoughts. We could object that Plato seems to see poetry's very characteristic strength as a deficiency.

We may question the assumption that our capacity to be rational, good-seeking agents is compromised by activities that stimulate us as poetry does. We might suggest that poetry is either harmless as far as our rational, ethical nature is concerned, or, more strongly, that only with the rounded, emotional grasp of the particular situations in which individuals can find themselves can we be fully human ethical agents.

None of these objections would move Plato, however, because in his conception of the good and healthy individual, the rational part which seeks to understand and act for the overall good must be what governs and must not have any competitors. This conception has been worked out extensively earlier in the *Republic*.

(iii)   The culmination of Plato's argument is what he calls the 'most serious charge' against poetry ($\boxed{\text{n}}$→ to $\boxed{\text{o}}$→).

What is this most serious charge?

The charge is really a variant of what has gone before. It is not just that imitative poetry appeals to a kind of person in whom the inferior, image-loving part predominates, it is that 'the best of us' succumb to the same powerful influence in an insidious fashion, and the rule of the rational, good-seeking part of us is undermined. To comprehend Plato's notion of the 'best' individuals we need to refer back to his conception of the healthy or just soul established in Book 4 of the *Republic*. There it was argued that each human being consists of a rational part, that seeks to understand and pursue the good, an appetitive part that has desires for things such as food, drink, and sex, and a spirited or emotional part that seeks honour and esteem and becomes angry when these are breached. The best person is the one in whom the rational part governs in alliance with the spirited emotions, with the appetites well regulated and subordinated to the pursuit of the good.

Now Plato argues that the pleasure we gain from poetry, and the distance the represented events have from our own lives, can lead us to think that our engagement with it is without consequence for the relationship of the parts of our soul in ordinary life. But this is false, he suggests. If we habitually approve a poem or drama in which X occurs, we will have a tendency to approve X – injustice, cowardice, lack of self-control, and so on – in our own lives too. This charge throws up the question to what extent the images portrayed by imitative poetry are insulated from the rest of our psyche. If there were not some carry-over from the fictional to the real emotional situation, it would perhaps be hard to account for the strong pull that fictions exert upon us. But we may suspect that Plato exaggerates our inability to separate approval of a poetic work from approval of its depicted contents. On the other hand, to this day there are those who are convinced that the occurrences in narratives that we know to be fictions can have a powerful and pernicious influence on our real-life attitudes.

Few would conclude with Plato that poetry should be banished and that the individual should resist its pleasures for the good of his or her soul – but then few are so confident as Plato about what constitutes the good for human beings. It is with that confidence, not with the total insensitivity to the arts that is sometimes attributed to him, that he invites (see $\boxed{\text{p}}\!\!\rightarrow$) a defence of poetry. Only if it can be shown that there is something wrong with his own arguments, and that poetry has a clear ethical benefit – enabling us to know better what is good and bad in human life or training us to live better – should we value it and make it a central part of our lives.

Introduction to Nietzsche

Friedrich Nietzsche (1844–1900) is regarded as one of the most influential thinkers and writers in the modern period. He began his career as a brilliant classical scholar and was always prone to contrast the culture and values of the ancient Greeks with those of the post-Christian period, extending into the Europe of his own day. In his later works, such as *On the Genealogy of Morality*, he mounts a scathing attack on the values of the morality that has dominated the Western tradition. The extract here is from his first book, *The Birth of Tragedy*, published in 1872, where his preoccupation is with the arts, the values they embody, and the place they have in culture.

Although it is primarily concerned with the origins of tragedy in ancient Greek culture, this book seriously damaged Nietzsche's reputation as a classical scholar. He had become a professor at the University of Basel at a prodigiously young age, but his intellectual predilections and his personality as a creative writer were already beginning to burst through the confines of academia. The style in which *The Birth of Tragedy* is written is distinctly unscholarly, high-flown, metaphorical and over-complicated, grouping together symbols and giving speculative psychological interpretations of historical phenomena. Nietzsche also imports in semi-digested fashion chunks of the philosophy of Arthur Schopenhauer (1788–1860) whose work he had been passionate about for some time. And, finally, the book is over-shadowed by the figure of Richard Wagner, into whose circle the young Nietzsche had been accepted as a friend and supporter. *The Birth of Tragedy*, whose full title is *The Birth of Tragedy out of the Spirit of Music*, culminates in an argument that Wagner's music dramas are the rebirth of art in the spirit of ancient tragedy that was killed by rationalistic philosophy at the end of the 5th century BC. The book's stylistic pretensions, propagandistic overtones and second-hand reliance on an ambitious metaphysical system make for a rich cocktail, and it is no wonder Nietzsche's colleagues were scandalized. Nietzsche's own retrospective judgement was almost as harsh. In 1886 in a Preface called 'Attempt at a Self-Criticism' he called the book 'impossible', and objected to it as badly written, over-influenced by Wagner and spoilt by too much Schopenhauerian terminology. To this day it remains uniquely hard to read, but uniquely rewarding as a vision of the value attaching to ancient Greek tragedy and a challenge to philosophy and the arts to recover some of that value by rethinking themselves.

The text here has been substantially exerpted, with the aim of revealing a set of constrasting symbols that give the work its underlying structure. First Nietzsche contrasts the deities Apollo and Dionysus, using them as symbols for cultural and psychological tendencies, and as the foundational principles of different art forms in the ancient world. Tragedy, he argues, arises from a confluence of the two tendencies: the Apollinian concerned with plastic values of beauty of form and superficial appearance, the Dionysian with trance-like abandon and loss of individuality in a higher unity. Finally, he introduces the figure of Socrates as the emblem of the rationalistic tendency in Greek culture which, he suggests, was responsible for destroying and replacing tragedy.

Friedrich Nietzsche, *The Birth of Tragedy* (extracts)

1

We shall have gained much for the science of aesthetics, once we perceive not merely by logical inference, but with the immediate certainty of vision, that the continuous development of art is bound up with the *Apollinian* and *Dionysian* duality – just as procreation depends on the duality of the sexes, involving perpetual strife with only periodically intervening reconciliations. The terms Dionysian and Apollinian we borrow from the Greeks, who disclose to the discerning mind the profound mysteries of their view of art, not, to be sure, in concepts, but in the intensely clear figures of their gods. Through Apollo and Dionysus, the two art deities of the Greeks, we come to recognize that in the Greek world there existed a tremendous opposition, in origin and aims, between the Apollinian art of sculpture, and the nonimagistic, Dionysian art of music. These two different tendencies run parallel to each other, for the most part openly at variance; and they continually incite each other to new and more powerful births, which perpetuate an antagonism, only superficially reconciled by the common term "art"; till eventually, by a metaphysical miracle of the Hellenic "will," they appear coupled with each other, and through this coupling ultimately generate an equally Dionysian and Apollinian form of art – Attic tragedy.

[b] → In order to grasp these two tendencies, let us first conceive of them as the separate art worlds of *dreams* and *intoxication*. These physiological phenomena present a contrast analogous to that existing between the Apollinian and the Dionysian....

[...] [O]ur innermost being, our common ground, experiences dreams with profound delight and a joyous necessity.

This joyous necessity of the dream experience has been embodied by the Greeks in their Apollo: Apollo, the god of all plastic energies, is at the same time the soothsaying god. He, who (as the etymology of the name indicates) is the "shining one," the deity of light, is also ruler over the beautiful illusion of the inner world of fantasy. The higher truth, the perfection of these states in contrast to the incompletely intelligible everyday world, this deep consciousness of nature, healing and helping in sleep and dreams, is at the same time the symbolical analogue of the soothsaying faculty and of the arts generally, which make life possible and worth living. But we must also include in our image of Apollo that delicate boundary which the dream image must not overstep lest it have a pathological effect (in which case mere appearance would deceive us as if it were crude reality). We must keep in mind that measured restraint, that freedom from the wilder emotions, that calm of the sculptor god. His eye must be "sunlike," as befits his origin; even when it is angry and distempered it is still hallowed by beautiful illusion. And so, in one sense, we might apply to Apollo the words of Schopenhauer when he speaks of the man wrapped in the veil of *māyā* (*Welt als Wille und Vorstellung*, I, p. 416): "Just as in a stormy sea that, unbounded in all directions, raises and drops mountainous waves, howling, a sailor sits in a boat and trusts in his frail bark: so in the midst of a world of torments the individual human being sits quietly, supported by and trusting in the *principium individuationis*." In fact, we might say of Apollo that in him the unshaken faith in this *principium* and the calm repose of the man wrapped up in it receive their most sublime expression; and we might call Apollo himself the glorious divine image of the *principium individuationis*, through whose gestures and eyes all the joy and wisdom of "illusion," together with its beauty, speak to us.

In the same work Schopenhauer has depicted for us the tremendous *terror* which seizes man when he is suddenly dumbfounded by the cognitive form of phenomena because the principle of sufficient reason, in one of its manifestations, seems to suffer an exception. If we add to this terror the blissful ecstasy that wells from the innermost depths of man, indeed of nature, at this collapse of the *principium individuationis*, we steal a glimpse into the nature of the *Dionysian*, which is brought home to us most intimately by the analogy of intoxication.

Either under the influence of the narcotic draught, of which the songs of all primitive men and peoples speak, or with the potent coming of spring that penetrates all nature with joy, these Dionysian emotions awake, and as they grow in intensity everything subjective vanishes into complete self-forgetfulness [...]

Under the charm of the Dionysian not only is the union between man and man reaffirmed, but nature which has become alienated, hostile, or subjugated, celebrates once more her reconciliation with her lost son, man. Freely, earth proffers her gifts, and peacefully the beasts of prey of the rocks and desert approach. The chariot of Dionysus is covered with flowers and garlands; panthers and tigers walk under its yoke. Transform Beethoven's "Hymn to Joy" into a painting; let your imagination conceive the multitudes bowing to the dust, awe-struck – then you will approach the Dionysian. Now the slave is a free man; now all the rigid, hostile barriers that necessity, caprice, or "impudent convention" have fixed between man and man are broken. Now, with the gospel of universal harmony, each one feels himself not only united, reconciled, and fused with his neighbor, but as one with him, as if the veil of *maya* had been torn aside and were now merely fluttering in tatters before the mysterious primordial unity.

In song and in dance man expresses himself as a member of a higher community; he has forgotten how to walk and speak and is on the way toward flying into the air, dancing. His very gestures express enchantment. Just as the animals now talk, and the earth yields milk and honey, supernatural sounds emanate from him, too: he feels himself a god, he himself now walks about enchanted, in ecstasy, like the gods he saw walking in his dreams. He is no longer an artist, he has become a work of art: in these paroxysms of intoxication the artistic power of all nature reveals itself to the highest gratification of the primordial unity. The noblest clay, the most costly marble, man, is here kneaded and cut, and to the sound of the chisel strokes of the Dionysian world-artist rings out the cry of the Eleusinian mysteries: "Do you prostrate yourselves, millions? Do you sense your Maker, world?"

2

Thus far we have considered the Apollinian and its opposite, the Dionysian, as artistic energies which burst forth from nature herself, *without the mediation of the human artist* – energies in which nature's art impulses are satisfied in the most immediate and direct way – first in the image world of dreams, whose completeness is not dependent upon the intellectual attitude or the artistic culture of any single being; and then as intoxicated reality, which likewise does not heed the single unit, but even seeks to destroy the individual and redeem him by a mystic feeling of oneness. With reference to these immediate art-states of nature, every artist is an "imitator," that is to say, either an Apollinian artist in dreams, or a Dionysian artist in ecstasies, or finally – as for example in Greek tragedy – at once artist in both dreams and ecstasies; so we may perhaps picture him sinking down in his Dionysian intoxication and mystical self-abnegation, alone and apart from the singing revelers, and we may imagine how, through Apollinian dream-inspiration, his own state, i.e., his oneness with the inmost ground of the world, is revealed to him in a *symbolical dream image*.

So much for these general premises and contrasts. Let us now approach the *Greeks* in order to learn how highly these *art impulses of nature* were developed in them. Thus we shall be in a position to understand and appreciate more deeply that relation of the Greek artist to his archetypes which is, according to the Aristotelian expression, "the imitation of nature." In spite of all the dream literature and the numerous dream anecdotes of the Greeks, we can speak of their *dreams* only conjecturally, though with reasonable assurance. If we consider the incredibly precise and unerring plastic power of their eyes, together with their vivid, frank delight in colors, we can hardly refrain from assuming even for their dreams (to the shame of all those born later) a certain logic of line and contour, colors and groups, a certain pictorial sequence reminding us of their finest bas-reliefs whose perfection would certainly justify us, if a comparison were possible, in designating the dreaming Greeks as Homers, and Homer as a dreaming Greek – in a deeper sense than that in which modern man, speaking of his dreams, ventures to compare himself with Shakespeare.

On the other hand, we need not conjecture regarding the immense gap which separates the *Dionysian Greek* from the Dionysian barbarian. From all quarters of the ancient world – to say nothing here of the modern – from Rome to Babylon, we can point to the existence of Dionysian festivals, types which bear, at best, the same relation to the Greek festivals which the bearded satyr, who borrowed his name and attributes from the goat, bears to Dionysus himself. In nearly every case these festivals centered in extravagant sexual licentiousness, whose waves overwhelmed all family life and its venerable traditions; the most savage natural instincts were unleashed, including even that horrible mixture of sensuality and cruelty which has always seemed to me to be the real "witches' brew." For some time, however, the Greeks were apparently perfectly insulated and guarded against the feverish excitements of these festivals, though knowledge of them must have come to Greece on all the routes of land and sea; for the figure of Apollo, rising full of pride, held out the Gorgon's head to this grotesquely uncouth Dionysian power – and really could not have countered any more dangerous force. It is in Doric art that this majestically rejecting attitude of Apollo is immortalized.

The opposition between Apollo and Dionysus became more hazardous and even impossible, when similar impulses finally burst forth from the deepest roots of the Hellenic nature and made a path for themselves: the Delphic god, by a seasonably effected reconciliation, now contented himself with taking the destructive weapons from the hands of his powerful antagonist. This reconciliation is the most important moment in the history of the Greek cult: wherever we turn we note the revolutions resulting from this event. The two antagonists were reconciled; the boundary lines to be observed henceforth by each were sharply defined, and there was to be a periodical exchange of gifts of esteem. At bottom, however, the chasm was not bridged over. But if we observe how, under the pressure of this treaty of peace, the Dionysian power revealed itself, we shall now recognize in the Dionysian orgies of the Greeks, as compared with the Babylonian Sacaea with their reversion of man to the tiger and the ape, the significance of festivals of world redemption and days of transfiguration. It is with them that nature for the first time attains her artistic jubilee; it is with them that the destruction of the *principium individuationis* for the first time becomes an artistic phenomenon.

The horrible "witches' brew" of sensuality and cruelty becomes ineffective; only the curious blending and duality in the emotions of the Dionysian revelers remind us – as medicines remind us of deadly poisons – of the phenomenon that pain begets joy, that ecstasy may wring sounds of agony from us. At the very climax of joy there sounds a cry of horror or a yearning lamentation for an irretrievable loss. In these Greek festivals, nature seems to reveal a sentimental trait; it is as if she were heaving a sigh at her dismemberment into individuals. The song and pantomime of such dually-minded revelers was something new and unheard-of in the Homeric–Greek world; and the Dionysian *music* in particular excited awe and terror. If music, as it would seem, had been known previously as an Apollinian art, it was so, strictly speaking, only as the wave beat of rhythm, whose formative power was developed for the representation of Apollinian states. The music of Apollo was Doric architectonics in tones, but in tones that were merely suggestive, such as those of the cithara. The very element which forms the essence of Dionysian music (and hence of music in general) is carefully excluded as un-Apollinian – namely, the emotional power of the tone, the uniform flow of the melody, and the utterly incomparable world of harmony. In the Dionysian dithyramb man is incited to the greatest exaltation of all his symbolic faculties;

something never before experienced struggles for utterance – the annihilation of the veil of *māyā*, oneness as the soul of the race and of nature itself. The essence of nature is now to be expressed symbolically; we need a new world of symbols; and the entire symbolism of the body is called into play, not the mere symbolism of the lips, face, and speech but the whole pantomime of dancing, forcing every member into rhythmic movement. Then the other symbolic powers suddenly press forward, particularly those of music, in rhythmics, dynamics, and harmony. To grasp this collective release of all the symbolic powers, man must have already attained that height of self-abnegation which seeks to express itself symbolically through all these powers – and so the dithyrambic votary of Dionysus is understood only by his peers. With what astonishment must the Apollinian Greek have beheld him! With an astonishment that was all the greater the more it was mingled with the shuddering suspicion that all this was actually not so very alien to him after all, in fact, that it was only his Apollinian consciousness which, like a veil, hid this Dionysian world from his vision.

3

To understand this, it becomes necessary to level the artistic structure of the *Apollinian culture*, as it were, stone by stone, till the foundations on which it rests become visible. First of all we see the glorious *Olympian* figures of the gods, standing on the gables of this structure. Their deeds, pictured in brilliant reliefs, adorn its friezes. We must not be misled by the fact that Apollo stands side by side with the others as an individual deity, without any claim to priority of rank. For the same impulse that embodied itself in Apollo gave birth to this entire Olympian world, and in this sense Apollo is its father. What terrific need was it that could produce such an illustrious company of Olympian beings?

Whoever approaches these Olympians with another religion in his heart, searching among them for moral elevation, even for sanctity, for disincarnate spirituality, for charity and benevolence, will soon be forced to turn his back on them, discouraged and disappointed. For there is nothing here that suggests asceticism, spirituality, or duty. We hear nothing but the accents of an exuberant, triumphant life in which all things, whether good or evil, are deified. And so the spectator may stand quite bewildered before this fantastic excess of life, asking himself by virtue of what magic potion these high-spirited men could have found life so enjoyable that, wherever they turned, their

eyes beheld the smile of Helen, the ideal picture of their own existence, "floating in sweet sensuality." But to this spectator, who has
already turned his back, we must say: "Do not go away, but stay and
hear what Greek folk wisdom has to say of this very life, which with
such inexplicable gaiety unfolds itself before your eyes.

g→ "There is an ancient story that King Midas hunted in the forest a
long time for the wise Silenus, the companion of Dionysus, without
capturing him. When Silenus at last fell into his hands, the king asked
what was the best and most desirable of all things for man. Fixed and
immovable, the demigod said not a word, till at last, urged by
the king, he gave a shrill laugh and broke out into these words:
'Oh, wretched ephemeral race, children of chance and misery, why
do you compel me to tell you what it would be most expedient for you
not to hear? What is best of all is utterly beyond your reach: not to be
born, not to *be*, to be *nothing*. But the second best for you is – to die
soon.' "

How is the world of the Olympian gods related to this folk wisdom? Even as the rapturous vision of the tortured martyr to his
suffering.

Now it is as if the Olympian magic mountain had opened before us
h→ and revealed its roots to us. The Greek knew and felt the terror and
horror of existence. That he might endure this terror at all, he had to
interpose between himself and life the radiant dream-birth of the
Olympians. That overwhelming dismay in the face of the titanic
powers of nature, the Moira enthroned inexorably over all knowledge, the vulture of the great lover of mankind, Prometheus, the
terrible fate of the wise Oedipus, the family curse of the Atridae
which drove Orestes to matricide: in short, that entire philosophy of
the sylvan god, with its mythical exemplars, which caused the down-
fall of the melancholy Etruscans – all this was again and again
overcome by the Greeks with the aid of the Olympian *middle world*
of art; or at any rate it was veiled and withdrawn from sight. It was in
order to be able to live that the Greeks had to create these gods from a
most profound need. Perhaps we may picture the process to ourselves
somewhat as follows: out of the original Titanic divine order of terror,
the Olympian divine order of joy gradually evolved through the
Apollinian impulse toward beauty, just as roses burst from thorny
bushes. How else could this people, so sensitive, so vehement in its
desires, so singularly capable of *suffering*, have endured existence, if it
had not been revealed to them in their gods, surrounded with a higher
glory? [...]

4

[...]

Up to this point we have simply enlarged upon the observation made at the beginning of this essay: that the Dionysian and the Apollinian, in new births ever following and mutually augmenting one another, controlled the Hellenic genius; that out of the age of "bronze," with its wars of the Titans and its rigorous folk philosophy, the Homeric world developed under the sway of the Apollinian impulse to beauty; that this "naïve" splendor was again over-whelmed by the influx of the Dionysian; and that against this new power the Apollinian rose to the austere majesty of Doric art and the Doric view of the world. If amid the strife of these two hostile principles, the older Hellenic history thus falls into four great periods of art, we are now impelled to inquire after the final goal of these developments and processes, lest perchance we should regard the last-attained period, the period of Doric art, as the climax and aim of these artistic impulses. And here the sublime and celebrated art of *Attic tragedy* and the dramatic dithyramb presents itself as the common goal of both these tendencies whose mysterious union, after many and long precursory struggles, found glorious consummation in this child – at once Antigone and Cassandra.

[...]

7

We must now avail ourselves of all the principles of art considered so far, in order to find our way through the labyrinth, as we must call it, of *the origin of Greek tragedy*. I do not think I am unreasonable in saying that the problem of this origin has as yet not even been seriously posed, to say nothing of solved, however often the ragged tatters of ancient tradition have been sewn together in various combinations and torn apart again. This tradition tells us quite unequivocally *that tragedy arose from the tragic chorus*, and was originally only chorus and nothing but chorus. Hence we consider it our duty to look into the heart of this tragic chorus as the real proto-drama, without resting satisfied with such arty clichés as that the chorus is the "ideal spectator" or that it represents the people in contrast to the aristocratic region of the scene. This latter explanation has a sublime sound to many a politician – as if the immutable moral law had been embodied by the democratic Athenians in the popular chorus, which always won out over the passionate excesses and extravagances of

The Southampton MA in Aesthetics

With the highest concentration of specialist aestheticians anywhere in the UK, Philosophy at Southampton is uniquely well placed to offer a rich and stimulating MA in Aesthetics. Our principal aestheticians are:

Christopher Janaway (well known for his work on contemporary aesthetics and on the aesthetics of Plato, Kant, Schopenhauer and Nietzsche)
Alex Neill (well known for his work on the philosophy of literature and tragedy and on the aesthetics of Hume and Schopenhauer)
Aaron Ridley (well known for his work on the philosophy of music and the aesthetics of Nietzsche and Collingwood)

Other members of the Department also have research interests in aesthetics, in areas including the philosophy of literature, the philosophy of music, and the aesthetics of Kierkegaard, Wittgenstein and Heidegger. As members of the School of Humanities, moreover, our Master's students also benefit from the opportunity to take units from programmes run elsewhere in the School, by, for example, the departments of English and Film. And, at University level, there are the advantages of an excellent theatre (the Nuffield), concert hall (the Turner-Sims) and art gallery (the Hansard).

Courses offered include: Tragedy; The Beautiful and The Sublime; Creativity and Genius; Hume and Kant on Aesthetic Judgement; Art and Emotion; The Nature of Art; Aesthetic Value and the Value of Music; Representation and Truth in the Arts. All students also write a Dissertation of 15,000-20,000 words.

Most of our Master's students, full- or part-time, have good degrees either in Philosophy or a related subject (such as English Literature or Art History), but applications from those with different educational backgrounds are also welcome, and will be considered on their merits. The MA programme has been designed both to offer a grounding in Aesthetics to those relatively new to the area and to extend and deepen the understanding of those who have already studied Aesthetics at undergraduate level; the programme is also designed to offer thorough preparation for those wishing to go on to do postgraduate research.

For further details, contact: Professor Christopher Janaway
                                  Philosophy, School of Humanities
                                  University of Southampton
                                  Southampton SO17 1BJ

                                  Tel: 023 8059 3424
                                  Email: cjanaway@soton.ac.uk

kings. This theory may be ever so forcibly suggested by one of Aristotle's observations; still, it has no influence on the original formation of tragedy, inasmuch as the whole opposition of prince and people – indeed the whole politico-social sphere – was excluded from the purely religious origins of tragedy. But even regarding the classical form of the chorus in Aeschylus and Sophocles, which is known to us, we should deem it blasphemy to speak here of intimations of "constitutional popular representation." From this blasphemy, however, others have not shrunk. Ancient constitutions knew of no constitutional representation of the people in *praxi*, and it is to be hoped that they did not even "have intimations" of it in tragedy.

Much more famous than this political interpretation of the chorus is the idea of A. W. Schlegel, who advises us to regard the chorus somehow as the essence and extract of the crowd of spectators – as the "ideal spectator." This view, when compared with the historical tradition that originally tragedy was only chorus, reveals itself for what it is – a crude, unscientific, yet brilliant claim that owes its brilliancy only to its concentrated form of expression, to the typically Germanic bias in favor of anything called "ideal," and to our momentary astonishment. For we are certainly astonished the moment we compare our familiar theatrical public with this chorus, and ask ourselves whether it could ever be possible to idealize from such a public something analogous to the Greek tragic chorus. We tacitly deny this, and now wonder as much at the boldness of Schlegel's claim as at the totally different nature of the Greek public. For we had always believed that the right spectator, whoever he might be, must always remain conscious that he was viewing a work of art and not an empirical reality. But the tragic chorus of the Greeks is forced to recognize real beings in the figures on the stage. The chorus of the Oceanides really believes that it sees before it the Titan Prometheus, and it considers itself as real as the god of the scene. But could the highest and purest type of spectator regard Prometheus as bodily present and real, as the Oceanides do? Is it characteristic of the ideal spectator to run onto the stage and free the god from his torments? We had always believed in an aesthetic public and considered the individual spectator the better qualified the more he was capable of viewing a work of art as art, that is, aesthetically. But now Schlegel tells us that the perfect, ideal spectator does not at all allow the world of the drama to act on him aesthetically, but corporally and empirically. Oh, these Greeks! we sigh; they upset all our aesthetics! But once accustomed to this, we repeated Schlegel's saying whenever the chorus came up for discussion.

Now the tradition, which is quite explicit, speaks against Schlegel. The chorus as such, without the stage – the primitive form of tragedy – and the chorus of ideal spectators do not go together. What kind of artistic genre could possibly be extracted from the concept of the spectator, and find its true form in the "spectator as such"? The spectator without the spectacle is an absurd notion. We fear that the birth of tragedy is to be explained neither by any high esteem for the moral intelligence of the masses nor by the concept of the spectator without a spectacle; and we consider the problem too deep to be even touched by such superficial considerations.

An infinitely more valuable insight into the significance of the chorus was displayed by Schiller in the celebrated Preface to his *Bride of Messina*, where he regards the chorus as a living wall that tragedy constructs around itself in order to close itself off from the world of reality and to preserve its ideal domain and its poetical freedom.

With this, his chief weapon, Schiller combats the ordinary conception of the natural, the illusion usually demanded in dramatic poetry. Although the stage day is merely artificial, the architecture only symbolical, and the metrical language ideal in character, nevertheless an erroneous view still prevails in the main, as he points out: it is not sufficient that one merely tolerates as poetic license what is actually the essence of all poetry. The introduction of the chorus, says Schiller, is the decisive step by which war is declared openly and honorably against all naturalism in art.

It would seem that to denigrate this view of the matter our would-be superior age has coined the disdainful catchword "pseudo-idealism." I fear, however, that we, on the other hand, with our present adoration of the natural and the real, have reached the opposite pole of all idealism, namely, the region of wax-work cabinets. There is an art in these, too, as there is in certain novels much in vogue at present; but we really should not be plagued with the claim that such art has overcome the "pseudo-idealism" of Goethe and Schiller.

It is indeed an "ideal" domain, as Schiller correctly perceived, in which the Greek satyr chorus, the chorus of primitive tragedy, was wont to dwell. It is a domain raised high above the actual paths of mortals. For this chorus the Greek built up the scaffolding of a fictitious *natural state* and on it placed fictitious *natural beings*. On this foundation tragedy developed and so, of course, it could dispense from the beginning with a painstaking portrayal of reality. Yet it is no arbitrary world placed by whim between heaven and earth; rather it is a world with the same reality and credibility that Olympus with its inhabitants possessed for the believing Hellene. The satyr, as the

Dionysian chorist, lives in a religiously acknowledged reality under the sanction of myth and cult. That tragedy should begin with him, that he should be the voice of the Dionysian wisdom of tragedy, is just as strange a phenomenon for us as the general derivation of tragedy from the chorus.

Perhaps we shall have a point of departure for our inquiry if I put forward the proposition that the satyr, the fictitious natural being, bears the same relation to the man of culture that Dionysian music bears to civilization. Concerning the latter, Richard Wagner says that it is nullified by music just as lamplight is nullified by the light of day. Similarly, I believe, the Greek man of culture felt himself nullified in the presence of the satyric chorus; and this is the most immediate effect of the Dionysian tragedy, that the state and society and, quite generally, the gulfs between man and man give way to an overwhelming feeling of unity leading back to the very heart of nature. The metaphysical comfort – with which, I am suggesting even now, every true tragedy leaves us – that life is at the bottom of things, despite all the changes of appearances, indestructibly powerful and pleasurable – this comfort appears in incarnate clarity in the chorus of satyrs, a chorus of natural beings who live ineradicably, as it were, behind all civilization and remain eternally the same, despite the changes of generations and of the history of nations.

With this chorus the profound Hellene, uniquely susceptible to the tenderest and deepest suffering, comforts himself, having looked boldly right into the terrible destructiveness of so-called world history as well as the cruelty of nature, and being in danger of longing for a Buddhistic negation of the will. Art saves him, and through art – life.

For the rapture of the Dionysian state with its annihilation of the ordinary bounds and limits of existence contains, while it lasts, a *lethargic* element in which all personal experiences of the past become immersed. This chasm of oblivion separates the worlds of everyday reality and of Dionysian reality. But as soon as this everyday reality re-enters consciousness, it is experienced as such, with nausea: an ascetic, will-negating mood is the fruit of these states.

In this sense the Dionysian man resembles Hamlet: both have once looked truly into the essence of things, they have *gained knowledge*, and nausea inhibits action; for their action could not change anything in the eternal nature of things; they feel it to be ridiculous or humiliating that they should be asked to set right a world that is out of joint. Knowledge kills action; action requires the veils of illusion: that is the doctrine of Hamlet, not that cheap wisdom of Jack the Dreamer who reflects too much and, as it were, from an excess of possibilities does not get around to action. Not reflection, no – true knowledge, an insight into the horrible truth, outweighs any motive for action, both in Hamlet and in the Dionysian man.

Now no comfort avails any more; longing transcends a world after death, even the gods; existence is negated along with its glittering reflection in the gods or in an immortal beyond. Conscious of the truth he has once seen, man now sees everywhere only the horror or absurdity of existence; now he understands what is symbolic in Ophelia's fate; now he understands the wisdom of the sylvan god, Silenus: he is nauseated.

Here, when the danger to his will is greatest, *art* approaches as a saving sorceress, expert at healing. She alone knows how to turn these nauseous thoughts about the horror or absurdity of existence into notions with which one can live: these are the *sublime* as the artistic taming of the horrible, and the *comic* as the artistic discharge of the nausea of absurdity. The satyr chorus of the dithyramb is the saving deed of Greek art; faced with the intermediary world of these Dionysian companions, the feelings described here exhausted themselves.

8

The satyr, like the idyllic shepherd of more recent times, is the off-spring of a longing for the primitive and the natural; but how firmly and fearlessly the Greek embraced the man of the woods, and how timorously and mawkishly modern man dallied with the flattering image of a sentimental, flute-playing, tender shepherd! Nature, as yet unchanged by knowledge, with the bolts of culture still unbroken – that is what the Greek saw in his satyr who nevertheless was not a mere ape. On the contrary, the satyr was the archetype of man, the embodiment of his highest and most intense emotions, the ecstatic reveler enraptured by the proximity of his god, the sympathetic companion in whom the suffering of the god is repeated, one who proclaims wisdom from the very heart of nature, a symbol of the sexual omnipotence of nature which the Greeks used to contemplate with reverent wonder.

The satyr was something sublime and divine: thus he had to appear to the painfully broken vision of Dionysian man. The contrived shepherd in his dress-ups would have offended him: on the uncon-cealed and vigorously magnificent characters of nature, his eye rested with sublime satisfaction; here the true human being was disclosed, the bearded satyr jubilating to his god. Confronted with him, the man of culture shriveled into a mendacious caricature.

Schiller is right about these origins of tragic art, too: the chorus is a living wall against the assaults of reality because it – the satyr chorus – represents existence more truthfully, really, and completely than the man of culture does who ordinarily considers himself as the only reality. The sphere of poetry does not lie outside the world as a fantastic impossibility spawned by a poet's brain: it desires to be just the opposite, the unvarnished expression of the truth, and must precisely for that reason discard the mendacious finery of that alleged reality of the man of culture.

The contrast between this real truth of nature and the lie of culture that poses as if it were the only reality is similar to that between the eternal core of things, the thing-in-itself, and the whole world of appearances: just as tragedy, with its metaphysical comfort, points to the eternal life of this core of existence which abides through the perpetual destruction of appearances, the symbolism of the satyr chorus proclaims this primordial relationship between the thing-in-itself and appearance. The idyllic shepherd of modern man is merely a counterfeit of the sum of cultural illusions that are allegedly nature; the Dionysian Greek wants truth and nature in their most forceful form – and sees himself changed, as by magic, into a satyr.

The reveling throng, the votaries of Dionysus jubilate under the spell of such moods and insights whose power transforms them before their own eyes till they imagine that they are beholding themselves as restored geniuses of nature, as satyrs. The later constitution of the chorus in tragedy is the artistic imitation of this natural phenomenon, though, to be sure, at this point the separation of Dionysian spectators and magically enchanted Dionysians became necessary. Only we must always keep in mind that the public at an Attic tragedy found itself in the chorus of the *orchestra*, and there was at bottom no opposition between public and chorus: everything is merely a great sublime chorus of dancing and singing satyrs or of those who permit themselves to be represented by such satyrs.

Now we are ready to understand Schlegel's formulation in a deeper sense. The chorus is the "ideal spectator" insofar as it is the only beholder, the beholder of the visionary world of the scene. A public of spectators as we know it was unknown to the Greeks: in their theaters the terraced structure of concentric arcs made it possible for everybody to actually *overlook* the whole world of culture around him and to imagine, in absorbed contemplation, that he himself was a chorist.

In the light of this insight we may call the chorus in its primitive form, in proto-tragedy, the mirror image in which the Dionysian man contemplates himself. This phenomenon is best made clear by imagining an actor who, being truly talented, sees the role he is supposed to play quite palpably before his eyes. The satyr chorus is, first of all, a vision of the Dionysian mass of spectators, just as the world of the stage, in turn, is a vision of this satyr chorus: the force of this vision is strong enough to make the eye insensitive and blind to the impression of "reality," to the men of culture who occupy the rows of seats all around. The form of the Greek theater recalls a lonely valley in the mountains: the architecture of the scene appears like a luminous cloud formation that the Bacchants swarming over the mountains behold from a height – like the splendid frame in which the image of Dionysus is revealed to them.

In the face of our learned views about elementary artistic processes, this artistic proto-phenomenon which we bring up here to help explain the tragic chorus is almost offensive, although nothing could be more certain than the fact that a poet is a poet only insofar as he sees himself surrounded by figures who live and act before him and into whose inmost nature he can see. Owing to a peculiar modern weakness, we are inclined to imagine the aesthetic proto-phenomenon in a manner much too complicated and abstract.

For a genuine poet, metaphor is not a rhetorical figure but a vicarious image that he actually beholds in place of a concept. A character is for him not a whole he has composed out of particular traits, picked up here and there, but an obtrusively alive person before his very eyes, distinguished from the otherwise identical vision of a painter only by the fact that it continually goes on living and acting. How is it that Homer's descriptions are so much more vivid than those of any other poet? Because he visualizes so much more vividly. We talk so abstractly about poetry because all of us are usually bad poets. At bottom, the aesthetic phenomenon is simple: let anyone have the ability to behold continually a vivid play and to live constantly surrounded by hosts of spirits, and he will be a poet; let anyone feel the urge to transform himself and to speak out of other bodies and souls, and he will be a dramatist.

The Dionysian excitement is capable of communicating this artistic gift to a multitude, so they can see themselves surrounded by such a host of spirits while knowing themselves to be essentially one with them. This process of the tragic chorus is the *dramatic* proto-phenomenon: to see oneself transformed before one's own eyes and to begin to act as if one had actually entered into another body, another character. This process stands at the beginning of the origin of drama. Here we have something different from the rhapsodist who does not become fused with his images but, like a painter, sees them outside himself as objects of contemplation. Here we have a surrender of individuality and a way of entering into another character. And this phenomenon is encountered epidemically: a whole throng experiences the magic of this transformation.

The dithyramb is thus essentially different from all other choral odes. The virgins who proceed solemnly to the temple of Apollo, laurel branches in their hands, singing a processional hymn, remain what they are and retain their civic names: the dithyrambic chorus is a chorus of transformed characters whose civic past and social status have been totally forgotten: they have become timeless servants of their god who live outside the spheres of society. All the other choral lyric poetry of the Hellenes is merely a tremendous intensification of the Apollinian solo singer, while in the dithyramb we confront a community of unconscious actors who consider themselves and one another transformed.

Such magic transformation is the presupposition of all dramatic art. In this magic transformation the Dionysian reveler sees himself as a satyr, *and as a satyr, in turn, he sees the god*, which means that in his metamorphosis he beholds another vision outside himself, as the Apollinian complement of his own state. With this new vision the drama is complete.

In the light of this insight we must understand Greek tragedy as the Dionysian chorus which ever anew discharges itself in an Apollinian world of images. Thus the choral parts with which tragedy is inter- laced are, as it were, the womb that gave birth to the whole of the so- called dialogue, that is, the entire world of the stage, the real drama. In several successive discharges this primal ground of tragedy radiates this vision of the drama which is by all means a dream apparition and to that extent epic in nature; but on the other hand, being the object- ification of a Dionysian state, it represents not Apollinian redemption through mere appearance but, on the contrary, the shattering of the individual and his fusion with primal being. Thus the drama is the Dionysian embodiment of Dionysian insights and effects and thereby separated, as by a tremendous chasm, from the epic.

The *chorus* of the Greek tragedy, the symbol of the whole excited Dionysian throng, is thus fully explained by our conception. Accus- tomed as we are to the function of our modern stage chorus, espe- cially in operas, we could not comprehend why the tragic chorus of the Greeks should be older, more original and important than the "action" proper, as the voice of tradition claimed unmistakably. And with this traditional primacy and originality we could not reconcile the fact that the chorus consisted only of humble beings who served – indeed, initially only of goatlike satyrs. Finally, there remained the riddle of the orchestra in front of the scene. But now we realize that the scene, complete with the action, was basically and originally thought of merely as a *vision*; the chorus is the only "reality" and generates the vision, speaking of it with the entire symbolism of dance, tone, and words. In its vision this chorus beholds its lord and master Dionysus and is therefore eternally the *serving* chorus: it sees how the god suffers and glorifies himself and therefore does not itself *act*. But while its attitude toward the god is wholly one of service, it is nevertheless the highest, namely the Dionysian, expression of *nature* and therefore pronounces in its rapture, as nature does, oracles and wise sayings: *sharing his suffering* it also shares something of his *wisdom* and proclaims the truth from the heart of the world. That is the origin of the fantastic and seemingly so offensive figure of the wise and rapturous satyr who is at the same time "the simple man" as opposed to the god – the image of nature and its strongest urges, even their symbol, and at the same time the proclaimer of her wisdom and art – musician, poet, dancer, and seer of spirits in one person. [. . .]

12

[. . .]

[L]et us pause here a moment to recall to our minds our previously described impression of the discordant and incommensurable elements in the nature of Aeschylean tragedy. Let us recall our surprise at the *chorus* and the *tragic hero* of that tragedy, neither of which we could reconcile with our own customs any more than with tradition – till we rediscovered this duality itself as the origin and essence of Greek tragedy, as the expression of two interwoven artistic impulses, *the Apollinian and the Dionysian*.

To separate this original and all-powerful Dionysian element from tragedy, and to reconstruct tragedy purely on the basis of an un-Dionysian art, morality, and world view – this is the tendency of Euripides as it now reveals itself to us in clear illumination.

In the evening of his life, Euripides himself propounded to his contemporaries the question of the value and significance of this tendency, using a myth. Is the Dionysian entitled to exist at all? Should it not be forcibly uprooted from Hellenic soil? Certainly, the poet tells us, if it were only possible: but the god Dionysus is too powerful; his most intelligent adversary – like Pentheus in the *Bacchae* – is unwittingly enchanted by him, and in this enchantment runs to meet his fate. The judgment of the two old men, Cadmus and Tiresias, seems also to be the judgment of the old poet: the reflection of the wisest individuals does not overthrow these old popular traditions, nor the perpetually self-propagating worship of Dionysus;

rather it is proper to display a diplomatically cautious interest in the presence of such marvelous forces – although the possibility remains that the god may take offense at such lukewarm participation, and eventually transform the diplomat – like Cadmus – into a dragon. This is what we are told by a poet who opposed Dionysus with heroic valor throughout a long life – and who finally ended his career with a glorification of his adversary and with suicide, like a giddy man who, to escape the horrible vertigo he can no longer endure, casts himself from a tower.

This tragedy was a protest against the practicability of his own tendency; but alas, it had already been put into practice! The marvel had happened: when the poet recanted, his tendency had already triumphed. Dionysus had already been scared from the tragic stage, by a demonic power speaking through Euripides. Even Euripides was, in a sense, only a mask: the deity that spoke through him was neither Dionysus nor Apollo, but an altogether newborn demon, called *Socrates*.

This is the new opposition: the Dionysian and the Socratic – and the art of Greek tragedy was wrecked on this. Though Euripides may seek to comfort us by his recantation, he does not succeed: the most magnificent temple lies in ruins. What does the lamentation of the destroyer profit us, or his confession that it was the most beautiful of all temples? And even if Euripides has been punished by being changed into a dragon by the art critics of all ages – who could be content with so miserable a compensation?

Let us now approach this *Socratic* tendency with which Euripides combated and vanquished Aeschylean tragedy.

We must now ask ourselves, what could be the aim of the Euripidean design, which, in its most ideal form, would wish to base drama exclusively on the un-Dionysian? What form of drama still remained, if it was not to be born of the womb of music, in the mysterious twilight of the Dionysian? Only *the dramatized epos* – but in this Apollinian domain of art the *tragic* effect is certainly unattainable. The subject matter of the events represented is not decisive; indeed, I suggest that it would have been impossible for Goethe in his projected *Nausikaa* to have rendered tragically effective the suicide of this idyllic being, which was to have completed the fifth act. So extraordinary is the power of the epic-Apollinian that before our eyes it transforms the most terrible things by the joy in mere appearance and in redemption through mere appearance. The poet of the dramatized epos cannot blend completely with his images any more than the epic rhapsodist can. He is still that calm, unmoved contemplation which sees the images *before* its wide-open eyes. The actor in this dramatized epos still remains fundamentally a rhapsodist: the consecration of the inner dream lies on all his actions, so that he is never wholly an actor.

How, then, is the Euripidean play related to this ideal of the Apollinian drama? Just as the younger rhapsodist is related to the solemn rhapsodist of old times. In the Platonic *Ion*, the younger rhapsodist describes his own nature as follows: "When I am saying anything sad, my eyes fill with tears; and when I am saying something awful and terrible, then my hair stands on end with fright and my heart beats quickly." Here we no longer remark anything of the epic absorption in mere appearance, or of the dispassionate coolness of the true actor, who precisely in his highest activity is wholly mere appearance and joy in mere appearance. Euripides is the actor whose heart beats, whose hair stands on end; as Socratic thinker he designs the plan, as passionate actor he executes it. Neither in the designing nor in the execution is he a pure artist. Thus the Euripidean drama is a thing both cool and fiery, equally capable of freezing and burning. It is impossible for it to attain the Apollinian effect of the epos, while, on the other hand, it has alienated itself as much as possible from Dionysian elements. Now, in order to be effective at all, it requires new stimulants, which can no longer lie within the sphere of the only two art-impulses, the Apollinian and the Dionysian. These stimulants are cool, paradoxical thoughts, replacing Apollinian contemplation – and fiery *affects*, replacing Dionysian ecstasies; and, it may be added, thoughts and affects copied very realistically and in no sense dipped into the ether of art.

So we see that Euripides did not succeed in basing the drama exclusively on the Apollinian, and his un-Dionysian tendency actually went astray and became naturalistic and inartistic. Now we should be able to come closer to the character of *aesthetic Socratism*, whose supreme law reads roughly as follows, "To be beautiful everything must be intelligible," as the counterpart to the Socratic dictum, "Knowledge is virtue." With this canon in his hands, Euripides measured all the separate elements of the drama – language, characters, dramaturgic structure, and choric music – and corrected them according to this principle.

The poetic deficiency and degeneration, which are so often imputed to Euripides in comparison with Sophocles, are for the most part products of this penetrating critical process, this audacious reasonableness.

The Euripidean *prologue* may serve as an example of the productivity of this rationalistic method. Nothing could be more uncongenial to the technique of our own stage than the prologue in the drama of Euripides. For a single person to appear at the outset of the play, telling us who he is, what precedes the action, what has happened so far, even what will happen in the course of the play, would be condemned by a modern playwright as a willful, inexcusable abandonment of the effect of suspense. We know everything that is going to happen; who would want to wait till it actually does happen? After all, we do not even have the exciting relation of a prophetic dream to a reality that comes to be later on. But Euripides did not think like that at all. The effect of tragedy never depended on epic suspense, on a fascinating uncertainty as to what is to happen now and afterward, but rather on the great rhetorical–lyrical scenes in which the passion and dialectic of the protagonist swelled to a broad and powerful current. Everything laid the ground for pathos, not for action: and whatever was not directed toward pathos was considered objectionable. But what interferes most with the hearer's pleasurable absorption in such scenes is any missing link, any gap in the texture of the background story. So long as the spectator has to figure out the meaning of this or that person, or the presuppositions of this or that conflict of inclinations and purposes, he cannot become completely absorbed in the activities and sufferings of the chief characters or feel breathless pity and fear.

Aeschylean–Sophoclean tragedy employed the most ingenious devices in the initial scenes to place in the spectator's hands, as if by chance, all the threads necessary for a complete understanding – a trait proving that noble artistry which, as it were, masks the *necessary* formal element and makes it appear accidental. Yet Euripides thought he observed that during these first scenes the spectator was so anxious to solve the problem of the background history that the poetic beauties and the pathos of the exposition were lost on him. So he put the prologue even before the exposition, and placed it in the mouth of a person who could be trusted: often some deity had to guarantee the plot of the tragedy to the public, to remove every doubt as to the reality of the myth – somewhat as Descartes could prove the reality of the empirical world only by appealing to the truthfulness of God and his inability to utter falsehood. Euripides makes use of this same divine truthfulness once more at the close of his drama, in order to reassure the public as to the future of his heroes; this is the task of the notorious *deus ex machina*. Between this epic preview and epic prospect lies the dramatic-lyric present, the "drama" proper.

Thus Euripides as a poet is essentially an echo of his own conscious knowledge; and it is precisely on this account that he occupies such a remarkable position in the history of Greek art. With reference to his critical-productive activity, he must often have felt as if he had to bring to life for drama the beginning of the essay of Anaxagoras: "In the beginning all things were mixed together; then came the under-standing and created order." Anaxagoras with his *"nous"* is said to have appeared among philosophers as the first sober person amid a crowd of drunken ones. Euripides may have conceived his relation to the other tragic poets in terms of a similar image. As long as the sole ruler and disposer of the universe, the *nous*, remained excluded from artistic activity, things were all mixed together in a primeval chaos: this was what Euripides must have thought; and so, as the first "sober" one among them, he had to condemn the "drunken" poets. Sophocles said of Aeschylus that he did what was right, though he did it unconsciously. This was surely not how Euripides saw it. He might have said that Aeschylus, *because* he created unconsciously, did what was *wrong*. The divine Plato, too, almost always speaks only ironic-ally of the creative faculty of the poet, insofar as it is not conscious insight, and places it on a par with the gift of the soothsayer and dream-interpreter: the poet is incapable of composing until he has become unconscious and bereft of understanding. Like Plato, Euripi-des undertook to show to the world the reverse of the "unintelligent" poet; his aesthetic principle that "to be beautiful everything must be conscious" is, as I have said, the parallel to the Socratic "to be good everything must be conscious." So we may consider Euripides as the poet of aesthetic Socratism.

Socrates, however, was that *second spectator* who did not compre-hend and therefore did not esteem the Old Tragedy; in alliance with him Euripides dared to be the herald of a new art. If it was this of which the older tragedy perished, then aesthetic Socratism was the murderous principle; but insofar as the struggle was directed against the Dionysian element in the older tragedy, we may recognize in Socrates the opponent of Dionysus. [. . .]

14

Let us now imagine the one great Cyclops eye of Socrates fixed on tragedy, an eye in which the fair frenzy of artistic enthusiasm had never glowed. To this eye was denied the pleasure of gazing into the Dionysian abysses. What, then, did it have to see in the "sublime and greatly lauded" tragic art, as Plato called it? Something rather unrea-sonable, full of causes apparently without effects, and effects appar-ently without causes; the whole, moreover, so motley and manifold that it could not but be repugnant to a sober mind, and a dangerous tinder for sensitive and susceptible souls. We know the only kind of poetry he comprehended: the *Aesopian fable*; and this he favored no

doubt with the smiling accommodation with which the good honest
Gellert sings the praise of poetry in the fable of the bee and the hen:

> *Poems are useful: they can tell*
> *The truth by means of parable*
> *To those who are not very bright.*

But to Socrates it seemed that tragic art did not even "tell the truth";
moreover, it addressed itself to "those who are not very bright," not to
the philosopher: a twofold reason for shunning it. Like Plato, he
reckoned it among the flattering arts which portray only the agreeable, not the useful; and therefore he required of his disciples abstin-
ence and strict separation from such unphilosophical attractions –
with such success that the youthful tragic poet Plato first burned his
poems that he might become a student of Socrates. But where uncon-
querable propensities struggled against the Socratic maxims, their
power, together with the impact of his tremendous character, was
still great enough to force poetry itself into new and hitherto unknown channels.

An instance of this is Plato, who in condemning tragedy and art in
general certainly did not lag behind the naïve cynicism of his master;
he was nevertheless constrained by sheer artistic necessity to create an
art form that was related to those forms of art which he repudiated.
Plato's main objection to the older art – that it is the imitation of a
phantom and hence belongs to a sphere even lower than the empirical
world – could certainly not be directed against the new art; and so we
find Plato endeavoring to transcend reality and to represent the idea
which underlies this pseudo-reality. Thus Plato, the thinker, arrived by
a detour where he had always been at home as a poet – at the point
from which Sophocles and the older art protested solemnly against
that objection. If tragedy had absorbed into itself all the earlier types
of art, the same might also be said in an eccentric sense of the Platonic
dialogue which, a mixture of all extant styles and forms, hovers
midway between narrative, lyric, and drama, between prose and
poetry, and so has also broken the strict old law of the unity of
linguistic form. This tendency was carried still further by the *Cynic*
writers, who in the greatest stylistic medley, oscillating between prose
and metrical forms, realized also the literary image of the "raving
Socrates" whom they represented in real life.

The Platonic dialogue was, as it were, the barge on which the
shipwrecked ancient poetry saved herself with all her children:
crowded into a narrow space and timidly submitting to the single
pilot, Socrates, they now sailed into a new world, which never tired of

looking at the fantastic spectacle of this procession. Indeed, Plato has given to all posterity the model of a new art form, the model of the *novel* – which may be described as an infinitely enhanced Aesopian fable, in which poetry holds the same rank in relation to dialectical philosophy as this same philosophy held for many centuries in relation to theology: namely, the rank of *ancilla*. This was the new position into which Plato, under the pressure of the demonic Socrates, forced poetry.

Here *philosophic thought* overgrows art and compels it to cling close to the trunk of dialectic. The *Apollinian* tendency has withdrawn into the cocoon of logical schematism; just as in the case of Euripides we noticed something analogous, as well as a transformation of the *Dionysian* into naturalistic affects. Socrates, the dialectical hero of the Platonic drama, reminds us of the kindred nature of the Euripidean hero who must defend his actions with arguments and counterarguments and in the process often risks the loss of our tragic pity; for who could mistake the *optimistic* element in the nature of dialectic, which celebrates a triumph with every conclusion and can breathe only in cool clarity and consciousness – the optimistic element which, having once penetrated tragedy must gradually overgrow its Dionysian regions and impel it necessarily to self-destruction – to the death-leap into the bourgeois drama. Consider the consequences of the Socratic maxims: "Virtue is knowledge; man sins only from ignorance; he who is virtuous is happy." In these three basic forms of optimism lies the death of tragedy. For now the virtuous hero must be a dialectician; now there must be a necessary, visible connection between virtue and knowledge, faith and morality; now the transcendental justice of Aeschylus is degraded to the superficial and insolent principle of "poetic justice" with its customary *deus ex machina*.

As it confronts this new Socratic-optimistic stage world, how does the *chorus* appear now, and indeed the whole musical-Dionysian substratum of tragedy? As something accidental, a dispensable vestige of the origin of tragedy; while we have seen that the chorus can be understood only as the *cause* of tragedy, and of the tragic in general. This perplexity in regard to the chorus already manifests itself in Sophocles – an important indication that even with him the Dionysian basis of tragedy is beginning to break down. He no longer dares to entrust to the chorus the main share of the effect, but limits its sphere to such an extent that it now appears almost co-ordinate with the actors, just as if it were elevated from the orchestra into the scene; and thus its character is, of course, completely destroyed, even if Aristotle favors precisely this theory of the chorus. This alteration in the position of the chorus, which Sophocles at any rate recommended by his practice and, according to tradition, even by a treatise, is the first step toward the *destruction* of the chorus, whose phases follow one another with alarming rapidity in Euripides, Agathon, and the New Comedy. Optimistic dialectic drives *music* out of tragedy with the scourge of its syllogisms; that is, it destroys the essence of tragedy, which can be interpreted only as a manifestation and projection into images of Dionysian states, as the visible symbolizing of music, as the dream-world of a Dionysian intoxication.

Commentary on Nietzsche

The opening sentence speaks of making advances in 'the science of aesthetics' if we realize that 'the continuous development of art is bound up with the *Apollinian* and the *Dionysian* duality'. The initial thought is that all art is either Apollinian or Dionysian in spirit, or a marriage or synthesis of the two. Nietzsche places Greek tragedy in the latter category, and seeks to explain its particular value as an art form in terms of its manifesting just this combination.

Apollo and Dionysus

Since the whole of *The Birth of Tragedy* is structured around this opposition between the figures of Apollo and Dionysus, it would seem wise to try to understand what the terms of the opposition are for Nietzsche, a task made unusually challenging by the rich set of images and associations in which they are enmeshed.

Try to list the most essential oppositions Nietzsche attaches to the pair Apollo–Dionysus in sections 1 and 2 of the text.

The markers $\boxed{a} \mapsto$ to $\boxed{f} \mapsto$ may be of assistance here, as they attempt to show places where Nietzsche makes the constrasts most explicit. We find first a split between two Greek gods. Apollo is the noble, Olympian god *par excellence*, associated with sun, light, appearance, and clarity. Dionysus on the other hand is a nature-god, whose worship is associated with trance, abandon, and ritual dance. But we find Nietzsche talking of 'tendencies' and 'forces' associated with these two figures. Firstly, before we even think of art, we are to recognize the Apollinian and the Dionysian as natural forces or drives. He gives us a key-word for each (at $\boxed{b} \mapsto$): *dream* and *intoxication*. It appears we have these two drives: to immerse ourselves in an alternative world of appearance and beauty, and to lose our sense of self in a drunken transport or trance in which we become conscious of an identity with nature as a whole.

Nietzsche gives one prominent explanation of his central dichotomy (at
⟨c⟩→ and ⟨d⟩→) which makes sense, if at all, only to someone aquainted with
the philosophy of Schopenhauer. The *principium individuationis* or principle
of individuation is what makes it possible for there to be distinct individuals.
In Schopenhauer's metaphysics there are no individuals in the world as it is in
itself. Space and time are required for individuation, and space and time,
according to his idealist position, do not exist in the world as it is in itself –
they do not exist without the experiencing subject, whose experience is
essentially organized by the forms of space and time. Nietzsche alludes to
this metaphysical system without much explanation, and only as a kind of
analogy or comparison we 'might' make.

The reader is best advised initially to concentrate on Nietzsche's contrast
between the individual and the whole from which he or she is separated out.
He is suggesting that we are both enchanted by the beauty of individual
appearance and form, and awed by the feeling of individuality and consciousness being dissolved into what he calls a primal Oneness. This latter feeling he
pictures as a kind of horror, but at the same time an intense rapture, in which
one feels united with other human beings and with nature as a whole.

The association of Dionysus with intoxicating ritual and loss of self leads
into another aspect of the Apollo–Dionysus distinction: a psychological split
between consciousness and self-control on the one hand, and the 'savage
natural instincts' lying beneath which can lead to sexual abandon and cruelty
(see ⟨f⟩→).

As regards art, Nietzsche's first important point is that these 'natural'
tendencies in human beings are also creative and give rise to forms of art:
on the one hand the plastic, primarily visual arts; on the other the non-visual
rapture-inducing form of music.

Pessimism and art

Nietzsche questions a traditional view of the Greek classical world as an age
of beauty, proportion, reason, and bright optimism. He locates in Greek
culture what he calls 'pessimism', which comes to light in section 3. The
Olympian deities, characteristic of the Homeric age, are, according to
Nietzsche, not so foundational as we might think in Greek culture. He
compares them to a radiant frieze on the top of a magnificent building (an
allusion to the Parthenon); but, if we dismantle this edifice 'stone by stone' we
find that its foundation is really something quite different.

> What, according to Nietzsche's text, was the motivating force behind the
> construction of the image-world of the Homeric gods?

The story of Silenus (⟨g⟩→) reveals a folk-tradition among the Greeks
according to which life is full of unredeemed suffering, something to be

lamented and left behind as soon as possible. How does this attitude relate to the splendour of the fictional world of Olympian deities and the Homeric heroes? According to the passage at $\boxed{h}$→ the beautiful appearance of the individual gods and heroes is a victory for artifice, illusion, creative art, over the terrors of existence. Only by aestheticizing their world, and placing between themselves and reality a radiant realm of dream-images, could the Greeks turn life into something they could affirm. The gods and heroes of the Homeric poems are 'a sublimation of suffering into beauty, the formation of a beautiful illusion to conceal the painful truth' (Silk and Stern, *Nietzsche on Tragedy*, 66). In Nietzsche's terms this marks a complete victory of Apollinian illusion over the terror and chaos that the Greek mind apprehended in reality.

The Homeric poems mark one earlier stage in the history of Greek poetry. As he announces at $\boxed{i}$→, Nietzsche will go on to say that the culmination of Greek artistic achievement is tragic poetry in its Attic form (Attica being the region of Greece in which Athens was situated, and the prime tragedians of that place and time being Aeschylus, Sophocles, and Euripides). Tragedy is the highest art form because it successfully unites the pre-existing Dionysian and the Apollinian tendencies.

The value of tragedy

It is in sections 7 and 8 that Nietzsche comes closest to a statement, or at any rate an evocation, of the way in which tragedy derives its value from a combination of the Dionysian and the Apollinian. Probably the most productive question to keep in mind here is as follows:

> What explanation can Nietzsche give of the *peculiar* value of Greek tragedy at its peak?

Greek tragedy at its peak is exemplified by the dramas of Aeschylus and Sophocles. Nietzsche constrasts them with the later writer Euripides, author of the *Bacchae, Medea*, and other dramas, suggesting that he corrupted and killed off the art form – a contrast which more recent writers have found unfair and unsubstantiated.

In Nietzsche's account tragedy originated as chorus: a communal dance-form with music, and this is its Dionysian element. The original form of the chorus was a ritual dance in honour of Dionysus, and the participants represented mythical satyrs, half-human creatures which for Nietzsche represent unity with nature and the exercise of powerful appetites that cannot be unleashed in the ordinary 'civilized' individual (see especially $\boxed{j}$→ and $\boxed{k}$→).

But tragedy has its Apollinian element, in that it represents individual characters, as if in a vision, dream, or illusion. These characters, Oedipus, Prometheus, Antigone, Medea, appeared on a stage which was raised above the circular floor of the amphitheatre. The chorus moved and sang in this circular space which Nietzsche refers to by its Greek name of *orchestra*. So there is both a physical and an artistic division between the two elements of classical tragedy.

The paragraph at [l]→ is enlightening as to Nietzsche's overall claims. Tragedy is 'the Dionysian chorus which ever anew discharges itself in an Apollinian world of images'. The acts and sufferings of the protagonists of the drama on stage arise out of the 'womb' provided by the communal, music-driven chorus. The chorus of fictitious natural beings witnesses the unfolding of the drama, and the audience witnesses it, but through an identification with the chorus, whereby they partake of something communal, unifying, and elemental that is the counterpoise to the individual character portrayed on stage.

Nietzsche returns to the theme of individuation. The tragic hero is symbolic of individuation, which is destroyed in the course of the drama; but the chorus, which lives on, symbolizes something primitive and enduring. So the experience of tragedy combines an imaginative submission to the illusion of individuality and an identification with a unity that transcends it. The whole drama makes tangible for us the thought that individual suffering is witnessed and even celebrated from a point of identification with a greater unity beyond the individual. Because of the nature of human life, the hero as individual must suffer and be destroyed. But through our identification with the primal unity of nature represented by the chorus, we can find this destruction fulfilling.

Hence, according to Nietzsche, in tragedy pessimism is embraced, not shunned. Purely Apollinian representation, as in the case of Homer, creates an illusion, screening off the essential metaphysical truth about the horrors of existence. Tragedy, because it always retains its Dionysian chorus, keeps the spectator always in contact with the elemental destructive forces that are beyond the individual, and affirms life, not by creating a beautiful illusion, but by taking a joy in the metaphysical reality that makes each individual of no consequence, and makes individual existence inescapably horrific. We become painfully aware of the vulnerability, and expendability, of ourselves as individuals, by contrast with this 'world-will' multiplying itself with such abandon. Seeing individuals as mere 'appearances' in contrast with the elemental force beneath enables us to feel the torment of our own existence. But feeling this through *art* makes life something justified and worthy of celebration.

The death of tragedy: Socrates and Socratism

Socrates, who is both a historical individual and the literary figure who dominates most of Plato's dialogues, is now introduced in a role parallel to that of Dionysus and Apollo: a symbol or emblem of something pervasive in Greek culture, and in human culture generally. Socrates stands for something distinct from both Dionysus and Apollo, as passages at [m]→, [n]→, [o]→, [p]→, and [q]→ should confirm.

What, for Nietzsche, does Socrates symbolize, and why is he destructive of tragedy?

In general Socrates stands for the principle that everything ought to be rationally investigated and rationally explained. This allows us to reflect that, from the beginning, neither the Apollinian nor the Dionysian has been symbolic of rationality. Further points are as follows:

1   The Socratic world-view (taken over by Plato) is optimistic, in that the person governed by his/her rational element will be the happiest, can hope to attain truth about the good, and eventually to leave behind the world of suffering altogether.
2   Plato's kind of philosophy is the very historical development which makes tragedy's full value inaccessible to us. If Nietzsche is right, it is no wonder that Plato fails to see any value in tragedy, because Socratic philosophy is established precisely to supersede it, by substituting for art's combination of dream-like illusion, primal rapture, and horrific realization, the supremacy of rational enquiry into an attainable good.

We can with some reason think that the mainstream of philosophical tradition, until very recently, has unquestioningly followed in the wake of this Platonic change in priorities. It might even be said that philosophy owes its self-definition to Plato's placing it in opposition to poetry. Arthur Danto, writing recently on these issues, makes the following observation:

> [Plato's attack on the arts] consists ... in rationalizing art, so that reason bit by bit colonizes the domain of feelings, the socratic dialogue being a form of dramatic representation in which the substance is reason exhibited as taming reality by absorbing it into concepts. Nietzsche refers to this as 'aesthetic Socratism,' the philosopher having so identified reason with beauty that nothing could be beautiful that is not rational. This, Nietzsche proposes, marks the death of tragedy, which finds a terrible beauty in irrationality.... And ever since this complex aggression, as profound a victory as philosophy has ever known or ever will know, the history of philosophy has alternated between the analytical effort to ephemeralize and hence defuse art, or to allow a degree of validity to art by treating it as doing what philosophy itself does, only uncouthly.   (Danto, *The Philosophical Disenfranchisement of Art*, p. 7)

Plato, we may recall, attacks poetry through the mouthpiece of Socrates in both its Apollinian and Dionysian aspects: he complains that it produces pleasing images without a proper basis in knowledge, and that its emotional pull on the spectators undermines the individual's rationality. Hence Nietzsche's assessment of the impact of Socratic thinking has some plausibility.

2

Aesthetics, Art, and Nature

Introduction to the Issues

We turn in this chapter to some recent writings that explore the relationships between the aesthetic and art and between the aesthetic and nature. Our selected authors work in opposite directions, Noël Carroll complaining that the concept of the aesthetic is too narrow to capture everything that is characteristic of our interest in art, Ronald Hepburn that our conception of the aesthetic is too much moulded by the attempt to characterize art, to the exclusion of looking properly at the aesthetics of nature. There is no contradiction in these two approaches. It can be the case both that our conception of art needs to be improved so as to embrace more than the aesthetic, and that our conception of the aesthetic needs to be improved so as to embrace more than art.

Symptomatic of these problems of scope is the fact that some people working in aesthetics object to that title and would rather call the subject the philosophy of art, while others resist this because they are not interested only in questions that arise concerning art. The pushing together of the concept of art and the concept of the aesthetic (sometimes conceived of as beauty) has a long history. A definitive moment in that history comes in Hegel's *Introductory Lectures on Aesthetics* where we find that the word 'aesthetics' has already (by approximately 1820) 'passed into common language' for the discipline which 'does not treat of beauty in general, but merely of *artistic* beauty'.

Such a discipline labours under the weight of a bundle of assumptions: that whatever is art is so because it has aesthetic value, that beauty is aesthetic value (or one important variety of it), and that any account of this aesthetic value must show why art in particular has value. Of course, there is beauty outside art, as even Hegel admits, but for aesthetics as traditionally conceived there is point in examining beauty only if we know from the outset that our understanding of art is to be enriched. In setting themselves the task of chipping away at this monolithic conception of art as aesthetic and the aesthetic as art, the authors in this chapter are hoping for a revision in the way aesthetics most traditionally conceives itself.

Introduction to Carroll

This essay by Noël Carroll was first published in 1986 and, written in the clear, argumentative style characteristic of recent analytical philosophy, it offers no problems of interpretation comparable with those we encountered in Chapter 1. Carroll is, at the time of writing, Professor of Philosophy at Temple University, Philadelphia. He is the author of the collection of essays *Beyond Aesthetics* (2001), from which this piece is taken, and of *Philosophy of Art: An Introduction* (1999).

The important work done in this piece is to set *art* and *the aesthetic* apart from one another. The writers Carroll discusses are representative of a long-lived and subtly influential view that the defining characteristic of art works is their aesthetic interest for us, that art works are designed to arouse aesthetic experiences or responses, and that works that are not so designed or that do not successfully arouse aesthetic experiences are either unsuccessful as art or are not art at all.

Understanding the aesthetic as definitive of art in this way has the corollary that one can discriminate, from among purported works of art, which are truly art and which are not. Carroll uses the famous examples from Marcel Duchamp: *Fountain*, the much-discussed signed urinal exhibited in 1917, and *L. H. O. O. Q.* and *L. H. O. O. Q. Shaved* (which are, respectively, the image of the Mona Lisa with a moustache added, and the same image with no moustache). It is easy to decry something as 'not really art', if one makes certain assumptions about what is definitive of art. Most readers will be able to supply other examples, perhaps more recent, of works that are broadly speaking 'conceptual', or at least not obviously designed for aesthetic response, and which have aroused this kind of controversy.

Carroll argues that if art does not have the sole function of bringing about aesthetic experiences, then works that do not seem to function in this way need not be excluded from the category of art. More positively, he argues that our engagement with art is frequently characterized by the task of interpretation, which can be 'gamelike' or a kind of 'play' for the observer or consumer of art.

Noël Carroll, 'Art and Interaction'

Ideas of the aesthetic figure largely in two crucial areas of debate in the philosophy of art. On the one hand, *the aesthetic* often plays a definitive role in characterizations of our responses to or interactions with artworks. That is, what is thought to be distinctive about our commerce with artworks is that these encounters are marked by aesthetic experiences, aesthetic judgments, aesthetic perceptions, and so forth. Furthermore, the use of aesthetic terminology in such accounts of our interactions with artworks is, most essentially, "experiential" or "perceptual" where those terms are generally understood by contrast to responses mediated by the application of concepts or reasoning.

Second, notions of the aesthetic are also mobilized in theories of the nature of art objects; the artwork, it is claimed, is an artifact designed to bring about aesthetic experiences and aesthetic perceptions, or to engender aesthetic attitudes, or to engage aesthetic faculties, et cetera. Thus, these two claims – that aesthetic responses distinguish our responses to art, and that art objects can be defined in terms of the aesthetic – though ostensibly independent, can, nevertheless, be connected by means of a neat, commonsensical approach that holds that what an object is can be captured through an account of its function. The art object is something designed to provoke a certain form of response, a certain type of interaction. The canonical interaction with art involves the aesthetic (however that is to be characterized). So the artwork is an object designed with the function of engendering aesthetic experiences, perceptions, attitudes, and so forth.

The purpose of this essay is to dispute both the thesis that aesthetic responses are definitive of our responses to artworks and the thesis that art is to be characterized exclusively in terms of the promotion of aesthetic responses. It will be argued against the first thesis that many of our entrenched forms of interaction with artworks – what may be neutrally designated as our art responses or art experiences – are not aesthetic in nature nor are they reducible to aesthetic responses or experiences. The argument here proceeds by enumerating and describing several of our nonaesthetic though eminently characteristic responses to art objects. That is, along with doing things like attending to the *brittleness* of a piece of choreography – a paradigmatic aesthetic response – we also contemplate artworks with an eye to discerning latent meanings and structures, and to determining the significance of an artwork in its art historical context. These art responses, often interpretive in nature, are, it will be claimed, as central as, and certainly no less privileged than, aesthetic responses in regard to our interactions with artworks.[1] Moreover, if an expanded view of the art response is defensible, then our concept of art, especially when construed functionally, must be broadened to countenance as art objects that are designed to promote characteristically appropriate art responses or art experiences distinct from aesthetic responses. And this, in turn, has consequences for attempts by theorists, armed with aesthetic definitions of art, who wish to exclude such objects as Duchamp's *Fountain* from the order of art.

This essay is motivated by a recent development in the philosophy of art, namely the popularity of aesthetic definitions of art. As is well known, the antidefinitional stance of post-World War II philosophers of art provoked a reaction formation called the Institutional Theory of Art.[2] Dissatisfaction with the Institutional Theory has, in turn, elicited several countermoves of which the aesthetic definition of art is one species. For though the Institutional Theory has been judged wanting in numerous respects, it has re-established the respectability of attempts to define art.

Examples of this development include articles such as "An Aesthetic Definition of Art" by Monroe Beardsley and "Toward an Aesthetic Account of the Nature of Art" by William Tolhurst.[3] These writers attempt to construct theories that discriminate between

---

[1]   Though throughout this essay I maintain that there is a strong tendency among philosophers of art to deploy notions of the aesthetic as definitive of our interactions with art, not all philosophers find the aesthetic to be a congenial idea. George Dickie, for example, challenges its use in his classic "The Myth of Aesthetic Attitude," in *American Philosophical Quarterly* 1:1 (Jan., 1964). Dickie challenges proponents of the aesthetic to find a plausible differentia between this concept as a prefix for experiences of art versus ordinary experiences. I am sympathetic with Dickie's reservations as well as with objections that worry about whether the usage of such notions as disinterest and freedom in characterizations of the aesthetic is ultimately coherent. However, for the purposes of this paper, I have not dwelt on these problems with aesthetic theories of art but rather, in a manner of speaking, have attempted to give the devil his due by generally proceeding as if such notions as disinterest could be rendered intelligibly while also wondering whether even with this concession aesthetic theories of art are acceptable. I am prone, especially in regard to what I later call "affect-oriented" characterizations, to think that the notion of the aesthetic is mythic. On the other hand, where the notion of aesthetic experiences is what I label above as "content-oriented," I think there is no problem in speaking of aesthetic experience, that is, of the experience of aesthetic and/or expressive qualities.

[2]   For an example of the anti-definitionalist stance, see Morris Weitz, "The Role of Theory in Aesthetics," *The Journal of Aesthetics and Art Criticism* 15:1 (Fall 1956). For an example of an Institutional Theory, see George Dickie, *Art and the Aesthetic: An Institutional Analysis* (Cornell University Press, 1974).

[3]   Monroe Beardsley, "An Aesthetic Definition of Art," in *What is Art?*, ed. Hugh Curtler (New York, 1983); W. Tolhurst, "Toward an Aesthetic Account of the Nature of Art," *The Journal of Aesthetics and Art Criticism* 42:3 (Spring 1984). Also, Harold Osborne's "What is a Work of Art?" *British Journal of Aesthetics* 21 (1981) represents another attempt at defining art in terms of aesthetic experience.

art and nonart by reference to aesthetic experience, which is taken as the canonical mode of our interaction with artworks. In this, I think that these authors are symptomatic of the tendency within much contemporary philosophy of art to equate the art experience with the aesthetic experience. Given this propensity, both articles define an artwork as an object produced with the intended function of fostering aesthetic experiences. Beardsley's statement of the theory is "An artwork is something produced with the intention of giving it the capacity to satisfy the aesthetic interest."[4] To have an aesthetic interest in an object, for Beardsley, is to have an interest in the aesthetic character of experience that a given object affords. Simply put, our aesthetic interest in an object is predicated on the possibility of our deriving aesthetic experiences from the object.

Tolhurst's statement of the aesthetic theory of art is more complex. As a rough indication of the way in which an aesthetic definition might go, Tolhurst writes

> A thing, x, is a work of art if and only if, there is a person, y, such that 1) y believed that x could serve as an object of (positive) aesthetic experiences, 2) y wanted x to serve as an object of (positive) aesthetic experiences, and 3) y's belief and desire caused y (in a certain characteristic way) to produce x, to create x, or to place x where x is, etc.[5]

Both Beardsley and Tolhurst are involved in the attempt to limit the range of things we shall count as art. Broadly speaking, this attempt is carried out by two maneuvers: invoking the condition that the producer of a putative artwork had an appropriate intention, which, in turn, is specified in terms of a plan to afford aesthetic experience. Given this twofold requirement, Beardsley believes that he can deny the status of art to such things as Edward T. Cone's "Poème symphonique" – a composition that involves one hundred metronomes running down – and to Duchamp's *Fountain*. In a similar gesture, Tolhurst thinks that Duchamp's *L.H.O.O.Q.* and *L.H.O.O.Q. Shaved* are not art. With such cases, Beardsley and Tolhurst believe that the artists could not possibly have been motivated by the intention of promoting aesthetic experience.

For the purposes of this essay I shall put the issue of the intentional component of the aesthetic theory of art somewhat to one side. I am more interested in the job that the concept of aesthetic experience is

---

[4] Beardsley, p. 21.
[5] Tolhurst, p. 265.

c → supposed to perform in the theories. It must be said that the commonsense approach of the aesthetic theory of art is very attractive. It conceives of the artwork as an object designed with a function, a function, moreover, that is connected with what a spectator can get out of an artwork in virtue of its facilitating or promoting certain types of responses or interactions. As a theory of art, it has the strength of acknowledging the mutual importance of the artist, the object, and the audience; it does not emphasize one element of the matrix of art over others in the manner of a Croce or a Collingwood with their preoccupations with the artist and his expression of intuitions.

d → Also, this type of theory puts its proponent in a strong position to systematically tackle further questions in the philosophy of art, such as what is the value of art and why are we interested in seeking out artworks? Clearly, the aesthetic theorist of art can answer that the value of art and the interest we have in pursuing artworks reside in whatever positive benefit there is in having the types of experiences and responses that art objects are designed to promote.

On the other hand, the delimitation of the relevant art experience to the aesthetic experience – the maneuver that gives the aesthetic theory of art much of its exclusionary thrust – appears to me to be a liability. The aesthetic definition of art privileges aesthetic experience to the exclusion of other nonaesthetic forms of interaction that the art object can be designed to promote. I shall argue that there is no reason for the aesthetic experience to be privileged in this way insofar as it seems to me that we cannot rule out other, nonaesthetic forms of response to art as illegitimate on the grounds that they are not aesthetic responses. Indeed, when discussing these other responses to works of art, I think I will be able to show that denying the status of art to such works as *L.H.O.O.Q.* and "Poème symphonique" is a mistake.

Before charting several forms of nonaesthetic responses to art, it will be helpful to clarify the notion of an aesthetic response to art. One problem here is that there are a number of different, ostensibly nonequivalent characterizations available. Let a sample suffice to initiate the discussion. Tolhurst intentionally refrains from characterizing aesthetic experience, though Beardsley, of course, has offered a number of accounts. Writing on aesthetic enjoyment, which as I take it is nothing but positive aesthetic experience, Beardsley has claimed that

> Aesthetic enjoyment is (by definition) the kind of enjoyment we obtain from the apprehension of a qualitatively diverse segment of the phenomenal field insofar as the discriminable parts are

unified into something of a whole that has a character (that is, regional qualities) of its own.[6]

[e] → This account offers what might be thought of as a content-oriented characterization of positive aesthetic experience. It is "content-oriented" because it stresses the properties of the object, here "regional qualities," to which attention is directed. This approach corresponds to J. O. Urmson's notion that what marks an aesthetic reaction is its attention to how things look and feel especially in terms of qualities such as appearing spacious, swift, strong, mournful, cheerful, and so on.[7] I will take it that one major variation of the aesthetic response approach – the content-oriented approach – designates a response as aesthetic when it takes as its focus the aesthetic or expressive or "qualitative" appearances of the object. I will argue that this leaves us with a particularly impoverished view of our customary reaction to art that has extremely problematic consequences for any theorist who would want to use aesthetic experience as definitive of the function, vis-à-vis the spectators' reaction, which artworks are designed to produce.

[f] → Beardsley has not always characterized aesthetic experience primarily by reference to content. Often he attempts to characterize aesthetic experience through the analysis of its internal-feeling-structure, which we might call an affect-oriented account of aesthetic experience. In recent essays, Beardsley has placed more weight than the previous quotation did on the affective features of aesthetic experience. In a formal statement of his criteria for aesthetic experience, one mirrored informally in *What is Art?*, Beardsley says that an experience has an aesthetic character if it has the first of the following features and at least three of the others. For Beardsley, the five relevant features of aesthetic experience are: object directedness, felt freedom, detached affect, active discovery, and wholeness, that is, a sense of integration as a person.[8] Apart from "active discovery," these criteria allude to affective attributes of experience. And even in the case of "active discovery" the criterion is a case of both content-oriented and affect-oriented considerations, for though said discoveries are achieved through seeing connections between percepts and meanings, such insights are to be accompanied by a sense of intelligibility.

[6]   Monroe Beardsley, "The Discrimination of Aesthetic Enjoyment," in *The Aesthetic Point of View*, ed. Michael Wreen and Donald Callen (Cornell University Press, 1982), p. 42.
[7]   J. O. Urmson, "What Makes a Situation Aesthetic," *Art and Philosophy*, ed. W. E. Kennick (New York, 1979), pp. 395–7.
[8]   Monroe Beardsley, "Aesthetic Experience," *The Aesthetic Point of View*, pp. 288–9.

There are many problems with this characterization of aesthetic experience. First, it is possible that either there is no experience that meets this account or, if this account can be read in a way that grants that some experiences meet it, then other-than-aesthetic experiences, for example, solving theorems in nonapplied mathematics, may also meet it. But, most important, it is clear that many of our typical responses to art will, under a rigorous reading of Beardsley's formula, not stand up as aesthetic, with the consequence that objects that support only certain typical but nonaesthetic interactions with art will not count as art. Of course, the desiderata canvassed in what I've called the content-approach and the predominantly affect-oriented approach do not reflect every belief about aesthetic experience found in the tradition; other beliefs will be mentioned in the ensuing discussion of nonaesthetic responses to art. However, frequent return to these two models of the aesthetic response will be useful in discussing typical nonaesthetic interactions with art.

g⟶ A great many of our typical, nonaesthetic responses to art can be grouped under the label of interpretation. Artists often include, imply, or suggest meanings in their creations, meanings and themes that are oblique and that the audience works at discovering. Mallarmé wrote

> To actually name an object is to suppress three-quarters of the sense of enjoyment of a poem, which consists in the delight of guessing one stage at a time: to *suggest* the object, that is the poet's dream.... There must always be a sense of the enigmatic in poetry, and that is the aim of literature.

And in a similar vein, John Updike says "I think books should have secrets as a bonus for the sensitive reader." These statements are by writers but there are artists in every artform who strive to incorporate oblique or hidden meanings or themes, and nonobvious adumbrations of the oblique themes in their work.[9] In Peter Hutchinson's interpretation of *Tonio Kroger*, we find an example of an oblique theme, that of the split personality, and of an adumbration thereof, the use of the character's name to convey, in a camouflaged way, extra inflection concerning the nature of the split personality. Hutchinson writes

---

[9] The practice of planting oblique meanings and themes in artworks that the audience is meant to discover occurs to varying degrees in different artforms, perhaps most frequently in literature and least frequently in orchestral music. But it has examples in every artform.

In *Tonio Kroger*, Mann's most famous early story, the eponymous hero bears features of two distinct qualities in his name: those of his artistic mother, and the more somber ones of his self-controlled father. It is his mother from whom Tonio has inherited his creative powers – she comes from "the South," a land lacking in self-discipline but rich in self-expression, and its qualities are symbolized in his Christian name (with its clear Italian ring). His father, on the other hand, the upright Northerner, the practical man of common sense and sound business acumen, bears a name suggestive of dullness and solidity (it derives from the Middle Low German 'Kroger,' a publican). The very sound of each component reinforces those ideas and explains the split in Tonio's character, the major theme of this Novelle.[10]

The presence of such obliquely presented themes and adumbrations occurs frequently enough, especially in certain genres, that audiences customarily search for hidden meanings that are likely to have been implanted in the artwork. Though Hutchinson's interpretation might be thought of as "professional," I think that it is reflective of one central way in which we, in general, have been trained to think, talk, and in short, respond to art. This training began when we were first initiated into the world of art in our earliest literature and art appreciation classes. Moreover, we have every reason to believe that our training in this matter supplies dependable guidelines for appropriate art responses since our early training is reinforced by the evident preoccupation with oblique meanings found in discussions of art by critics, scholars, and connoisseurs in newspapers, journals, and learned treatises. And clearly our training and behavior regarding the search for hidden meanings are not beside the point since artists, steeped in the same hermeneutical traditions that spectators practice, have often put oblique meanings in their works precisely so that we, excited by the challenge, exercise our skill and ingenuity, our powers of observation, association, and synthesis in order to discover oblique themes and to trace their complex adumbrations.

With certain forms of interpretation, the spectator's relation to the artwork is gamelike. The spectator has a goal, to find a hidden or oblique theme (or an oblique adumbration of one), which goal the spectator pursues by using a range of hermeneutical strategies, which, in turn, place certain epistemological constraints on his or her activity. This interpretive play is something we have been trained in since grammar school, and it is a practice that is amplified and publicly

[10]   Peter Hutchinson, *Games Authors Play* (London, 1983), p. 80.

endorsed by the criticism we read. The obliqueness of the artist's presentation of a theme confronts the audience with an obstacle that the audience voluntarily elects to overcome. How the artist plants this theme and how the audience goes about discovering it – in terms of distinctive forms of reasoning and observation – are primarily determined by precedent and tradition, though, of course, the tradition allows for innovation both in the area of artmaking and of interpretation. Within this gamelike practice, when we discover a hidden theme we have achieved a success, and we are prone, all things being equal, to regard our activity as rewarding insofar as the artwork has enabled us to apply our skills to a worthy, that is, challenging, object. But this type of interpretive play, though characteristic of our interaction with artworks, and rewarding, exemplifies neither the content-oriented form, nor the affect-oriented form of aesthetic response.

Though so far I have only spoken of the interpretation of obliquely presented meanings, it should be noted that our interpretive, nonaesthetic responses also include the discernment of latent structures. That is, when we contemplate art, we often have as a goal, upon which we may expend great effort, figuring out the way in which a given painting or musical composition works. In the presence of an artwork, we characteristically set ourselves to finding out what its structure is as well as often asking the reason for its being structured that way. Or, if we sense that an artwork has a certain effect, for example, the impression of the recession of the central figure in Malevich's *Black Quadrilateral*, we examine the formal arrangement and principles that bring this effect about.[11] Again, this is something we have been trained to do and something that pervades the discussion of art in both informal and professional conversation. Indeed, some radical formalists might hold that understanding how a work works is the only legitimate interest we should have in art and the only criterion of whether our response to art is appropriate. This seems an unduly narrow recommendation given art as we know it. My claim is only that identifying the structure or structures of a work – seeing how it works – is, like the identification of a hidden meaning, one criterion of a successful interaction with art. Moreover, this form of interaction is not "aesthetic," as that is normally construed, but it should not, for that reason, be disregarded as a characteristic and appropriate mode of participating with artworks.

---

[11] For a reproduction of *Black Quadrilateral* see *The Russian Avant-Garde: The George Costakis Collection*, ed. Angelica Zander Rudenstine (New York, 1981), p. 256.

So far two types of interpretive play have been cited as examples of characteristic responses to art that tend to be overlooked when philosophers of art accord a privileged position to aesthetic responses as the canonical model of our interaction with art. And if interpretation is ignored as an appropriate art response while only aesthetic experience is so countenanced, and if art is identified in relation to the promotion of appropriate responses, then objects devoted exclusively to engendering interpretive play will be artistically disenfranchised. But, of course, one may wonder whether it is correct to claim, as I have, that the philosophers of art tend to ignore the importance of interpretation. For much of the literature in the field concerns issues of interpretation. This, admittedly, is true in one sense. However, it must be added that the attention lavished on interpretation in the literature is not focused on interpretive play as a characteristic form of the experience of interacting with artworks but rather revolves around epistemological problems, for example, are artist's intentions admissible evidence; can interpretations be true or are they merely plausible; and so forth. This epistemological focus, moreover, tends to take critical argument as its subject matter. Thus, the fact that philosophers have such epistemological interests in interpretation does not vitiate the point that interpretive play is an ingredient in our characteristic experience of artworks which philosophers, by privileging the aesthetic, have effectively bracketed from the art experience proper. Indeed, within the philosophical tradition, the kind of intellective responses I have cited under the rubric of interpretation are not part of the experience, proper, of art. Hume, for example, tells us that though good sense is necessary for the correct functioning of taste, it is not part of taste.[12] Rather, the picture he suggests is that the prior operation of the understanding, engaged in doing things like identifying the purpose and related structure of the artwork, puts us in a position to undergo, subsequently, the central experience of the work, namely, for Hume, a feeling of pleasure.

This citation of Hume provides us with one reason why philosophers are tempted to exclude interpretive play from the art experience proper. The essential experience of art, for them, is a matter of feeling pleasure either of the undifferentiated Humean sort or of the disinterested Kantian variety. Interpretive activity, on the other hand, it might be said, has no obvious connection with pleasure. But I'm not so sure of this.

---

[12]   David Hume, "Of the Standard of Taste," *Art and Philosophy*, p. 495. This view of Hume in regard to intellection is discussed in my "Hume's Standard of Taste," *The Journal of Aesthetics and Art Criticism* 43:2 (Winter 1984).

I have asserted that art spectatorship is a practice, a practice linked with other practices, such as artmaking, within the institution of the artworld. I follow MacIntyre when he writes that

> By a "practice" I am going to mean any coherent and complex form of socially established cooperative human activity through which goods internal to that form of activity are realized in trying to achieve those standards of excellence which are appropriate to, and partially definitive of, that form of activity, with the result that human powers to achieve excellence, and human conceptions of the ends and goods involved, are systematically extended.[13]

Within the practice of art spectatorship, among the goals of the enterprise, we find the making of interpretations of various sorts. Finding hidden meanings and latent structures are goods internal to the activity of art spectatorship. Pursuit of these goals in our encounters with artworks occupies large parts of our experience of artworks. Our interpretations can succeed or fail. They can be mundane or excellent. When our interpretations succeed, we derive the satisfaction that comes from the achievement of a goal against an established standard of excellence. That is, satisfaction is connected with success, within the practice of art spectatorship, when we are able to detect a latent theme or form in an artwork. Moreover, I see no reason to deny that this type of satisfaction is a type of pleasure even though it differs from the type of pleasurable sensation, or thrill, or beauteous rapture that theorists often appear to have in mind when speaking of aesthetic experience. The exercise of the skills of art spectatorship is its own reward within our practice. This is not to say that interpretive play is the only source of pleasure, but only that it is a source of pleasure. Thus, the worry that interpretive play is remote from pleasure should supply no grounds for excluding interpretive play from our characterization of the art experience proper.

Apart from the argument that interpretive play is not connected with pleasure, there may be other motives behind the tendency not to include interpretive play in the account of the art experience proper. One concern might be that interpretive play is not essential or fundamental to the art experience because it fails to differentiate the interaction with art from other experiences. In this context, the putative virtue of the notion of the aesthetic experience of art is that it can say how our experiences of art differ from other types of experience. The

---

13   Alasdair MacIntyre, *After Virtue* (University of Notre Dame Press, 1981), p. 175.

proponent of the aesthetic experience approach might argue that the interpretive play I refer to regarding the art response is not different in kind from that activity in which a cryptographer indulges.

Of course, it is not clear that aesthetic-experience accounts can do the differentiating work they are supposed to do. First, those versions of aesthetic experience that rely on notions of detachment and disinterest may just be implausible. Second, even an account as detailed as Beardsley's affect-oriented one doesn't differentiate the aesthetic experience of art from all other activities. For example, assuming that there are acts of disinterested attention, Beardsley's affect-oriented account might not differentiate aesthetic experience from the mathematician's experience of solving a problem that is divorced from practical application. So if the argument against including interpretive play in our account of the art experience is that interpretive play does not differentiate that experience from other kinds whereas the notion of aesthetic experience does, then we can say that neither of the putatively competing accounts succeeds at the task of essentially differentiating the art experience. Thus, essentially differentiating the art experience from others might not be a desideratum in our characterizations of it.

I suspect that since art evolved over a long period of time and through the interactions of many different cultures, it may support a plurality of interests such that the art experience is comprised of a plurality of activities of which having aesthetic experiences of some sort is one, while engaging in interpretive play is another. There are undoubtedly more activities than only these two. Furthermore, it may be the case that none of the multiple types of interactions that comprise the art experience is unique to encounters with art. Of course, this might be granted at the same time that the proponent of the aesthetic theory urges that nevertheless aesthetic experience is a necessary component of any experience of art whereas other responses, like interpretive play, are not. At the point, the aesthetic theorist will have to show that aesthetic experience is such a necessary component. And, at least for those who hold an aesthetic definition of art, that will not be easy to do without begging the question. Suppose my counterexample to the notion that aesthetic experience is a necessary component of every art experience is Duchamp's *Fountain*. I note that it is an object placed in a situation such that it has an oblique significance that supports a great deal of interpretive play. But it does not appear to promote the kinds of response that theorists call aesthetic. So it affords an art experience that is not an aesthetic one. Moreover, the interpretive play available in contemplating *Fountain* involves an art experience of a very high degree of intensity for its kind. The aesthetic theorist can attempt to block this counterexample by saying that *Fountain* is not an artwork and that an interpretive response to it, therefore, is not even an experience of art. But one can only do this by asserting that aesthetic experience is definitive of art and of what can be experienced as art. Yet that begs the question insofar as it presupposes that a work designed to provoke and promote interpretive play cannot be art because interpretive play is not a criterion of the kind of experience appropriate to art.

One might argue that interpretive play is not fundamental to the art experience in the sense that it is not the original purpose for which the works we call art were created. But this faces problems from two directions. First, hermeneutics has been around for a long time and may even predate our notion of taste. Second, if one makes this argument with aesthetic experience in mind, can we be so certain that promoting aesthetic experience was the original purpose for which many of the more historically remote objects we call art were made? Moreover, if it is claimed that many of the ancient or medieval artifacts we call art at least had a potentially aesthetic dimension, it must be acknowledged that most of the self-same objects also possessed a symbolizing dimension that invited interpretive play.

Perhaps it will be argued that interpretive play is inappropriate to the art response proper. This tack seems to me an implausible one since all the evidence – our training in art appreciation and the behavior of the majority of our leading connoisseurs – points in the direction of suggesting that interpretative play is one of the central and esteemed modes of the practice of art spectatorship. Indeed, how would one go about showing that a behavior as deeply entrenched and as widely indulged in a practice as interpretive play in art spectatorship is inappropriate to the practice? Practices are human activities constituted by traditionally evolved purposes and ways of satisfying those purposes. The active traditions of such practices determine what is appropriate to a practice both in terms of the ends and means of the practice. Thus, in art, the continuing tradition of interpretation establishes the appropriateness of the kinds of hermeneutical responses that we have been discussing.

One might try to show the inappropriateness of interpretive play as an art response by arguing that it interferes with some deeper goal of the practice of art. But what could that be? Perceiving aesthetic properties might be one candidate. However, in some cases interpretive play may, in fact, enhance the perception of aesthetic qualities. Nor does this suggest that interpretive play is subservient to the goal of perceiving qualities. For in some further instances, perceiving qualities may be valuable for the way in which it enables the discovery of a richer interpretation, while in other cases the interpretive play and the aesthetic response may remain independent of one another, supplying spectators with separate focii of interest in the work. Of course, proponents of the aesthetic approach may assert that theirs is the only proper response to art, but that, as I have, I hope, shown, is only an assertion.

I think that it is obvious that the types of activities I have used, so far, to exemplify interpretive play diverge from what was earlier called the content-oriented version of the aesthetic approach. There the notion was that an aesthetic response to art was one that was directed at the qualitative features of the object, such as its perceptible or expressive features. And though interpretation may, in different ways, sometimes be involved with aesthetic responses, it should be clear that interpretive play is not equivalent to aesthetic or expressive apprehension both because it is not evident that interpretation is an element in all instances of aesthetic perception, and because the objects of interpretive play extend beyond aesthetic and expressive qualities to themes and their adumbrations, and to structures and their complications.

But what about the affect-oriented variant of the aesthetic approach? First, it should be noted that many of the candidates in this area rely centrally on a characterization of aesthetic experience that rests on notions such as disinterested pleasure or detachment from practical interest. But one may successfully engage in interpretive play without being devoid of practical interest – one may be a critic whose reputation has been built on clever interpretations. So interpretive play differs from aesthetic experience as the latter is typically explicated.

But the Beardsleyan affect-oriented account of aesthetic experience is more detailed than many of its predecessors and it seems to have room for interpretive play. That is, in later versions of his account of aesthetic experience, Beardsley includes a new feature to the characterization of aesthetic experience – namely, active discovery – which is not included in previous accounts, either his own or, to my knowledge, those of others. By the inclusion of active discovery, it may be felt that interpretive play has been successfully wedded to aesthetic experience.

I disagree. For even in Beardsley's new variant, a response still requires much more than active discovery to amount to an aesthetic experience. It would also have to be at least object-directed as well as meeting two of the following three criteria: afford a sense of felt freedom, detached affect, or a sense of wholeness. But surely we could, via interpretive play, engage in active discovery without felt freedom – that is, the absence of antecedent concerns – and without detached affect – that is, emotional distance. Imagine a Marxist literary critic, pressed by a deadline to finish her paper on the hidden reactionary meaning of a Balzac novel. Nor does it seem likely that interpretive play often correlates with Beardsley's criterion of wholeness, that is, a sense of integration as a person. Indeed, I suspect that this is a rather unusual concomitant to expect of many interactions with art. And, furthermore, many instances of interpretive play may not meet the requirement of object directedness. A work like Duchamp's *Fountain* surely supports a great amount of interpretive play although most, if not all, of this can be derived from attention to the art historical context in which it was placed rather than to the object itself.

Even Beardsley's account of the element of active discovery, as it is involved in the art response, has an affective component. For under the rubric of active discovery, he not only has in mind that we actively make connections but that this be accompanied by a feeling of intelligibility. One is uncertain here whether this feeling of intelligibility is simply seeing a connection or whether it is something more. If the former, then it is true of every interpretive insight. But if it is the latter, which is a more likely reading given Beardsley's overall program, I am not sure that a sense of intelligibility accompanies every interpretive insight. I may come to realize that *The Turn of the Screw* is structured to support at least two opposed interpretations but that doesn't result in a sense of intelligibility.

What these considerations are meant to show is that even with the inclusion of active discovery in Beardsley's formula, interpretive play remains a mode of response to art that is independent of and not subsumable under aesthetic experience. Often, instances of interpretive play will not amount to full-blown, Beardsleyan-type aesthetic experiences because they will not score appreciably in terms of the criteria he requires over and above active discovery. And it may also be the case that instances of interpretive play may not even count as examples of Beardsleyan active discovery because they will not result in the appropriate sense of intelligibility.

But interpretive play nevertheless still remains a characteristic form of interaction with artworks. And, *pace* aesthetic theorists of art, I think that if we encounter an object designed to support interpretive play, even though it affords no aesthetic experience or aesthetic perception, then we have *a* reason to believe it is an artwork. Of course, an aesthetic theorist might try to solve this problem by saying that interpretive play, sans any particular affect or perceptual focus, is a sufficient condition for calling a response "aesthetic."

However, this move involves abandoning not only the letter but also the spirit of the aesthetic approach, for the tradition has always used the idea of the "aesthetic" to single out a dimension of interaction with objects that is bound up with perceptual experience, affective experience, or a combination thereof. In short, to assimilate interpretive play as a mode of aesthetic experience misses the point of what people were trying to get at by use of the notion of the "aesthetic."

One key feature of the notion of the aesthetic, mentioned by Beardsley and others,[14] is object directedness. In this light, having aesthetic experiences or aesthetic perceptions is, in large measure, a matter of focusing our attention on the artwork that stands before us. The implicit picture of spectatorship that this approach suggests is of an audience consuming artworks atomistically, one at a time, going from one monadic art response to the next. But this hardly squares with the way in which those who attend to art with any regularity or dedication either respond to or have been trained to respond to art. Art – both in the aspect of its creation and its appreciation – is a combination of internally linked practices, which, to simplify, we may refer to as a single practice. Like any practice,[15] art involves not only a relationship between present practitioners but a relationship with the past. Artmaking and artgoing are connected with traditions. As artgoers we are not only interested in the artwork as a discrete object before us – the possible occasion for an aesthetic experience – but also as an object that has a place in the tradition. Entering the practice of art, even as an artgoer, is to enter a tradition, to become apprised of it, to be concerned about it, and to become interested in its history and its ongoing development. Thus, a characteristic response to art, predictably enough, is, given an artwork or a series of artworks, to strive to figure out and to situate their place within the tradition, or within the historical development and/or tradition of a specific art form or genre. This implies that important aspects of our interaction with artworks are not, strictly speaking, object directed, but are devoted to concerns with issues outside the object. We don't concentrate on the object in splendid isolation: our attention fans out to enable us to see the place of the art object within a larger, historical constellation of objects. Nor is this attending to the historical context of the object undertaken to enhance what would be traditionally construed as our aesthetic experience. Rather, our wider ambit of attention is motivated by the art appreciator's interest in the tradition

---

[14] Jerome Stolnitz, "The Aesthetic Attitude," *Introductory Readings in Aesthetics*, ed. John Hospers (New York, 1969), pp. 17–27.
[15] MacIntyre, p. 181.

at large. Yet this deflection of attention from the object is not an aesthetic aberration. It is part of what is involved with entering a practice with a living tradition.

To be interested in the tradition at large is to be interested in its development and in the various moves and countermoves that comprise that development. For example, encountering one of Morris Louis's *Unfurleds*, we may remark upon the way in which it works out a problematic of the practice of painting initiated by the concern of Fauvists and Cubists with flatness. The painting interests us not only for whatever aesthetic perceptions it might promote, but also for the way in which it intervenes in an ongoing painterly dialectic about flatness. To be concerned with the significance of the painting within the tradition of modern art is not inappropriate, but rather is a characteristic response of an appreciator who has entered the practice of art. From one artwork to the next, we consider the way in which a new work may expand upon the dialectic or problematic present in earlier works. Or, a later work may, for example, amplify the technical means at the disposal of a given artform for the pursuit of its already established goals. So we may view a film such as Griffith's *The Birth of a Nation* as the perfection of primitive film's commitment to narration. Such an interest in *The Birth of a Nation* is neither the viewpoint of an antiquarian, a filmmaker, or a film specialist. It is rather the response of any film appreciator who has entered the practice of film spectatorship.

Confronted with a new artwork, we may scrutinize it with an eye to isolating the ways in which it expands upon an existing artworld dialectic, solves a problem that vexed previous artists, seizes upon a hitherto unexpected possibility of the tradition, or amplifies the formal means of an artform in terms of the artform's already established pursuits. But a new artwork may also stand to the tradition by way of making a revolutionary break with the past. A new artwork may emphasize possibilities not only present in, but actually repressed by, preceding styles; it may introduce a new problematic; it may repudiate the forms or values of previous art. When Tristan Tzara composed poems by randomly drawing snippets of words from a hat, he was repudiating the Romantic poet's valorization of expression, just as the Romantic poet had repudiated earlier poet's valorization of the representation of the external world in favor of a new emphasis on the internal, subjective world. Tzara's act wasn't random; it made perfect sense in the ongoing dialogue of art history. Concerned with the tradition at large, we as spectators review artworks in order to detect the tensions or conflicts between artistic generations, styles, and programs. We interpret stylistic choices and gambits as repudiations and gestures of rejection by later artworks of earlier ones. This is often much like the interpretation of a hidden meaning; however, it requires attention outside the work to its art historical context. The significance we identify is not so much one hidden in the work as one that emerges when we consider the work against the backdrop of contesting styles and movements. Call it the dramatic meaning of the artwork. But as participants in a tradition, we are legitimately interested in its historical development and especially in its dramatic unfolding. Recognizing the dramatic significance of an artwork as it plays the role of antagonist or protagonist on the stage of art history is not incidental to our interest in art but is an essential element of immersing ourselves in the tradition. Following the conflicts and tensions within the development of art history is as central a component of the practice of art spectatorship as is having aesthetic experiences.

The "other directed," as opposed to the "object directed," interpretive play we characteristically mobilize when interacting with art takes other appropriate forms than those of detecting stylistic amplifications and repudiations. For example, we may wish to contemplate lines of influence or consider changes of direction in the careers of major artists. These concerns as well are grounded in our interests, as participants, in an evolving tradition. However, rather than dwell on these, I would rather turn to a proposal of the way in which the detection of a repudiation – insofar as it is an important and characteristic interpretive response to art – can enable us to short-circuit the dismissal, by aesthetic theorists of art, of such works as Duchamp's *Fountain*.

Let us grant that Duchamp's *Fountain* does not afford an occasion for aesthetic experiences or aesthetic perceptions as those are typically and narrowly construed. Nevertheless, it does propose a rich forum for interpretive play. Its placement in a certain artworld context was designed to be infuriating, on the one hand, and enigmatic and puzzling on the other. Confronted by *Fountain*, or by reports about its placement in a gallery, one asks what it means to put such an object on display at an art exhibition. What is the significance of the object in its particular social setting? And, of course, if we contemplate *Fountain* against the backdrop of art history, we come to realize that it is being used to symbolize a wealth of concerns. We see it to be a contemptuous repudiation of that aspect of fine art that emphasizes craftsmanship in favor of a re-emphasis of the importance of ideas to fine art. One might also gloss it as a gesture that reveals the importance of the nominating process, which George Dickie analyzed, of the institution of the artworld. And so on.

Now my point against aesthetic theorists of art is that even if *Fountain* does not promote an aesthetic interaction, it does promote an interpretive interaction. Moreover, an interpretive interaction, including one of identifying the dialectical significance of a work in the evolution of art history, is as appropriate and as characteristic a response to art as an aesthetic response. Thus, since *Fountain* encourages an appropriate and characteristic art response, we have an important reason to consider it to be a work of art even if it promotes no aesthetic experience.

Aesthetic theorists hold that something is art if it has been designed to function in such a way as to bring about certain appropriate responses to art. This seems to be a reasonable strategy. However, such theorists countenance only aesthetic responses as appropriate. Yet there are other characteristic and appropriate responses to art. And if an object supports such responses to an appreciable degree, then I think that gives us reason to call the object art.

One objection to my reclamation of *Fountain* might be that my model of the standard artgoer is unacceptable. It might be said that someone involved in trying to decipher the moves and countermoves of artists within the historically constituted arena of the artworld is not the standard spectator but a specialist or an art historian. My response to this is to deny that I am speaking of specialists and to urge that I take as my model someone who attends to art on some regular basis, and who is an informed viewer, one who "keeps up" with art without being a professional critic or a professor of art. It is the responses of such spectators that should provide the data for philosophers of art concerned to discuss the experience of art.

On the other hand, I am disquieted by the implicit picture that aesthetic theories project of the standard artgoer. For them, it would appear, the spectator is one who goes from one encounter with art to the next without attempting to connect them. Such a person, for example, might read a novel every year or so, hear a concert occasionally, and go to an art exhibition whenever he or she visits New York. But why should the casual viewer of art be our source for characterizing the art experience? If we want to characterize what it is to respond to baseball appropriately, would we look to the spectator who watches one game every five years? Of course, this is an *ad hominem* attack. Aesthetic theorists don't say that we should use such casual artgoers as our model of the standard spectator. Nevertheless, there is something strange about their standard viewer, namely, that he or she responds to each work of art monadically, savoring each aesthetic experience as a unitary event and not linking that event to a history of previous interactions with artworks. As a matter of fact,

I think this picture is inaccurate. Such an artgoer would be as curious as the dedicated baseball spectator who attends games for whatever excitement he can derive from the contest before him and who does not contemplate the significance of this game in terms of the past and future of the practice of baseball.

The aesthetic theorist may, of course, admit that interpretive responses to the hidden meanings, dramatic significance, and latent structures are appropriate within the practice of spectatorship. But he might add that they are not basic because the practice of art spectatorship would never have gotten off the ground nor would it continue to keep going if artworks did not give rise to aesthetic experiences. Our desire for aesthetic pleasure is the motor that drives the art institution. These are, of course, empirical claims. Possibly aesthetic pleasure is what started it all, although it is equally plausible to think that the pleasure of interpretation could have motivated and does motivate spectatorship. But, in any case, this debate is probably beside the point. For it is likely that both the possibility of aesthetic pleasure and the pleasure of interpretation motivate artgoing, and that interacting with artworks by way of having aesthetic perceptions and making interpretations are both appropriate and equally basic responses to art.

My dominant thesis has been that there are more responses, appropriate to artworks, than aesthetic responses. I have not given an exhaustive catalogue of these but have focused upon various types of interpretive responses. This raises the question of whether or not something like the aesthetic definition of art, amplified to incorporate a more catholic view of the appropriate experiences art avails us, couldn't be reworked in such a way that the result would be an adequate theory of art. The theory might look like this: "A work of art is an object designed to promote, in some appreciable magnitude, the having of aesthetic perceptions, or the making of various types of interpretations, or the undertaking of whatever other appropriate responses are available to spectators."

Attractive as this maneuver is, I doubt it will work. It does not seem to me that any given type of response is necessary to having an appropriate interaction with the artwork. With some artworks, we may only be able to respond in terms of aesthetic perceptions while with others only interpretive responses are possible. Nor, by the way, does any particular response supply us with sufficient grounds for saying something is a work of art. Cars are designed to impart aesthetic perceptions but they are not typically artworks, while we might interpret one artist throwing soup in another artist's face as the repudiation of a tradition without counting the insult as art. Likewise an encoded military document with a hidden message is not art despite the interpretive play it might engender.

At the same time, if we are trying to convince someone that something is an artwork, showing that it is designed to promote one or more characteristic art interactions – whether aesthetic or interpretive – supplies *a* reason to regard the object as art. Suppose we are arguing about whether comic book serials like *The Incredible Hulk*, *Spiderman*, and the *Fantastic Four* are art. And suppose we agree that such exercises do not afford aesthetic experiences of any appreciable magnitude. But, nevertheless, suppose I argue that these comic books contain hidden allegories of the anxieties of adolescence, such that those allegories are of a complexity worthy of decipherment. At that point, we have *a* reason to regard the comics as art, and the burden of proof is on the skeptic who must show that the alleged allegories are either merely fanciful concoctions of mine or are so transparent that it is outlandish to suppose that they warrant a response sophisticated enough to be counted as an interpretation.

Commentary on Carroll

Within the first five paragraphs of this essay we have a clear statement of its author's purpose (see a |→) and the 'tendency within much contemporary philosophy of art' that he sets out to challenge (b |→), a tendency that we may call the 'aesthetic theory' of art.

> Before attacking the aesthetic theory, Carroll concedes that it has certain merits. What are they?

The attractive features of the aesthetic theory should not be so great as to challenge Carroll's own position before he has presented it. On the other hand, there would be little interest in persuading people away from a theory with little to be said for it. At c |→ and d |→ Carroll sketches general advantages of the aesthetic theory: its inclusion of roles for artist, audience and art object, all attaching to a single central function of art, and its potential for giving a clear answer to the question about the value of art.

Given that the issues will be whether aesthetic experience belongs within the function of art, and whether our experience of art can be characterized exclusively in terms of aesthetic experience, we should look for some explanation of what this aesthetic experience is supposed to be.

> What characterization does Carroll offer of aesthetic experience (or aesthetic response)?

At $\boxed{e}\!\!\rightarrow$ and $\boxed{f}\!\!\rightarrow$ Carroll divides accounts of aesthetic experience into two kinds: what he calls 'content-oriented' and 'affect-oriented' characterizations. The first concerns ways in which things that we perceive may appear to us as having some kind of unified quality or character – spacious, swift, strong, mournful are given as examples. The second concerns ways in which we are said to feel when undergoing an aesthetic response to something. Aesthetic experience is an elusive notion, and many writers have avoided giving a characterization of it. Even so, one may question whether the characterizations here, taken from Beardsley, are entirely perspicuous or intuitive.

Perhaps the details of aesthetic experience theory may not matter too much for Carroll's case against it. For his objection is, in effect, to any theory that equates our characteristic experience of art with an affective response to phenomenal properties. Later he characterizes the tradition he is opposing in just such broad terms: 'a dimension of interaction with objects that is bound up with perceptual experience, affective experience, or a combination thereof' (see $\boxed{m}\!\!\rightarrow$). So aesthetic experience, at least roughly, is a way of responding with a kind of feeling, presumably pleasurable, to experiences of seeing and hearing things (and possibly, though less centrally, perceiving them with the other senses).

The onus is now on Carroll to say what element of our experience of art is excluded by the aesthetic experience theorists. The paragraphs marked $\boxed{g}\!\!\rightarrow$, $\boxed{h}\!\!\rightarrow$, and $\boxed{i}\!\!\rightarrow$ give the beginning of his account; later, the paragraph marked $\boxed{n}\!\!\rightarrow$ gives some further considerations. His allegation is first and foremost that aesthetic experience theorists ignore types of response that people commonly, and appropriately, have to art works.

> ## What are the 'typical, nonaesthetic responses to art' that Carroll itemizes?

He mentions interpretation of hidden meanings and oblique themes, identification of structure in a work, and figuring out of an artwork's relation to other works and traditions of art (or 'following the conflicts and tensions within the development of art history'). It is not controversial to claim any of these as typical reponses to art, nor is it meant to be: all are descriptions of ordinary practices that anyone familiar with what Carroll calls 'artgoing' will recognize.

Carroll has located several aspects of understanding or interpreting art. The last, that of locating the object to which we attend within art history, contrasts with a feature of the 'aesthetic experience' tradition that was not mentioned at the outset: that it tends to imagine the observer's confrontation with an art work as 'atomistic', isolated from thoughts or interpretations of other works. This is perhaps suggested by the traditional emphasis on immediate phenomenal qualities and an affective response to them, though it is not clear that any aesthetic experience theory of art must conceive artgoing as consisting of disconnected series of experiences of individual art objects.

In the paragraphs marked $\boxed{q}\!\rightarrow$ and $\boxed{r}\!\rightarrow$ Carroll contrasts two pictures of the 'standard artgoer'. Do you agree with his judgement as to which is more plausible?

A possible rejoinder to Carroll here would be that someone can have a valuable, isolated confrontation with an art object. Some opera-goers are in the auditorium for the first time, some for the first and last time, without knowing or caring about the history of opera. We cannot, admittedly, legislate that their experience of the work is as rewarding as that of the historically aware member of the audience. But nor can we legislate that as a 'casual viewer' their experience of the opera must be shallow and unrewarding. That said, one may agree that Carroll's connection-making artgoer is a more realistic proposition than the one he contrasts it with.

Though in summary fashion, we have now effectively presented most of what Carroll positively argues for in this piece. What has he shown? At various places he states his conclusion more or less as follows: interpretive interaction is as appropriate and as characteristic a response to art as aesthetic interaction (see $\boxed{p}\!\rightarrow$; compare $\boxed{o}\!\rightarrow$, $\boxed{s}\!\rightarrow$, and $\boxed{t}\!\rightarrow$). This seems a balanced and not especially bold conclusion: it implicitly concedes that there is such a thing as aesthetic experience, and that it is appropriate and characteristic of our response to art works. Perhaps, it might be felt, this gives the aesthetic experience theorist some space for a counter-attack.

Carroll imagines some objections to his case on the part of the aesthetic experience theorist. What are they, and does he have effective replies to them?

There are perhaps three chief objections that are worth mentioning:

1   That Carroll's notion of interpretive interaction is not distinctive of interaction with art works, but applies to many other situations as well (see $\boxed{j}\!\rightarrow$).
2   That, while interpretive interaction with art works may be frequent and appropriate, it is not essential to the function of art in the way that aesthetic interaction can be claimed to be (see $\boxed{k}\!\rightarrow$).
3   That what Carroll has described is, after all, just a species of aesthetic interaction rather than something distinct from it.

(1) There are two clear responses to the first objection: it is unclear why the fact that a kind of interaction is undergone with things other than art disqualifies it from a central place in an account of our interaction with art. Secondly, it is unclear that aesthetic responses, however specified, are had exclusively in interaction with art works, rather with other artefacts, nature,

and human beings. So aesthetic interaction is in no way more exclusive to art than Carroll's types of interaction.

(2) Carroll sees this line of objection as begging the question. He gives an example of an art work in which the appropriate forms of interaction do not include that of aesthetic experience – Duchamp's *Fountain*, or some other work. In order to dispute his claim, the aesthetic experience theorist would either have to show that aesthetic interaction is after all an appropriate form of interaction with the work, or that the work is not art. But on what would the second approach be founded? It would be question-begging to say that *Fountain* is not art because it does not give rise to aesthetic experience. But is this the only possible line of thought here?

> Could there be some other, non-question-begging reason for not describing *Fountain* as an art work?

Sometimes it is thought that to be an art work, an object must have resulted from some extraordinary kind of activity, some special exercise of skill and talent, or some especially insightful or emotionally sensitive state of mind. If *Fountain* failed to be an art work by such criteria as these, then the challenge for Carroll would be to find some work which did not fail these criteria, and so was an art work, but to which aesthetic experience was not the most appropriate response. There may or may not be such works. However, note that this argument has now changed the dialectical position. Carroll was asking only whether the theorist who makes the providing of aesthetic experience an essential function of art can give a good reason why *Fountain* is not art. Someone who thinks skilfulness or expressiveness are criteria for something's being art is a different kind of theorist, whom Carroll is not seeking to argue with at this point.

(3) At $\boxed{1}\!\!\rightarrow$ Carroll touches on this objection: that what he has labelled as 'interpretive play' is 'in fact' part of, or a type of, aesthetic response. We should beware of prejudging this issue by implicitly collapsing the meaning of 'aesthetic response' into something uninformative like 'appropriate response to a work of art'. But one might hold out for the idea that interpreting the hidden meanings, structures, and art-historical connections of works of art is not really something distinct from responding affectively to the perceptual experience of them, but an extension or part of such a response.

It is perhaps an odd idea that we can or should simply respond with positive feeling to an isolated object of immediate perceptual experience, with no input from our interpretations of its meaning, structure, or situation in history. But need we jettison aesthetic experience from our account of art just because that notion of what we might call 'pure' aesthetic experience does not embrace all our typical responses to art? Why not work out a way in which aesthetic experience, still conceived as an affective response to an object with which we have an experiential encounter, can include and be enhanced by the kinds of interpretive activity Carroll identifies?

A final point is that there may well be, as Carroll suggests, other characteristic ways of interacting with art works that do not fall easily into either the aesthetic or the interpretive patterns here discussed. An example from narrative and dramatic art (and straying again onto the territory Plato is interested in) might be emotional interaction with the doings and sufferings of fictional characters, through which we gain rewarding insights into ethical issues. Indeed, it might be thought that there cannot in principle be a limit to the kinds of interaction that are appropriate and fruitful to works of art, because, as history reminds us, art is always renewing itself and surprising its audiences into new forms of interaction. And, on the side of Carroll's argument here, someone who thought that whatever forms of experience it became appropriate to have towards art works must always be counted as aesthetic would have emptied the term 'aesthetic' of most of its significance.

Introduction to Hepburn

R. W. Hepburn was for many years Professor of Moral Philosophy at the University of Edinburgh, and wrote extensively on aesthetics and philosophy of religion. The present piece was included in his collection 'Wonder' and Other Essays: Eight Studies in Aesthetics and Neighbouring Fields (1984), but was first published in 1966. In places the essay has a certain period feel to it, since it reflects British philosophy of the 1950s and 1960s, with its concern for 'linguistic and conceptual analysis', and some particular conceptions as to which art works and art theories are of prime interest. Nevertheless, the clarity of Hepburn's argument and the richness of his insights make this piece of enduring interest. Since he wrote it there has been something of a resurgence of interest in the aesthetics of nature, and the present essay is often cited as a forerunner by those working in this field today.

The question is whether philosophers who think about questions of aesthetics have tended to neglect the aesthetic experience of nature. And if they have, as Hepburn alleges, whether there is anything distinctive about the aesthetic experience of nature that remains theoretically unexplored. Some of the background assumptions Hepburn makes are shared with Carroll. He mentions the expression theory of art as one that is 'in eclipse' but can usefully be contrasted with more recent thinking. Carroll suggested that the expression theory (associated with Collingwood, whom we encounter in chapter 4 below) placed a one-sided emphasis on the states of mind of the artist in its account of what was definitive about art, at the expense of the object and the audience's response. Hepburn makes a parallel criticism, to the effect that the expression theory cannot adapt itself easily to the case of nature, where it is not usually supposed that natural objects are an expression or communication on the part of any mind. We shall also find in the background a familiar received view about what constitutes 'pure' aesthetic experience – the idea of a perceptual encounter with an individual object, unmediated by context or interpretation. Carroll argued that this does not best capture much of our experiential interaction with art works; Hepburn argues that it does not capture our aesthetic interaction with nature either.

R. W. Hepburn, 'Contemporary Aesthetics and the Neglect of Natural Beauty' (extracts)

Open an eighteenth-century work on aesthetics, and the odds are it will contain a substantial treatment of the beautiful, the sublime, the picturesque in nature.[1] Its treatment of art may be secondary and derivative, not its primary concern. Although the nineteenth century could not be said to repeat these same emphases, they certainly reappear in some impressive places, in Ruskin's *Modern Painters*, for instance – a work that might have been entitled, no less accurately, 'How to look at nature and enjoy it aesthetically'. In our own day, however, writings on aesthetics attend almost exclusively to the arts and very rarely indeed to natural beauty, or only in the most perfunctory manner. Aesthetics is even *defined* by some mid-century writers as 'the philosophy of art', 'the philosophy of criticism', analysis of the language and concepts used in describing and appraising art objects.[2]

[a]→   Why has this curious shift come about? For part of the answer we have to look not to philosophers' theories but to some general shifts in aesthetic taste itself. This is a legitimate procedure, since, despite the difference of logical level between them, judgements of taste and the theorizing of aesthetics exert unmistakable influences upon one another. Relevant facts, then, are these: that – for all the cult of the open

[1]   By 'nature' I shall mean all objects that are not human artefacts. This will, of course, include living creatures. I can afford to ignore for the purposes of this study the many possible disputes over natural objects that have received a marked, though limited, transformation at man's hands.
[2]   H. Osborne defines beauty as the 'characteristic and peculiar excellence of works of art' (*Theory of Beauty*, 1952). Compare M. C. Beardsley in *Aesthetics*, 1958: 'There would be no problems of aesthetics, in the sense in which I propose to mark out this field of study, if no one ever talked about works of art.'

air, the caravans, camps and excursions in the family car – serious aesthetic concern with nature is today rather a rare phenomenon. If we regard the Wordsworthian vision as the great peak in the recent history of the subject, then we have to say that the ground declined very sharply indeed from that extraordinary summit, and that today we survey it from far below. In one direction it quickly declined to the deeps of the romantics' own 'dejection' experiences, and in another to the forced ecstasies and hypocrisies of a fashionable and trivialized nature-cult. At its most deeply felt the Wordsworthian experience brought a rekindling of a religious imagination for some who found it no longer sustained by the traditional dogmas. But a still more radical loss of religious confidence came to undermine the undogmatic Wordsworthian experience itself.

The vanishing of the sense that nature is man's 'educator', that its beauties communicate more or less specific morally ennobling messages, this is only one aspect of the general (and much anatomized) disappearance of a rationalist faith in nature's thorough-going intelligibility and its ultimate endorsement of human visions and aspirations. The characteristic image of contemporary man, as we all know, is that of a 'stranger', encompassed by a nature, which is indifferent, unmeaning and 'absurd'.

The work of the sciences, too, has tended to increase bewilderment and loss of nerve over the aesthetic interpretation of nature. Microscope and telescope have added vastly to our perceptual data; the forms of the ordinary landscape, ordinarily interpreted, are shown up as only a selection from countless different scales.

It is not surprising that (with a few exceptions) the artists themselves have turned from imitation and representation to the sheer creation of new objects, rewarding to contemplate in their own right. If they are expressive of more than purely formal relationships, then that 'more' tends to be not the alien external landscape but the inner landscape of the human psyche.

On the theoretical level, there are other and distinctive reasons for the neglect of natural beauty in aesthetics itself, especially an aesthetic that seeks to make itself increasingly rigorous. One such reason is that if we are aiming at an entirely general account of aesthetic excellence, this account cannot make essential reference to experience of (or imitation of) nature; since there are arts like music which are devoid of any such reference. Some writers have been impressed by the fact that certain features of aesthetic experience are quite unobtainable in nature – a landscape does not minutely control the spectator's response to it as does a successful work of art; it is an unframed ordinary object, in contrast to the framed, 'esoteric', 'illusory' or 'virtual' character of the art object. And so the artefact is taken as the aesthetic object *par excellence*, and the proper focus of study.

Although it is now very much in eclipse, the last widely accepted unified aesthetic system was the expression theory. No single new system has taken its place; and some of its influences are still with us. The expression theory is a *communication* theory: it must represent aesthetic experience of nature either as a communication from the Author of Nature, which it rarely does, or else (rather awkwardly) as the discovery that nature's shapes and colours can with luck serve as expressive vehicles of human feeling, although never constructed for that end.[3] The theory most readily copes with artefacts, not natural objects; with successful interpersonal communication, not the contemplation of sheer entities *as* entities. Although some very recent aesthetic analyses provide instruments that could be used to redress the lopsidedness of these emphases, they have not yet been applied extensively to this task.[4]

We may note, finally, that linguistic or conceptual analysts have been understandably tempted to apply their techniques first and foremost to the arguments, counter-arguments and manifestos lying to hand in the writings of critics of the arts. In the case of natural beauty, however, such a polemical critical literature scarcely exists. The philosopher must first work out his own detailed and systematic account of the aesthetic enjoyment of nature. And this he has so far been slow, or reluctant, to do.

Having outlined the situation, the neglect of the study of natural beauty, I now want to argue that the neglect is a very bad thing: bad, because aesthetics is steered off from examining an important and richly complex set of relevant data; and bad because when a set of human experiences is ignored in a theory relevant to them, they tend to be rendered less readily available as experiences. If we cannot find sensible-sounding language in which to describe them – language of a piece with the rest of our aesthetic talk – the experiences are felt, in an embarrassed way, as off-the-map; and, since off the map, seldom visited. This result is specially unfortunate, if for some other reasons the experiences are already hard to achieve – in some of their varieties at least. What, then, can contemporary aesthetics say on the topic of natural beauty?

[3] For Croce's view, see Croce, *Aesthetic* (tr. Ainslie), part 1, ch. 13.
[4] I am thinking, for example, of the recent insistence that even the art-object is primarily *object*, that it must not be approached simply as a clue to its creator's states of mind. See Beardsley *passim*, especially the earlier sections. I discuss some aspects of this 'anti-intentionalism' later in this chapter.

This essay has begun with some general remarks; it will move gradually towards more specific and limited issues. These various topics are not so intimately related as to be links in a single chain of argument, but the later discussions make frequent and essential reference back to points made earlier. I see this movement between the poles of general and specific, long-shot and analytical close-up, as always legitimate, indeed necessary, for the writer on aesthetics. He is ill-advised to do *nothing but* general surveying, or his work would be too loosely and remotely related to the particularities of actual aesthetic experiences. But concentration upon analysis alone can be equally unfortunate. It may prevent even an intelligent choosing of cruces for the analysis itself, and make it impossible to see the bearing of the analysis upon the inquiry as a whole, far less upon the related fields of ethics and the philosophy of mind.

d→ If I am right that systematic description is one main lack in the treatment of our subject, my first obligation may well be to supply some account of the varieties of aesthetic experience of nature. But
e→ their variety is immense, and mere cataloguing would be tedious. I shall suggest, therefore, two principles of selection that may throw together some samples interesting in themselves and useful for our subsequent arguments.

f→ First, we have already remarked that art-objects have a number of general characteristics not shared by objects in nature. It would be useful if we could show (and I think we can) that the absence of certain of these features is not merely negative or privative in its effect, but can contribute positively and valuably to the aesthetic experience of nature. A good specimen is the degree to which the spectator can be involved in the natural aesthetic situation itself. On occasion he may confront natural objects as a static, disengaged observer; but far more typically the objects envelop him on all sides. In a forest, trees surround him; he is ringed by hills, or he stands in the midst of a plain. If there is movement in the scene, the spectator may himself be in motion, and his motion may be an important element in his aesthetic experience. Think, for instance, of a glider pilot, delighting in a sense of buoyancy, in the balancing of the air-currents that hold him aloft. This sort of involvement is well expressed by Barbara Hepworth:

> What a different shape and 'being' one becomes lying on the sand with the sea almost above from when standing against the wind on a sheer high cliff with seabirds circling patterns below one. (*Carvings and Drawings*, London: Lund Humphries, 1952, ch. 4)

We have not only a mutual involvement of spectator and object, but also a reflexive effect by which the spectator experiences *himself* in an unusual and vivid way; and this difference is not merely noted, but dwelt upon aesthetically. The effect is not unknown to art, especially architecture. But it is both more intensely realized and pervasive in nature-experience – for we are *in* nature and a part *of* nature; we do not stand over against it as over against a painting on a wall.

If this study were on a larger scale, we should have to analyse in detail the various senses of 'detachment' and 'involvement' that are relevant here. This would prove a more slippery investigation than in the case of art-appreciation; but a rewarding one. Some sort of detachment there certainly is, in the sense that I am not *using* nature, manipulating it or calculating how to manipulate it. But I am both actor and spectator, ingredient in the landscape and lingering upon the sensations of being thus ingredient, rejoicing in their multifariousness, playing actively with nature, and letting nature, as it were, play with me and my sense of myself.

My second specimen is very similar, but, I think, worth listing separately. Though by no means all art-objects have frames or pedestals, they share a common character in being *set apart* from their environment, and set apart in a distinctive way. We might use the words 'frame' and 'framed' in an extended sense, to cover not only the physical boundaries of pictures but all the various devices employed in the different arts to prevent the art-object being mistaken for a natural object or for an artefact without aesthetic interest. Our list of frames, in this wide sense, would include the division between the stage-area and audience-area in the theatre, the concert-convention that the only aesthetically relevant sounds are those made by the performers, the layout of a page in a book of poems, where typography and spacing set the poem apart from the titles, page-numbers, critical apparatus and footnotes. Such devices are best thought of as aids to the recognition of the formal *completeness* of the art-objects themselves, their ability to sustain aesthetic interest, an interest that is not crucially dependent upon the relationships between the object and its general environment. Certainly, its environment may enhance or weaken its effect; and we may even see parts of the environment in a new way as a result of contemplating an art-object. But this does not affect the central point, that these works of art are first and foremost bounded objects, that their aesthetic characteristics are determined by their internal structure, the interplay of their elements.

In contrast, natural objects are 'frameless'. This is in some ways a disadvantage aesthetically; but there are some remarkable compensating advantages. Whatever lies beyond the frame of an art-object cannot normally become part of the aesthetic experience relevant to it. A chance train-whistle cannot be integrated into the music of a string quartet; it merely interferes with its appreciation. But where there is no frame, and where nature is our aesthetic object, a sound or visible intrusion from beyond the original boundaries of our attention can challenge us to integrate it in our overall experience, to modify that experience so as to make room for it. This of course, *need* not occur; we may shut it out by effort of will, if it seems quite unassimilable. At any rate, our creativity is challenged, set a task; and when things go well with us, we experience a sudden expansion of imagination that can be memorable in its own right.

> And, when there came a pause
> Of silence such as baffled his best skill:
> Then sometimes, in that silence, while he hung
> Listening, a gentle shock of mild surprise
> Has carried far into his heart the voice
> Of mountain torrents;
> (Wordsworth, *There was a Boy*)

If the absence of 'frame' precludes full determinateness and stability in the natural aesthetic object, it at least offers in return such unpredictable perceptual surprises; and their mere possibility imparts to the contemplation of nature a sense of adventurous openness.[5]

Something more definite can be said on the determinate and indeterminate in this connection. In, say, a painting, the frame ensures that each element of the work is determined in its perceived qualities (including emotional qualities) by a limited and definite context. Colour modifies colour and form modifies form; yet the frame supplies a boundary to all relevant modifiers, and, thus, any given colour or shape can be seen in a successful painting to have a determinate, contextually controlled character. Obviously, this is one kind of determinateness that cannot be achieved with natural objects; and that for several reasons. To consider only one of them: the aesthetic impact made upon us by, say, a tree, is part-determined by the context we

---

[5] I have taken care not to set out the above contrast between 'framed' and 'unframed' as a contrast between *all* art-objects and *all* natural objects considered aesthetically; for not every art-object has a frame, even in the extended sense I have used above. Works of architecture, for instance, are like natural objects, in that we can set no limits to the viewpoints from which they can properly be regarded, nor can we decree where the aesthetically relevant context of a building ends. A church or castle, seen from several miles away, may dominate, and determine how we see a whole landscape. The contrast between framed and frameless can none the less be made for very many types of aesthetic object – for enough at least to justify the general points made in the text.

include in our view of it. A tree growing on a steep hill-slope, bent far over by the winds, may strike us as tenacious, grim, strained. But from a greater distance, when the view includes numerous similar trees on the hillside, the striking thing may be a delightful, stippled patterned slope, with quite different emotional quality – quixotic or cheery. So with any aesthetic quality in nature; it is always provisional, correctable by reference to a different, perhaps wider context, or to a narrower one realized in greater detail. 'An idyllic scene? But you haven't noticed that advancing, though still distant, thundercloud. Now you have noticed it, and the whole scene takes on a new, threatened, ominous look.' In positive terms this provisional and elusive character of aesthetic qualities in nature creates a restlessness, an alertness, a search for ever new standpoints, and for more comprehensive gestalts. Of this restlessness and of this search I shall, very shortly, have more to say.

My last point on the present topic is this. We can distinguish, in a rough and ready way, between the particular aesthetic impact of an object, whether natural or artefact, and certain general 'background' experiences that are common to a great many aesthetic situations and are of aesthetic value in themselves. With an art-object, there is the exhilarating activity of coming to grasp its intelligibility as a perceptual whole. We find built-in guides to interpretation, and contextual controls for our response. We are aware of these features as having been expressly put there by its creator. Now I think we can create a nearly parallel but interestingly different background experience when our object is not an artefact but an natural one. Again, it is a kind of exhilaration, in this case a delight in the fact that the forms of the natural world *offer scope* for the exercise of the imagination, that leaf pattern chimes with vein pattern, cloud form with mountain form and mountain form with human form. On a theistic view this begets a distinctive sort of wonderment at the 'artistry' of God. On a naturalistic view it can beget at least no less wonderment at this uncontrived adaptation. Indeed, when nature is pronounced to be 'beautiful' – not in the narrower sense of that word, which contrasts 'beautiful' with 'picturesque' or 'comic', but in the wide sense equivalent to 'aesthetically excellent' – an important part of our meaning is just this, that nature's forms do provide this scope for imaginative play. For that is surely not analytically true; it might have been otherwise.

I have been arguing that certain important differences between natural objects and art-objects should not be seen as entailing the aesthetic unimportance of the former, that (on the contrary) several of these differences furnish grounds for distinctive and valuable types of aesthetic experience of nature. These are types of experience that art cannot provide to the same extent as nature, and which in some cases it cannot provide at all.

Supposing that a person's aesthetic education fails to reckon with these differences, supposing it instils in him the attitudes, the tactics of approach, the expectations proper to the appreciation of art-works only, we may be sure that such a person will either pay very little aesthetic heed to natural objects, or else will heed them in the wrong way. He will look – and of course look in vain – for what can be found and enjoyed only in art. Furthermore, one cannot be at all certain that he will seriously ask himself whether there might be other tactics, other attitudes and expectations more proper and more fruitful for the aesthetic appreciation of nature. My sampling of these 'differences', therefore, is not merely an introductory exercise in distinction-making. It has the polemical purpose of showing that unless these distinctions are reckoned with both in aesthetic education and theorizing, one can neither intelligently pursue nor adequately comprehend experience of natural beauty, save only in its most rudimentary forms.

So much for the listing of neglects and omissions. I want now to turn to something more constructive, and to take as a starting-point certain recurrent and *prima facie* attractive ways in which natural beauty has in fact been attended to and described, both in the past and present. I say 'as a starting-point', because I do not plan to examine in detail specific philosophical theories that have incorporated them. Rather, we shall take note of those approaches, the characteristic vocabulary that goes with them, and enquire how far (if at all) they point to an aesthetic of natural beauty that could be viable today.

Accounts of natural beauty sometimes focus upon the contemplating of single natural objects in their individuality and uniqueness (for an example – Pepita Haezrahi's analysis of the aesthetic contemplation of a single falling leaf (*The Contemplative Activity*, Ch. 2)). Other writers, with greater metaphysical daring – or rashness – speak of the enjoyment of natural beauty as tending towards an ideal of 'oneness with nature' or as leading to the disclosure of 'unity' in nature. The formulations vary greatly and substantially among themselves; but the vocabulary of unity, oneness as the key aesthetic principle, is a recurrent theme.

There are strong influences in contemporary British philosophy that prompt one to have the fullest sympathy with a particularist approach to natural beauty – as the contemplation of individual objects with their aesthetically interesting perceptual qualities; and to have very little sympathy for the more grandiose, speculative and quasi-mystical language of 'oneness with or in nature'. Yet it seems to me that we do

not have here one good and one bad aesthetic approach, the first sane
and the second absurd. Rather, we have two poles or well-separated
landmarks between which lies a range of aesthetic possibilities; and in
the mapping of this range those landmarks will play a valuable,
perhaps a necessary role.

We must begin by bluntly denying the universal need for unity,
unity of form, quality, structure or of anything else. We can take
aesthetic pleasure in sheer plurality, in the stars of the night sky, in a
bird song without beginning, middle or end.[6]

And yet to make unity, in some sense, one's key concept need not be
simply wrong-headed or obscurantist. Nor do we have to say, rather
limply, that there are two distinct and unrelated types of aesthetic
excellence, one that contemplates individual uniqueness and the other
– no better or worse – that aims at some grand synthesis. I want to
argue that there are certain incompletenesses in the experience of the
isolated particular, that produce a *nisus* towards the other pole, the
pole of unity. Accuracy, however, will require us to deny that there is a
single type of unification or union; there are several notions to be
distinguished within the ideal, and the relations between them are
quite complex.

One such direction of development we have already noticed;
namely, the *nisus* towards more and more comprehensive or adequate
survey of the context that determines the perceived qualities of a
natural object or scene. Our motives are, in part, the desire for a
certain integrity or 'truth' in our aesthetic experience of nature; and of
this more shortly. In part also we are prompted by our awareness that
in all aesthetic experience it is contextual complexity that, more than
any other single factor, makes possible the minute discrimination of
emotional qualities; and such discrimination is accorded high aesthetic value. It is largely the pursuit of such value that moves us to
accept what I called 'the challenge to integrate' – to take notice of and
to accept as aesthetically relevant some shape or sound that initially
lies outside the limit of our attention. 'Challenge' was not, I think, an
over-dramatic word to use. For we can contrast the stereotyped
experiences of the aesthetically apathetic and unadventurous person
with the rich and subtly diversified experiences of the aesthetically
courageous person. His courage consists in his refusal to heed only
those features of a natural object or scene that most readily come
together in a familiar pattern or which yield a comfortingly generalized emotional quality. It also involves taking the repeated risk of
drawing a blank, of finding oneself unable to hold the various

<hr/>

[6] Compare A. C. Montefiore, in *Mind*, LXVIII (1959), pp. 563 ff.

elements together as a single object of contemplation, or to elicit any significant aesthetic experience from them at all.

The expansion of context may be a spatial expansion, but it does not have to be spatial. What else can it be? When we contemplate a natural object, we may see it not as sand-dune or rock but simply as a coloured shape. If this is difficult, we can look at the world upside down, with our head between our legs. But although an aesthetic view of an object will strive to shake free of conventional and deadening conceptualizings, that is not to say that *all* interpreting, all 'seeings as...' are lapses to the non-aesthetic. We ought not to accept a dichotomy of 'pure aesthetic contemplation' – 'impure admixture of associations'. Suppose I am walking over a wide expanse of sand and mud. The quality of the scene is perhaps that of wild, glad emptiness. But suppose I bring to bear upon the scene my knowledge that this is a tidal basin, the tide being out. The realization is not aesthetically irrelevant. I see myself now as walking on what is for half the day sea-bed. The wild glad emptiness may be tempered by a disturbing weirdness.

This sort of experience can readily be related to the movement we were examining, the movement towards more complex and comprehensive synopses. In addition to spatial extension (or sometimes instead of it), we may aim at enriching the interpretative element, taking this not as theoretical 'knowledge about' the object or scene, but as helping to determine the aesthetic impact it makes upon us. 'Unity' here plays a purely 'regulative' role. Nature is not a 'given whole', nor indeed is knowledge about it. But in any case, there are practical, psychological limits to the expansion process; a degree of complexity is reached, beyond which there will be no increase in discrimination of perceptual or emotional qualities: rather the reverse.

A second movement away from contemplation of uninterpreted particulars is sometimes known as the 'humanizing' or the 'spiritualizing' of nature. I shall merely note its existence and relevance here, for there have been a good many accounts of it in the history of aesthetics. Coleridge said that 'Art is...the power of humanizing nature, of infusing the thoughts and passions of man into everything which is the object of his contemplation'. And Hegel, that the aim of art is 'to strip the external world of its inflexible foreignness'.[7] What is here said about art is no less true of aesthetic experience of nature itself. Imaginative activity is working for a *rapprochement* between

---

[7] S. T. Coleridge, *Biographia Literaria*, vol. II; G. W. F. Hegel, *Introduction* to the Berlin Aesthetics Lectures of the 1820s, E.T. T. M. Knox (ed. C. Karelis), Oxford, 1979, p. 31.

the spectator and his aesthetic object: unity is again a regulative notion, a symbol of the unattainable complete transmutation of brute extenal nature into a mirror of the mind.

By developing and qualifying the 'humanization' ideal we can come to see yet a third aspect of the *nisus* towards unity. A person who contemplates natural objects aesthetically may sometimes find that their emotional quality is describable in the vocabulary of ordinary human moods and feelings – melancholy, exuberance, placidity. In many cases, however, he will find that they are not at all accurately describable in such terms. A particular emotional quality can be roughly *analogous* to some nameable human emotion, desolation for instance; but the precise quality of desolation revealed in some waste or desert in nature may be quite distinctive in timbre and intensity. To put this another way: one may go to nature to find shapes and sounds that can be taken as the embodiment of human emotion, and in so far as this occurs, nature is felt to be humanized. But instead of nature being humanized, the reverse may happen. Aesthetic experience of nature may be experience of a range of emotion that the human scene, by itself, untutored and unsupplemented, could not evoke. To extend the scope of these remarks, recall once again our quotation from Barbara Hepworth (p. 85). To be 'one' with nature in that sense was to realize vividly one's place in the landscape, as a form among its forms. And this is not to have nature's 'foreignness' or otherness overcome, but in contrast, to allow that otherness free play in the modifying of one's everyday sense of one's own being.

In this domain, again, we need not confine ourselves to the contemplating of naked uninterpreted particulars. In a leaf-pattern I may 'see' also blood-vessel patterns, or the patterns of branching, forked lightning: or all of these. In a spiral nebula pattern I may see the pattern of swirling waters or whirling dust. I may be aware of a network of affinities, of analogous forms, that spans the inorganic or the organic world, or both. My experience has a quality of *multum in parvo*.[8] This is not necessarily a 'humanizing' of nature; it may be more like a 'naturizing' of the human observer. If, with T. S. Eliot, one sees 'The dance along the artery / The circulation of the lymph' as 'figured in the drift of stars', something of the aesthetic qualities of the latter (as we perceive them) may come to be transferred to the former. Supposing that by this kind of aesthetic experience nature is felt to lose some of its 'foreignness', that may be because we have ourselves

---

[8] On such analogies and affinities among natural forms, see G. Kepes, *The New Landscape in Art and Science*. Chicago, 1956.

become foreign to our everyday, unexamined notion of ourselves, and not through any assimilation of nature's forms to pre-existent notions, images or perceptions.

A fourth class of approaches to the ideal of 'unity' is itself rather heterogeneous; but we can characterize its members as follows. They are, once again, concerned less with the specific content of particular aesthetic experiences than with what we have called the 'background' quality of emotions and attitudes, common to a great many individual experiences. In their case the background is a sense of reconciliation, suspension of conflict, and of being in that sense at one with the aesthetic object. This particular sort of 'at-one-ness' could hardly be present in art-experience, since it requires that the aesthetic object should be at the same time the natural environment or some part of it. This is the same environment from which we wrest our food, from which we have to protect ourselves in order to live, which refuses to sustain our individual lives beyond a limited term, and to which we are finally 'united' in a manner far different from those envisaged in the aesthetic ideals of 'unity': 'Rolled round in earth's diurnal course With rocks and stones and trees.' To attain, and sustain, the relevant detachment from such an environment in order to savour it aesthetically is in itself a fair achievement, an achievement which suffuses the aesthetic experiences themselves with that sense of reconciliation. A cease-fire has been negotiated in our struggle with nature.

There is immense variety in the ways in which this can manifest itself in individual experience. The objects of nature may look to us as if their *raison d'être* were precisely that we should celebrate their beauty. As Rilke put it: 'Everything beckons to us to perceive it.' Or, the dominant stance may be that of benediction: the Ancient Mariner 'blesses' the watersnakes at his moment of reconciliation.

The fourth type of unity-ideal is different from our first three specimens. The first three quest after unity in the particular aesthetic perception itself: the attainment of complex unified synopses, the grasping of webs of affinities and so on. The fourth, however, could arise in the contemplation of what is itself quite *un*-unified in the above senses, the night sky again, or a mass of hills with no detectable pattern to unite them. It is more strictly a concomitant, or a by-product of an aesthetic experience that we are already enjoying, an experience in which there may have been no synoptic grasping of patterns, relating of forms or any other sort of unifying.

I suspect that someone who tried to construct a comprehensive aesthetic theory with 'unity' as its sole key concept would obtain his comprehensiveness only by equivocating or punning over the meaning of the key expression, only by sliding or slithering from one of its many senses to another. When one sense is not applicable, another may well be. The fourth sense in particular can be relevant to vivid aesthetic experience of any natural object or collection of objects whatever.

So much the worse, we may conclude, for such a theory *qua* monolithic. But to say that is not to imply that our study has yielded only negative results. This is only one of several areas in aesthetics where we have to resist the temptation to work with a single supreme concept and must replace it by a *cluster* of related key concepts. Yet, in searching out the relevant key-concepts, the displaced single concept may yet be a useful guide – as it is in the present case. We should be ill-advised, however, to take this cluster of unity-concepts as by itself adequate for all explanatory purposes. Our analysis started with the contemplation of an individual natural object in all its particularity. This was not a mere starting-point, to be left behind in the pursuit of our 'unities'. On the contrary, aesthetic experience remains tethered to that concern with the particular, even if on a long rope. The rope is there, although the development and vitality of that experience demand that it be stretched to the full. The pull of the rope is felt, when the expanding and complicating of our synopses reaches the point beyond which we shall have not more but less fine discrimination of perceptual quality. It is felt again, when we risk the blurring and negating of natural forms as we really perceive them, in an anxious attempt to limit our experience of nature to the savouring of stereotyped and well-domesticated emotional qualities. It is even relevant to our fourth type of unity-ideal: for the sense of reconciliation is not an independent and autonomous aesthetic experience, but hangs entirely upon the occurrence of particular experiences of particular aesthetically interesting natural objects.

Up to this point my aim has been chiefly to describe some varieties of aesthetic experience of nature. From these we may make the following inferences. (i) Although some important features of art-experience are unattainable in nature, that by no means entitles the aesthetician to confine his studies to art; for even these points of apparent privation can yield types of aesthetic experience that are well worth analysis. (ii) Accounts of natural beauty that take 'unity' as their central concept are often metaphysically extravagant and unperceptive of ambiguities in their claims. Nevertheless, a cautious aesthetician would be unwise to let this extravagance deflect him from patiently teasing out the numerous and important strands of experience that originally prompted these accounts.

Although recent aesthetics has been little concerned with natural beauty as such, in the course of its analysis of *art*-experience, it has frequently made comparisons between our aesthetic approach to art-objects and to objects in nature. It has made these comparisons at crucial points in argument, and in several different sorts of context. But what has not been asked – or adequately answered – is whether the comparing has been fairly done; whether, in particular, the account of nature-experience, given or presupposed, is an adequate or distorted account. Our discussion so far has furnished us with useful data.

A substantial part of recent aesthetics has been the criticism of the expression theory of art. Right at the centre of this criticism is the denial that we need concern ourselves with discovering the intention or the actual feelings or intuitions of the artist, when we try to appreciate or to appraise his artefact. The expression theory saw the artefact as the middle link in communication from artist to spectator; the critics of the theory see the artefact first and foremost as an object with certain properties, properties which are, or should be, aesthetically interesting, worth contemplating, and which in their totality control and guide the spectator's response. This change of emphasis chimes in well with the desire for a 'scientific' criticism (the properties are *there* in the artefact, the object), and with the anti-psychologistic mood of current British and American philosophy (the work of art is not an 'imaginary' one: and we are not probing behind it to its creator's states of soul).

Clearly this is an aesthetic approach that reduces the gulf between art-object and natural object. Both are to be approached primarily as individual, self-contained entities, exciting to contemplate by virtue of the objective properties they can be seen to possess.[9] But, let us ask, how far can we accept this comparison? Critics of the critics have pointed out some deficiencies. They have insisted, for instance, upon the irreducible relevance of linguistic, social and cultural context to the interpretation of a poem. The identical words might constitute *two* poems, not one, if we read them in two different contexts.[10] We

[9] This account is highly general and schematic. I have said nothing about the basic differences among the arts themselves, which make the 'aesthetic object' in (say) music so unlike that in literature or that again in architecture. My account as it stands is most immediately relevant to the visual arts, especially sculpture; but what is said about overall trends and emphases has extension beyond those.
[10] H. S. Eveling argues that we should have a clash of competing criteria in such a situation. We should want to say 'same words, same poem': but, knowing how differently we shall interpret the words, according to the context in which we read them, we also want to say, 'one set of words but two poems' ('Composition and Criticism', *Proc. Arist. Soc.* LIX (1959), pp. 213–32).

p→ could extend this criticism as follows. Suppose we have two perceptually identical objects, one an artefact and the other natural. They might be a 'carved stone' of Arp and a naturally smoothed stone; a carving in wood and a piece of fallen timber. Or they might be identical in pattern, though not in material; for example, a rock face with a particular texture and markings, and an abstract expressionist painting with the same texture and the same markings. If we made the most of the *rapprochement*, we should have to say that we had in each of these cases essentially *one* aesthetic object. (Although numerically two, the pair would be no more aesthetically different from one another than two engravings from the same block.) Yet this would be a misleading conclusion. If we knew them for what they are – as artefact or natural object – we should certainly attend differently to them. As we look at the rock face in nature, we may realize imaginatively the geological pressures and turmoils that produced its pattern. The realizing of these need not be a piece of extra-aesthetic reflection: it may determine for us how we see and respond to the object itself. If we interpreted and responded to the abstract painting in the same way (assuming, of course, that it is a thoroughgoing abstract and not the representation of a rock face!), our interpretation would this time be merely whimsical, no more controlled or stabilised than a seeing of faces in the fire.[11] If we arbitrarily restricted aesthetic experience both of nature and art to the contemplating of uninterpreted shapes and patterns, we could, of course, have the *rapprochement*. But we have seen good reason for refusing so to restrict it in the case of nature-experience, whatever be the case with art.

q→ Take another example. Through the eye-piece of a telescope I see the spiral nebula in Andromeda. I look next at an abstract painting in a circular frame that contains the identical visual pattern. My responses are not alike, even if each is indisputably aesthetic. My awareness that the first shapes are of enormous and remote masses of matter in motion imparts to my response a strangeness and solemnity that are not generated by the pattern alone. The abstract pattern may indeed impress by reminding me of various wheeling and swirling patterns in nature. But there is a difference between taking the pattern as that sort of reminder, and, on the other hand, brooding on this impressive instantiation of it in the nebula. Furthermore, a point already made about the emotive 'background' to aesthetic experience

---

[11] It is a weakness of some abstract painting that it sacrifices almost all the devices by which the spectator's response can be controlled and given determinateness. In the case of natural objects one is free to rely upon 'controls' external to the object – as in the present example. But even if the artist makes his artefacts very like natural objects, our knowledge that they are in fact artificial and 'framed' prevents us relying, in their case, upon such external controls.

is relevant here again. Where we confront what we know to be a human artefact – say a painting – we have no special shock at the mere discovery that there are patterns here which delight perception; we know that they have been put there, though certainly we may be astonished at their particular aesthetic excellences. With a natural object, however, such surprise can figure importantly in our overall response, a surprise that is probably the greater the more remote the object from our everyday environment.

$\boxed{r}\rightarrow$ A more lighthearted but helpful way of bringing out these points is to suppose ourselves confronted by a small object, which, for all we know, may be natural or may be an artefact. We are set the task of regarding it aesthetically. I suppose that we might cast upon it an uneasy and embarrassed eye. How shall we approach it? Shall we, for instance, see in its smoothness the slow mindless grinding of centuries of tides, or the swifter and mindful operation of the sculptor's tools? Certainly, we can enjoy something of its purely formal qualities on either reckoning; but even the savouring of these is affected by non-formal factors that diverge according to the judgement we make about its origin.

To sum up this argument. On the rebound from a view of art as expression, as language, and the work of art as the medium of communication between artist and spectator, some recent aesthetics has been urging that the artefact is, first and foremost, an object among objects. The study of art is primarily the study of such objects, their observable qualities, their organization. This swing from intention to object has been healthful on the whole, delivering aesthetics and criticism from a great deal of misdirected labour. But it has countered the paradoxes of expressionism with paradoxes, or illuminating exaggerations, of its own. Differences between object and object need to be reaffirmed: indiscernibly different poems or carvings become discernibly different when we reckon with their aesthetically relevant cultural contexts; and the contextual controls that determine how we contemplate an object in nature are different from those that shape our experience of art. In other words, we have here a central current issue in aesthetics that cannot be properly tackled without a full-scale discussion of natural beauty.

Commentary on Hepburn

Hepburn's first task is to establish that there has been a neglect of the aesthetics of nature up until his time of writing, that is the middle part of the twentieth century. He says that some writers even define aesthetics as 'the philosophy of art', which is probably still true today. Hepburn gives some non-theoretical reasons why there is less interest in the aesthetic in nature (from $\boxed{a}\mapsto$), and some theoretical reasons (from $\boxed{b}\mapsto$). More important, however, are his diagnosis of why such neglect matters (at $\boxed{c}\mapsto$) and his ensuing suggestions about what positive distinctive features the aesthetic experience of nature has (from $\boxed{d}\mapsto$ onwards).

> Do you find convincing Hepburn's diagnosis (at $\boxed{c}\mapsto$) of why the neglect of nature is 'a bad thing' in aesthetics?

A sceptical response here might be as follows. If the theory of aesthetics concentrates heavily on our experiences of art, that is surely because such experiences are rich, varied, and prominent in our culture; but if aesthetic experience of nature is, by contrast, 'less readily available', from what point of view is the aesthetic experience of nature important? If the majority of human beings fail to find nature of any particular interest aesthetically, and our prevailing conceptions of the aesthetic do not adapt well to it, why are we to be faulted for not placing nature at the centre of aesthetic investigation? Hepburn has an interesting point that the failure to include some activity in a theory can marginalize that activity in practice. But is aesthetic experience of nature so marginal as this passage might imply? To answer this we have to think what is included under 'aesthetic experience of nature', or (apparently equivalent for Hepburn) experience of 'natural beauty'.

> What counts as an aesthetic experience of nature?

Hepburn's examples include trees, clouds, forests, beaches, mountains, and other landscape environments; also birdsong, a single sand dune, the night sky, patterns in a leaf, geological formations. These are different cases where we find rewarding or satisfying the contemplation of something that is not manmade but that exists naturally.

We might perhaps add, as fairly familiar, the collecting and displaying of butterflies and seashells, the experience of the appearance and behaviour of animals, and the enjoyment of flowers (though if they are cultivated and arranged in gardens an element of 'artistry' creeps into our response to them). Such a list suggests that aesthetic interest in nature is, in fact, common and widespread.

However, the examples we have chosen raise issues of a subtle kind, which Hepburn's discussion highlights. The notion of enjoying the contemplation of a single object detached, perhaps physically removed, from its environment, or even, as I have said, intentionally displayed to an audience, might be derivative from a traditional conception of an encounter with an art object – it may be to treat a bit of nature as if it were a kind of art work, a seashell as if it were a miniature sculpture, say, or a cloud as if it were a cloud in a painting. And a careful look at Hepburn's examples will show that he is after experiences which are truly distinctive responses *to nature*, and cannot easily be encompassed by a theory of aesthetic experience that originates with art objects.

At [e]→ Hepburn announces that he will apply two principles of selection in order to choose from among the many varieties of aesthetic experience of nature. What do these two principles of selection amount to in practice?

On a first reading it is difficult to discern what the two 'principles' are and where they are operative in Hepburn's argument. He does not refer back to them as principles. However, once one sees the overall structure of his piece, it becomes clear what he means. In summing up much later at [o]→ he recounts two points: (i) that aesthetic experience of nature is of interest despite, or perhaps because of, its lacking some features that characterize the experience of art; (ii) that there are various notions of striving towards 'unity' that capture valuable aspects of our experience of nature. These, I would suggest, are the two principles, or categories, that Hepburn has used to select the kinds of example that he considers. The first category occupies Hepburn's argument from [f]→ until [h]→ in the text; the second runs from [h]→ until [o]→.

Features lacking in aesthetic experience of nature

What two features does Hepburn locate under this heading?

The two features are the 'detachment' of the spectator and the 'framing' of the experienced object: in the case of nature the spectator is 'involved' in what he or she is experiencing and it is not demarcated by a frame. Recent art practice has perhaps narrowed the gap between nature and art in both respects. Artists have taken to making installations into which the spectator enters, moves about, and participates, or vast structures such as a fence covering hundreds of kilometers of territory (Christo), or works that are made of naturally growing and changing materials and merge into their environments (Andy Goldsworthy). In such cases there is a deliberate frustration of the attempt to detach oneself as a static spectator or to detach the art work from its surroundings as a discrete object of attention.

These more recent trends in art do, however, serve to illuminate one of Hepburn's points. Precisely by challenging the theoretical paradigm of the framed object contemplated by a detached spectator, they show that this paradigm exists and is strong. So these reflections on art provide more of an extension to Hepburn's position than a challenge.

At [g]→ Hepburn claims that with any aesthetic quality in nature 'it is always provisional, correctable by reference to a different, perhaps wider context, or to a narrower one realized in greater detail'. To what extent does this differentiate nature from art?

This would seem to be a feature of our recognition of the qualities of art as well. Just as we experience Hepburn's tree differently if we see it in isolated fashion or as part of a wider pattern, so we could appreciate some features of a medieval mass setting, for example, by noting the differences between it and more familiar post-Renaissance music, but it would likely take on a different character if heard against the background of closely contemporary pieces, earlier works by the same composer, and so on. So this feature does not really seem to differentiate the cases of nature and art.

Strivings towards unity in the experience of nature

When discussing this topic (in the section running from [h]→ to [o]→) Hepburn uses the Latin word *nisus*, meaning a striving or attempt to attain a goal. There are perhaps some problems for the reader with this section of the argument. For one thing, having identified two poles of experience, that of the isolated particular and that of unity, Hepburn groups together four different phenomena under his notion of a *nisus* towards unity, or rather three phenomena and one heterogeneous group of further phenomena (see [n]→). (Dare we say that this is not a very unified notion of unity?) Secondly, with some of the experiences he mentions, many readers may find it hard to grasp what is meant. Not everyone will have had an experience that they could confidently describe as 'allowing nature's otherness free play in the modifying of one's everyday sense of one's own being', for instance.

Consider in turn the types of experience Hepburn describes as manifesting a striving towards unity. Which of them are plausible descriptions? Which of them clearly differentiate the experience of nature from the experience of art?

The notion of embedding the object in a context, rather than contemplating it in isolation, is familiar from the case of art. Many of the considerations advanced by Carroll above in support of the notion of interpretive play and against that of atomistic art consumption, are relevant here. Hepburn rejects the notion of a 'pure aesthetic contemplation' ([k]→) in which interpretation plays no role. But he has something in common with the kind of 'aesthetic experience' theorist Carroll argues against, to the extent that he thinks of interpretive activity as subordinate to the aesthetic experience as such, which is a perceptual encounter 'free of conventional and deadening conceptualiz-ings' in which we integrate a complexity of sights and sounds (see $\boxed{i}{\mapsto}$ and $\boxed{j}{\mapsto}$).

What then is distinctive about the experience of *nature* here? Perhaps the absence of clear boundaries that establish what is object and what is context, and the absence of intentions that have led to the production of the object. But arguably the difference between art and nature here is only one of degree; and it cannot be assumed with too much confidence that art works have only one relevant context against which they are to be inter-preted, or that the intentions of the artist are definitive in constraining the interpretations we may make of them. (For more on this topic see chapter 5 below.)

Hepburn completes his discussion of the tendency towards unity in the experience of nature by introducing the notions of 'humanizing' nature, 'naturizing' the human observer, and of 'reconciliation' with nature.

> Do these descriptions by Hepburn fit experiences of nature that any aes-thetic theory must account for?

We may worry that such experiences could be had only by someone primed in advance by some specific set of assumptions about nature and their place within it. For example, Hepburn says (at $\boxed{m}{\mapsto}$), 'one may go to nature to find shapes and sounds that can be taken as the embodiment of human emotion'. One may, but what if one does not? Again (see $\boxed{1}{\mapsto}$), one cannot find the external world to be stripped of 'its inflexible foreignness', unless one already has some grounds to think of the world as foreign in certain ways. One cannot feel oneself as undergoing a 'ceasefire' with nature, unless one begins by thinking of oneself in conflict with it. It would be rash to deny that there are such experiences as Hepburn describes. The question is whether a theory of aesthetic experience in general is deficient if it does not treat them as central. (The use of examples from Coleridge and Hegel and the reference to a 'Wordsworthian vision' in the second paragraph of the essay suggest that Hepburn may have a conception of the aesthetic heavily influenced by Ro-manticism. It is not, of course, required of every aesthetic theory that it fall in line with the preoccupations of any particular art movement or period in intellectual history.)

Cases of perceptually indistinguishable objects

Hepburn here considers a number of thought-experiments somewhat similar in kind to those presented by Arthur Danto and much discussed in recent aesthetics literature (see chapter 5 below). Three parallel examples – a stone, a spiral formation, and an indeterminate small object – are given in the para-graphs $\boxed{p}{\mapsto}$, $\boxed{q}{\mapsto}$, and $\boxed{r}{\mapsto}$. All the cases concern two objects that are indistinguishable by way of perception, but which, allegedly, we would consider to differ from one another aesthetically.

> Consider any or all of these cases. Would the knowledge that an object is natural rather than a product of human labour (or vice versa) alter the aesthetic experience we have of it?

There is a temptation to say that our aesthetic experience would not be altered by such knowledge, that an object would be found aesthetically satisfying or interesting in just the same way before and after the discovery that it is natural rather than artificial – or at least that it ought to be. There is a notion of aesthetic experience being spoiled or corrupted by knowledge about the object. Hepburn argues that this notion is mistaken – a verdict borne out by much recent work in aesthetics – and he implies that it has persisted because too little attention has been paid to the differences between aesthetic experience of art and aesthetic experience of nature.

3

Aesthetic Judgements

Introduction to the Issues

What happens when we offer the opinion that a work of art, of whatever kind, is a good work of art, or that it is aesthetically good, or that it is beautiful? All of these – which I am not assuming to be equivalent – are ways of making an aesthetic judgement about a work of art. There are numerous other forms in which we might make such judgements. We might say of a poem or piece of visual art that 'it works' or is 'just right' aesthetically. In all these cases we seem to be making a statement that attributes a value to the work and which we regard as true. In fact, as the previous chapter should have alerted us, aesthetic judgements are not just made about works of art. We frequently make them about objects in nature too. For that matter, we also make such judgements about cars, hairstyles, jewellery, lap-tops, and so on. So the question about judgements attributing aesthetic value goes much wider than art.

Many questions arise already: are such statements genuinely true or false? What is it for a work of art to have an aesthetic value: is its beauty, or its aesthetic goodness, a property that a work has? If so, what kind of property would it be, and how would it relate to other kinds of property the object has, such as its physical properties or its colours?

The two extracts chosen to introduce this theme are from eighteenth-century texts so fundamental in the history of aesthetics that it is hard to imagine studying the subject without some engagement with them. It is fair to say that both Hume and Kant belong to the tradition in aesthetics that Carroll was reacting against in the previous chapter: the tradition according to which there is a peculiar, isolable experience of responding with a positive feeling to the perceptual experience of an object, which results in a judgement that the object is beautiful or has aesthetic value. Or at least, both have been regarded as belonging to that tradition by later theorists on both sides of the argument about 'pure aesthetic experience.'

Here the emphasis will be on the question of judgement. Hume and Kant face essentially the same problem about judgements of aesthetic value: a mismatch between their evidential basis and the apparent truth-claim that they make on that basis. When judging that a thing is 'just right' aesthetically, what confirms our initial judgement is simply our own subjective experience. There appears to be a kind of pleasure or liking that I feel when I see or hear this thing, and that liking is the evidence on which I pronounce the thing to have aesthetic value.

Yet usually, as Kant puts it, I behave *as if* this aesthetic value were object-ively present as a property in the object itself. So I am not just saying that I like it, rather that there is, as it were, something remarkable *there* in the object that I expect you to see as well. Nevertheless I cannot prove or demonstrate that to you. Your aesthetic judgement must be based on your feeling a similar liking for your own experience.

Much aesthetic discourse implicitly accepts that there are aesthetic stand-ards. It is permissible to say 'This new opera really is poor' or 'That poem is better than any of these others (hence we award it first prize).' These are not merely expressions of like and dislike – or at least we do not usually behave as if they are. We think that people making judgements can be right or wrong about these matters, and that disputes between judgers are genuine disputes, not just a matter of preference. Yet where does the standard of rightness come from, if judges have to rely solely on their own subjective response?

There are two tempting ways to think of solving the problem of aesthetic judgements:

1   To say that they are nothing more than personal expressions of like and dislike – then the question of how they can have objective validity would not arise.
2   To say that we can recognize aesthetic value by working to some set of general *principles*, of the kind 'Everything with features F, G, and H, is aesthetically good' which can be applied to the case of some particular thing that one discovers to possess these features.

Kant argues that we should resist both temptations. There are no general principles of taste; but aesthetic judgements are not mere expressions of personal liking. Hume speaks of principles, but it is somewhat obscure what he thinks they might be and how they might operate. Both are in search of a way to understand subjective likes and dislikes as a proper basis for inter-subjective judgements.

Introduction to Hume

David Hume (1711–76) is acknowledged as one of the greatest philosophers to have written in the English language. The works of Hume most studied by philosophers are his *Treatise of Human Nature* and his two *Enquiries* concerning human understanding and the principles of morals. Hume was an all-round philosopher who made important contributions to epistemology, metaphysics, philosophy of mind, ethics, and the philosophy of religion. His essay 'Of the Standard of Taste' was first published in 1757. One Hume scholar has referred to it as a 'condensed, derivative essay of under twenty pages'. The derivativeness (from certain then prominent French writers on the arts) will not be apparent to most readers today, but the essay is certainly short and condensed, appearing to leave many deep questions unanswered. It has provoked much debate in recent aesthetics, and is regarded as the most important work in aesthetics before Kant. Indeed, though it has been traditional to take Kant's work as the founding document for aesthetics as a subject, many would say that Hume's essay raised essentially the same questions thirty years earlier, and perhaps did so more deftly and more provocatively. The essay is valuable for this reason alone, whatever the degree to which Hume's answers are found convincing.

David Hume, 'Of the Standard of Taste'

The great variety of Taste, as well as of opinion, which prevails in the world, is too obvious not to have fallen under every one's observation. Men of the most confined knowledge are able to remark a difference of taste in the narrow circle of their acquaintance, even where the persons have been educated under the same government, and have early imbibed the same prejudices. But those, who can enlarge their view to contemplate distant nations and remote ages, are still more surprized at the great inconsistence and contrariety. We are apt to call *barbarous* whatever departs widely from our own taste and apprehension: But soon find the epithet of reproach retorted on us. And the highest arrogance and self-conceit is at last startled, on observing an equal assurance on all sides, and scruples, amidst such a contest of sentiment, to pronounce positively in its own favour.

As this variety of taste is obvious to the most careless enquirer; so will it be found, on examination, to be still greater in reality than in appearance. The sentiments of men often differ with regard to beauty and deformity of all kinds, even while their general discourse is the same. There are certain terms in every language, which import blame, and others praise; and all men, who use the same tongue, must agree in their application of them. Every voice is united in applauding elegance, propriety, simplicity, spirit in writing; and in blaming fustian, affectation, coldness, and a false brilliancy: But when critics come to particulars, this seeming unanimity vanishes; and it is found, that they had affixed a very different meaning to their expressions. In all matters of opinion and science, the case is opposite: The difference among men is there oftener found to lie in generals than in particulars; and to be less in reality than in appearance. An explanation of the terms commonly ends the controversy; and the disputants are surprized to find, that they had been quarrelling, while at bottom they agreed in their judgment.

Those who found morality on sentiment, more than on reason, are inclined to comprehend ethics under the former observation, and to maintain, that, in all questions, which regard conduct and manners, the difference among men is really greater than at first sight it appears. It is indeed obvious, that writers of all nations and all ages concur in applauding justice, humanity, magnanimity, prudence, veracity; and in blaming the opposite qualities. Even poets and other authors, whose compositions are chiefly calculated to please the imagination, are yet found from HOMER down to FENELON, to inculcate the same moral precepts, and to bestow their applause and blame on the same virtues and vices. This great unanimity is usually ascribed to the influence of plain reason; which, in all these cases, maintains similar sentiments in all men, and prevents those controversies, to which the abstract sciences are so much exposed. So far as the unanimity is real, this account may be admitted as satisfactory: But we must also allow that some part of the seeming harmony in morals may be accounted for from the very nature of language. The word *virtue*, with its equivalent in every tongue, implies praise; as that of *vice* does blame: And no one, without the most obvious and grossest impropriety, could affix reproach to a term, which in general acceptation is understood in a good sense; or bestow applause, where the idiom requires disapprobation. HOMER's general precepts, where he delivers any such, will never be controverted; but it is obvious, that, when he draws particular pictures of manners, and represents heroism in ACHILLES and prudence in ULYSSES, he intermixes a much greater degree of ferocity in the former, and of cunning and fraud in the latter, than FENELON would admit of. The sage ULYSSES in the GREEK poet seems to delight in lies and fictions, and often employs them without any necessity or even advantage: But his more scrupulous son, in the FRENCH epic writer, exposes himself to the most imminent perils, rather than depart from the most exact line of truth and veracity.

The admirers and followers of the ALCORAN insist on the excellent moral precepts interspersed throughout that wild and absurd performance. But it is to be supposed that the ARABIC words, which correspond to the ENGLISH, equity, justice, temperance, meekness, charity, were such as, from the constant use of that tongue, must always be taken in a good sense; and it would have argued the greatest ignorance, not of morals, but of language, to have mentioned them with any epithets, besides those of applause and approbation. But would we know, whether the pretended prophet had really attained a just sentiment of morals? Let us attend to his narration; and we shall soon find, that he bestows praise on such instances of treachery, inhumanity, cruelty, revenge, bigotry, as are utterly incompatible with civilized society. No steady rule of right seems there to be attended to; and every action is blamed or praised, so far only as it is beneficial or hurtful to the true believers.

The merit of delivering true general precepts in ethics is indeed very small. Whoever recommends any moral virtues, really does no more than is implied in the terms themselves. That people, who invented the word *charity*, and used it in a good sense, inculcated more clearly and much more efficaciously, the precept, *be charitable*, than any pretended legislator or prophet, who should insert such a *maxim* in his writings. Of all expressions, those, which, together with their other meaning, imply a degree either of blame or approbation, are the least liable to be perverted or mistaken.

It is natural for us to seek a *Standard of Taste*; a rule, by which the various sentiments of men may be reconciled; at least, a decision afforded, confirming one sentiment, and condemning another.

There is a species of philosophy which cuts off all hopes of success in such an attempt, and represents the impossibility of ever attaining any standard of taste. The difference, it is said, is very wide between judgment and sentiment. All sentiment is right; because sentiment has a reference to nothing beyond itself, and is always real, wherever a man is conscious of it. But all determinations of the understanding are not right; because they have a reference to something beyond themselves, to wit, real matter of fact; and are not always conformable to that standard. Among a thousand different opinions which different men may entertain of the same subject, there is one, and but one, that is just and true; and the only difficulty is to fix and ascertain it. On the contrary, a thousand different sentiments, excited by the same object, are all right: Because no sentiment represents what is really in the object. It only marks a certain conformity or relation between the object and the organs or faculties of the mind; and if that conformity did not really exist, the sentiment could never possibly have being. Beauty is no quality in things themselves: It exists merely in the mind which contemplates them; and each mind perceives a different beauty. One person may even perceive deformity, where another is sensible of beauty; and every individual ought to acquiesce in his own sentiment, without pretending to regulate those of others. To seek the real beauty, or real deformity, is as fruitless an enquiry, as to pretend to ascertain the real sweet or real bitter. According to the disposition of the organs, the same object may be both sweet and bitter; and the proverb has justly determined it to be fruitless to dispute concerning tastes. It is very natural, and even quite necessary, to extend this axiom to mental, as well as bodily taste; and thus common sense, which is so often at variance with philosophy, especially with the sceptical kind, is found, in one instance at least, to agree in pronouncing the same decision.

e⟶ But though this axiom, by passing into a proverb, seems to have attained the sanction of common sense; there is certainly a species of common sense which opposes it, at least serves to modify and restrain it. Whoever would assert an equality of genius and elegance between OGILBY and MILTON, or BUNYAN and ADDISON, would be thought to defend no less an extravagance, than if he had maintained a mole-hill to be as high as TENERIFFE, or a pond as extensive as the ocean. Though there may be found persons, who give the preference to the former authors; no one pays attention to such a taste; and we pronounce without scruple the sentiment of these pretended critics to be absurd and ridiculous. The principle of the natural equality of tastes is then totally forgot, and while we admit it on some occasions, where the objects seem near an equality, it appears an extravagant paradox, or rather a palpable absurdity, where objects so disproportioned are compared together.

f⟶ It is evident that none of the rules of composition are fixed by reasonings *a priori*, or can be esteemed abstract conclusions of the understanding, from comparing those habitudes and relations of ideas, which are eternal and immutable. Their foundation is the same with that of all the practical sciences, experience; nor are they any thing but general observations, concerning what has been univer-

g⟶ sally found to please in all countries and in all ages. Many of the beauties of poetry and even of eloquence are founded on falsehood and fiction, on hyperboles, metaphors, and an abuse or perversion of terms from their natural meaning. To check the sallies of the imagination, and to reduce every expression to geometrical truth and

exactness, would be the most contrary to the laws of criticism; because it would produce a work, which, by universal experience, has
[h]→ been found the most insipid and disagreeable. But though poetry can never submit to exact truth, it must be confined by rules of art, discovered to the author either by genius or observation. If some negligent or irregular writers have pleased, they have not pleased by their transgressions of rule or order, but in spite of these transgressions: They have possessed other beauties, which were conformable to just criticism; and the force of these beauties has been able to overpower censure, and give the mind a satisfaction superior to the disgust arising from the blemishes. ARIOSTO pleases; but not by his monstrous and improbable fictions, by his bizarre mixture of the serious and comic styles, by the want of coherence in his stories, or by the continual interruptions of his narration. He charms by the force and clearness of his expression, by the readiness and variety of his inventions, and by his natural pictures of the passions, especially those of the gay and amorous kind: And however his faults may diminish our satisfaction, they are not able entirely to destroy it. Did our pleasure really arise from those parts of his poem, which we denominate faults, this would be no objection to criticism in general: It would only be an objection to those particular rules of criticism, which would establish such circumstances to be faults, and would represent them as univer-
[i]→ sally blameable. If they are found to please, they cannot be faults; let the pleasure, which they produce, be ever so unexpected and unaccountable.

[j]→   But though all the general rules of art are founded only on experience and on the observation of the common sentiments of human nature, we must not imagine, that, on every occasion, the feelings of men will be conformable to these rules. Those finer emotions of the mind are of a very tender and delicate nature, and require the concurrence of many favourable circumstances to make them play with facility and exactness, according to their general and established principles. The least exterior hindrance to such small springs, or the least internal disorder, disturbs their motion, and confounds the operation of the whole machine. When we would make an experiment of this nature, and would try the force of any beauty or deformity, we must choose with care a proper time and place, and bring the fancy to a suitable situation and disposition. A perfect serenity of mind, a recollection of thought, a due attention to the object; if any of these circumstances be wanting, our experiment will be fallacious, and we shall be unable to judge of the catholic and universal beauty.
[k]→ The relation, which nature has placed between the form and the sentiment, will at least be more obscure; and it will require greater

accuracy to trace and discern it. We shall be able to ascertain its influence not so much from the operation of each particular beauty, as from the durable admiration, which attends those works, that have survived all the caprices of mode and fashion, all the mistakes of ignorance and envy.

l→ The same HOMER, who pleased at ATHENS and ROME two thousand years ago, is still admired at PARIS and at LONDON. All the changes of climate, government, religion, and language, have not been able to obscure his glory. Authority or prejudice may give a temporary vogue to a bad poet or orator; but his reputation will never be durable or general. When his compositions are examined by posterity or by foreigners, the enchantment is dissipated, and his faults appear in their true colours. On the contrary, a real genius, the longer his works endure, and the more wide they are spread, the more sincere is the admiration which he meets with. Envy and jealousy have too much place in a narrow circle; and even familiar acquaintance with his person may diminish the applause due to his performances: But when these obstructions are removed, the beauties, which are naturally fitted to excite agreeable sentiments, immediately display their energy; and while the world endures, they maintain their authority over the minds of men.

m→ It appears then, that, amidst all the variety and caprice of taste, there are certain general principles of approbation or blame, whose influence a careful eye may trace in all operations of the mind. Some particular forms or qualities, from the original structure of the internal fabric, are calculated to please, and others to displease; and if they fail of their effect in any particular instance, it is from some apparent defect or imperfection in the organ. A man in a fever would not insist on his palate as able to decide concerning flavours; nor would one, affected with the jaundice, pretend to give a verdict with regard to colours. In each creature, there is a sound and a defective
n→ state; and the former alone can be supposed to afford us a true standard of taste and sentiment. If, in the sound state of the organ, there be an entire or a considerable uniformity of sentiment among men, we may thence derive an idea of the perfect beauty; in like manner as the appearance of objects in day-light, to the eye of a man in health, is denominated their true and real colour, even while colour is allowed to be merely a phantasm of the senses.

o→ Many and frequent are the defects in the internal organs, which prevent or weaken the influence of those general principles, on which
p→ depends our sentiment of beauty or deformity. Though some objects, by the structure of the mind, be naturally calculated to give pleasure, it is not to be expected, that in every individual the pleasure will be

equally felt. Particular incidents and situations occur, which either throw a false light on the objects, or hinder the true from conveying to the imagination the proper sentiment and perception.

One obvious cause, why many feel not the proper sentiment of beauty, is the want of that *delicacy* of imagination, which is requisite to convey a sensibility of those finer emotions. This delicacy every one pretends to: Every one talks of it; and would reduce every kind of taste or sentiment to its standard. But as our intention in this essay is to mingle some light of the understanding with the feelings of sentiment, it will be proper to give a more accurate definition of delicacy, than has hitherto been attempted. And not to draw our philosophy from too profound a source, we shall have recourse to a noted story in DON QUIXOTE.

q⟶ It is with good reason, says SANCHO to the squire with the great nose, that I pretend to have a judgment in wine: This is a quality hereditary in our family. Two of my kinsmen were once called to give their opinion of a hogshead, which was supposed to be excellent, being old and of a good vintage. One of them tastes it; considers it; and after mature reflection pronounces the wine to be good, were it not for a small taste of leather, which he perceived in it. The other, after using the same precautions, gives also his verdict in favour of the wine; but with the reserve of a taste of iron, which he could easily distinguish. You cannot imagine how much they were both ridiculed for their judgment. But who laughed in the end? On emptying the hogshead, there was found at the bottom, an old key with a leathern thong tied to it.

The great resemblance between mental and bodily taste will easily teach us to apply this story. Though it be certain, that beauty and deformity, more than sweet and bitter, are not qualities in objects, but r⟶ belong entirely to the sentiment, internal or external; it must be allowed, that there are certain qualities in objects, which are fitted by nature to produce those particular feelings. Now as these qualities may be found in a small degree, or may be mixed and confounded with each other, it often happens, that the taste is not affected with such minute qualities, or is not able to distinguish all the particular flavours, amidst the disorder, in which they are presented. Where the organs are so fine, as to allow nothing to escape them; and at the same time so exact as to perceive every ingredient in the composition: This we call delicacy of taste, whether we employ these terms in the literal or metaphorical sense. Here then the general rules of beauty are of use; being drawn from established models, and from the observation of what pleases or displeases, when presented singly and in a high degree: And if the same qualities, in a continued composition and in a

smaller degree, affect not the organs with a sensible delight or uneasi-
ness, we exclude the person from all pretensions to this delicacy. To
s ⊢→ produce these general rules or avowed patterns of composition is like
finding the key with the leathern thong; which justified the verdict of
SANCHO's kinsmen, and confounded those pretended judges who had
condemned them. Though the hogshead had never been emptied, the
taste of the one was still equally delicate, and that of the other equally
dull and languid: But it would have been more difficult to have proved
the superiority of the former, to the conviction of every by-stander. In
like manner, though the beauties of writing had never been methodized,
or reduced to general principles; though no excellent models had ever
been acknowledged; the different degrees of taste would still have
subsisted, and the judgment of one man been preferable to that of
another; but it would not have been so easy to silence the bad critic,
who might always insist upon his particular sentiment, and refuse to
t ⊢→ submit to his antagonist. But when we show him an avowed principle
of art; when we illustrate this principle by examples, whose operation,
from his own particular taste, he acknowledges to be conformable to
the principle; when we prove, that the same principle may be applied to
the present case, where he did not perceive or feel its influence: He must
conclude, upon the whole, that the fault lies in himself, and that he
wants the delicacy, which is requisite to make him sensible of every
beauty and every blemish, in any composition or discourse.

   It is acknowledged to be the perfection of every sense or faculty, to
perceive with exactness its most minute objects, and allow nothing to
escape its notice and observation. The smaller the objects are, which
become sensible to the eye, the finer is that organ, and the more
elaborate its make and composition. A good palate is not tried by
strong flavours; but by a mixture of small ingredients, where we are
still sensible of each part, notwithstanding its minuteness and its
confusion with the rest. In like manner, a quick and acute perception
of beauty and deformity must be the perfection of our mental taste;
nor can a man be satisfied with himself while he suspects, that any
excellence or blemish in a discourse has passed him unobserved. In
this case, the perfection of the man, and the perfection of the sense or
feeling, are found to be united. A very delicate palate, on many
occasions, may be a great inconvenience both to a man himself and
u ⊢→ to his friends: But a delicate taste of wit or beauty must always be a
desirable quality; because it is the source of all the finest and most
innocent enjoyments, of which human nature is susceptible. In this
decision the sentiments of all mankind are agreed. Wherever you can
ascertain a delicacy of taste, it is sure to meet with approbation; and
the best way of ascertaining it is to appeal to those models and

principles, which have been established by the uniform consent and experience of nations and ages.

But though there be naturally a wide difference in point of delicacy between one person and another, nothing tends further to encrease and improve this talent, than *practice* in a particular art, and the frequent survey or contemplation of a particular species of beauty. When objects of any kind are first presented to the eye or imagination, the sentiment, which attends them, is obscure and confused; and the mind is, in a great measure, incapable of pronouncing concerning their merits or defects. The taste cannot perceive the several excellencies of the performance; much less distinguish the particular character of each excellency, and ascertain its quality and degree. If it pronounce the whole in general to be beautiful or deformed, it is the utmost that can be expected; and even this judgment, a person, so unpractised, will be apt to deliver with great hesitation and reserve. But allow him to acquire experience in those objects, his feeling becomes more exact and nice: He not only perceives the beauties and defects of each part, but marks the distinguishing species of each quality, and assigns it suitable praise or blame. A clear and distinct sentiment attends him through the whole survey of the objects; and he discerns that very degree and kind of approbation or displeasure, which each part is naturally fitted to produce. The mist dissipates, which seemed formerly to hang over the object: The organ acquires greater perfection in its operations; and can pronounce, without danger of mistake, concerning the merits of every performance. In a word, the same address and dexterity, which practice gives to the execution of any work, is also acquired by the same means, in the judging of it.

So advantageous is practice to the discernment of beauty, that, before we can give judgment on any work of importance, it will even be requisite, that that very individual performance be more than once perused by us, and be surveyed in different lights with attention and deliberation. There is a flutter or hurry of thought which attends the first perusal of any piece, and which confounds the genuine sentiment of beauty. The relation of the parts is not discerned: The true characters of style are little distinguished: The several perfections and defects seem wrapped up in a species of confusion, and present themselves indistinctly to the imagination. Not to mention, that there is a species of beauty, which, as it is florid and superficial, pleases at first; but being found incompatible with a just expression either of reason or passion, soon palls upon the taste, and is then rejected with disdain, at least rated at a much lower value.

It is impossible to continue in the practice of contemplating any order of beauty, without being frequently obliged to form *comparisons* between the several species and degrees of excellence, and estimating their proportion to each other. A man, who has had no opportunity of comparing the different kinds of beauty, is indeed totally unqualified to pronounce an opinion with regard to any object presented to him. By comparison alone we fix the epithets of praise or blame, and learn how to assign the due degree of each. The coarsest daubing contains a certain lustre of colours and exactness of imitation, which are so far beauties, and would affect the mind of a peasant or Indian with the highest admiration. The most vulgar ballads are not entirely destitute of harmony or nature; and none but a person, familiarized to superior beauties, would pronounce their numbers harsh, or narration uninteresting. A great inferiority of beauty gives pain to a person conversant in the highest excellence of the kind, and is for that reason pronounced a deformity: As the most finished object, with which we are acquainted, is naturally supposed to have reached the pinnacle of perfection, and to be entitled to the highest applause. One accustomed to see, and examine, and weigh the several performances, admired in different ages and nations, can alone rate the merits of a work exhibited to his view, and assign its proper rank among the productions of genius.

But to enable a critic the more fully to execute this undertaking, he must preserve his mind free from all *prejudice*, and allow nothing to enter into his consideration, but the very object which is submitted to his examination. We may observe, that every work of art, in order to produce its due effect on the mind, must be surveyed in a certain point of view, and cannot be fully relished by persons, whose situation, real or imaginary, is not conformable to that which is required by the performance. An orator addresses himself to a particular audience, and must have a regard to their particular genius, interests, opinions, passions, and prejudices; otherwise he hopes in vain to govern their resolutions, and inflame their affections. Should they even have entertained some prepossessions against him, however unreasonable, he must not overlook this disadvantage; but, before he enters upon the subject, must endeavour to conciliate their affection, and acquire their good graces. A critic of a different age or nation, who should peruse this discourse, must have all these circumstances in his eye, and must place himself in the same situation as the audience, in order to form a true judgment of the oration. In like manner, when any work is addressed to the public, though I should have a friendship or enmity with the author, I must depart from this situation; and considering myself as a man in general, forget, if possible, my individual being and my peculiar circumstances. A person influenced by prejudice, complies not with this condition; but obstinately maintains his natural position, without placing himself in that point of view, which the performance supposes. If the work be addressed to persons of a different age or nation, he makes no allowance for their peculiar views and prejudices; but, full of the manners of his own age and country, rashly condemns what seemed admirable in the eyes of those for whom alone the discourse was calculated. If the work be executed for the public, he never sufficiently enlarges his comprehension, or forgets his interest as a friend or enemy, as a rival or commentator. By this means, his sentiments are perverted; nor have the same beauties and blemishes the same influence upon him, as if he had imposed a proper violence on his imagination, and had forgotten himself for a moment. So far his taste evidently departs from the true standard; and of consequence loses all credit and authority.

It is well known, that in all questions, submitted to the understanding, prejudice is destructive of sound judgment, and perverts all operations of the intellectual faculties: It is no less contrary to good taste; nor has it less influence to corrupt our sentiment of beauty. It belongs to *good sense* to check its influence in both cases; and in this respect, as well as in many others, reason, if not an essential part of taste, is at least requisite to the operations of this latter faculty. In all the nobler productions of genius, there is a mutual relation and correspondence of parts; nor can either the beauties or blemishes be perceived by him, whose thought is not capacious enough to comprehend all those parts, and compare them with each other, in order to perceive the consistence and uniformity of the whole. Every work of art has also a certain end or purpose, for which it is calculated; and is to be deemed more or less perfect, as it is more or less fitted to attain this end. The object of eloquence is to persuade, of history to instruct, of poetry to please by means of the passions and the imagination. These ends we must carry constantly in our view, when we peruse any performance; and we must be able to judge how far the means employed are adapted to their respective purposes. Besides, every kind of composition, even the most poetical, is nothing but a chain of propositions and reasonings; not always, indeed, the justest and most exact, but still plausible and specious, however disguised by the colouring of the imagination. The persons introduced in tragedy and epic poetry, must be represented as reasoning, and thinking, and concluding, and acting, suitably to their character and circumstances; and without judgment, as well as taste and invention, a poet can never hope to succeed in so delicate an undertaking. Not to mention, that the same excellence of faculties which contributes to the improvement of reason, the same clearness of conception, the same exactness of distinction, the same vivacity of apprehension, are essential to the operations of true taste, and are its infallible concomitants. It seldom, or never happens, that a man of sense, who has experience in any art, cannot judge of its beauty; and it is no less rare to meet with a man who has a just taste without a sound understanding.

Thus, though the principles of taste be universal, and nearly, if not entirely the same in all men; yet few are qualified to give judgment on any work of art, or establish their own sentiment as the standard of beauty. The organs of internal sensation are seldom so perfect as to allow the general principles their full play, and produce a feeling correspondent to those principles. They either labour under some defect, or are vitiated by some disorder; and by that means, excite a sentiment, which may be pronounced erroneous. When the critic has no delicacy, he judges without any distinction, and is only affected by the grosser and more palpable qualities of the object: The finer touches pass unnoticed and disregarded. Where he is not aided by practice, his verdict is attended with confusion and hesitation. Where no comparison has been employed, the most frivolous beauties, such as rather merit the name of defects, are the object of his admiration. Where he lies under the influence of prejudice, all his natural sentiments are perverted. Where good sense is wanting, he is not qualified to discern the beauties of design and reasoning, which are the highest and most excellent. Under some or other of these imperfections, the generality of men labour; and hence a true judge in the finer arts is observed, even during the most polished ages, to be so rare a character: Strong sense, united to delicate sentiment, improved by practice, perfected by comparison, and cleared of all prejudice, can alone entitle critics to this valuable character; and the joint verdict of such, wherever they are to be found, is the true standard of taste and beauty.

But where are such critics to be found? By what marks are they to be known? How distinguish them from pretenders? These questions are embarrassing; and seem to throw us back into the same uncertainty, from which, during the course of this essay, we have endeavoured to extricate ourselves.

But if we consider the matter aright, these are questions of fact, not of sentiment. Whether any particular person be endowed with good sense and a delicate imagination, free from prejudice, may often be the subject of dispute, and be liable to great discussion and enquiry: But that such a character is valuable and estimable will be agreed in by all mankind. Where these doubts occur, men can do no more than in other disputable questions, which are submitted to the understanding: They must produce the best arguments, that their invention suggests to them; they must acknowledge a true and decisive standard to exist somewhere, to wit, real existence and matter of fact; and they must have indulgence to such as differ from them in their appeals to this standard. It is sufficient for our present purpose, if we have proved, that the taste of all individuals is not upon an equal footing, and that some men in general, however difficult to be particularly pitched upon, will be acknowledged by universal sentiment to have a preference above others.

But in reality the difficulty of finding, even in particulars, the standard of taste, is not so great as it is represented. Though in speculation, we may readily avow a certain criterion in science and deny it in sentiment, the matter is found in practice to be much more hard to ascertain in the former case than in the latter. Theories of abstract philosophy, systems of profound theology, have prevailed during one age: In a successive period, these have been universally exploded: Their absurdity has been detected: Other theories and systems have supplied their place, which again gave place to their successors: And nothing has been experienced more liable to the revolutions of chance and fashion than these pretended decisions of science. The case is not the same with the beauties of eloquence and poetry. Just expressions of passion and nature are sure, after a little time, to gain public applause, which they maintain for ever. ARISTOTLE, and PLATO, and EPICURUS, and DESCARTES, may successively yield to each other: But TERENCE and VIRGIL maintain an universal, undisputed empire over the minds of men. The abstract philosophy of CICERO has lost its credit: The vehemence of his oratory is still the object of our admiration.

Though men of delicate taste be rare, they are easily to be distinguished in society, by the soundness of their understanding and the superiority of their faculties above the rest of mankind. The ascendant, which they acquire, gives a prevalence to that lively approbation, with which they receive any productions of genius, and renders it generally predominant. Many men, when left to themselves, have but a faint and dubious perception of beauty, who yet are capable of relishing any fine stroke, which is pointed out to them. Every convert to the admiration of the real poet or orator is the cause of some new conversion. And though prejudices may prevail for a time, they never unite in celebrating any rival to the true genius, but yield at last to the force of nature and just sentiment. Thus, though a civilized nation may easily be mistaken in the choice of their admired philosopher, they never have been found long to err, in their affection for a favourite epic or tragic author.

But notwithstanding all our endeavours to fix a standard of taste, and reconcile the discordant apprehensions of men, there still remain two sources of variation, which are not sufficient indeed to confound all the boundaries of beauty and deformity, but will often serve to produce a difference in the degrees of our approbation or blame. The one is the different humours of particular men; the other, the particular manners and opinions of our age and country. The general principles of taste are uniform in human nature: Where men vary in their judgments, some defect or perversion in the faculties may commonly be remarked; proceeding either from prejudice, from want of practice, or want of delicacy; and there is just reason for approving one taste, and condemning another. But where there is such a diversity in the internal frame or external situation as is entirely blameless on both sides, and leaves no room to give one the preference above the other; in that case a certain degree of diversity in judgment is unavoidable, and we seek in vain for a standard, by which we can reconcile the contrary sentiments.

A young man, whose passions are warm, will be more sensibly touched with amorous and tender images, than a man more advanced in years, who takes pleasure in wise, philosophical reflections concerning the conduct of life and moderation of the passions. At twenty, OVID may be the favourite author; HORACE at forty; and perhaps TACITUS at fifty. Vainly would we, in such cases, endeavour to enter into the sentiments of others, and divest ourselves of those propensities, which are natural to us. We choose our favourite author as we do our friend, from a conformity of humour and disposition. Mirth or passion, sentiment or reflection; whichever of these most predominates in our temper, it gives us a peculiar sympathy with the writer who resembles us.

One person is more pleased with the sublime; another with the tender; a third with raillery. One has a strong sensibility to blemishes, and is extremely studious of correctness: Another has a more lively feeling of beauties, and pardons twenty absurdities and defects for one elevated or pathetic stroke. The ear of this man is entirely turned towards conciseness and energy; that man is delighted with a copious, rich, and harmonious expression. Simplicity is affected by one; ornament by another. Comedy, tragedy, satire, odes, have each its partizans, who prefer that particular species of writing to all others. It is plainly an error in a critic, to confine his approbation to one species or style of writing, and condemn all the rest. But it is almost impossible not to feel a predilection for that which suits our particular turn and disposition. Such preferences are innocent and unavoidable, and can never reasonably be the object of dispute, because there is no standard by which they can be decided.

y →   For a like reason, we are more pleased, in the course of our reading, with pictures and characters, that resemble objects which are found in our own age or country, than with those which describe a different set of customs. It is not without some effort, that we reconcile ourselves to the simplicity of ancient manners, and behold princesses carrying water from the spring, and kings and heroes dressing their own victuals. We may allow in general, that the representation of such manners is no fault in the author, nor deformity in the piece; but we are not so sensibly touched with them. For this reason, comedy is not easily transferred from one age or nation to another. A FRENCHMAN or ENGLISHMAN is not pleased with the ANDRIA of TERENCE, or CLITIA of MACHIAVEL; where the fine lady, upon whom all the play turns, never once appears to the spectators, but is always kept behind the scenes, suitably to the reserved humour of the ancient GREEKS and modern ITALIANS. A man of learning and reflection can make allowance for these peculiarities of manners; but a common audience can never divest themselves so far of their usual ideas and sentiments, as to relish pictures which no wise resemble them.

But here there occurs a reflection, which may, perhaps, be useful in examining the celebrated controversy concerning ancient and modern learning; where we often find the one side excusing any seeming absurdity in the ancients from the manners of the age, and the other refusing to admit this excuse, or at least, admitting it only as an apology for the author, not for the performance. In my opinion, the proper boundaries in this subject have seldom been fixed between the contending parties. Where any innocent peculiarities of manners are represented, such as those above mentioned, they ought certainly to be admitted; and a man, who is shocked with them, gives an evident proof of false delicacy and refinement. The poet's *monument more durable than brass*, must fall to the ground like common brick or clay, were men to make no allowance for the continual revolutions of manners and customs, and would admit of nothing but what was suitable to the prevailing fashion. Must we throw aside the pictures of our ancestors, because of their ruffs and fardingales? But where the ideas of morality and decency alter from one age to another, and where vicious manners are described, without being marked with the proper characters of blame and disapprobation; this must be allowed to disfigure the poem, and to be a real deformity. I cannot, nor is it proper I should, enter into such sentiments; and however I may excuse the poet, on account of the manners of his age, I never can relish the composition. The want of humanity and of decency, so conspicuous in the characters drawn by several of the ancient poets, even sometimes by HOMER and the GREEK tragedians, diminishes considerably the merit of their noble performances, and gives modern authors an advantage over them. We are not interested in the fortunes and sentiments of such rough heroes: We are displeased to find the limits of vice and virtue so much confounded: And whatever indulgence we may give to the writer on account of his prejudices, we cannot prevail on ourselves to enter into his sentiments, or bear an affection to characters, which we plainly discover to be blameable.

The case is not the same with moral principles, as with speculative opinions of any kind. These are in continual flux and revolution. The son embraces a different system from the father. Nay, there scarcely is any man, who can boast of great constancy and uniformity in this particular. Whatever speculative errors may be found in the polite writings of any age or country, they detract but little from the value of those compositions. There needs but a certain turn of thought or imagination to make us enter into all the opinions, which then prevailed, and relish the sentiments or conclusions derived from them. But a very violent effort is requisite to change our judgment of manners, and excite sentiments of approbation or blame, love or hatred, different from those to which the mind from long custom has been familiarized. And where a man is confident of the rectitude of that moral standard, by which he judges, he is justly jealous of it, and will not pervert the sentiments of his heart for a moment, in complaisance to any writer whatsoever.

Of all speculative errors, those, which regard religion, are the most excusable in compositions of genius; nor is it ever permitted to judge of the civility or wisdom of any people, or even of single persons, by the grossness or refinement of their theological principles. The same good sense, that directs men in the ordinary occurrences of life, is not hearkened to in religious matters, which are supposed to be placed altogether above the cognizance of human reason. On this account, all the absurdities of the pagan system of theology must be overlooked by every critic, who would pretend to form a just notion of ancient poetry; and our posterity, in their turn, must have the same indulgence to their forefathers. No religious principles can ever be imputed as a fault to any poet, while they remain merely principles, and take not such strong possession of his heart, as to lay him under the imputation of *bigotry* or *superstition*. Where that happens, they confound the sentiments of morality, and alter the natural boundaries of vice and virtue. They are therefore eternal blemishes, according to the principle abovementioned; nor are the prejudices and false opinions of the age sufficient to justify them.

It is essential to the ROMAN catholic religion to inspire a violent hatred of every other worship, and to represent all pagans, mahometans, and heretics as the objects of divine wrath and vengeance. Such sentiments, though they are in reality very blameable, are considered as virtues by the zealots of that communion, and are represented in their tragedies and epic poems as a kind of divine heroism. This bigotry has disfigured two very fine tragedies of the FRENCH theatre, POLIEUCTE and ATHALIA; where an intemperate zeal for particular modes of worship is set off with all the pomp imaginable, and forms the predominant character of the heroes. "What is this," says the sublime JOAD to JOSABET, finding her in discourse with MATHAN, the priest of BAAL, "Does the daughter of DAVID speak to this traitor? Are you not afraid, lest the earth should open and pour forth flames to devour you both? Or lest these holy walls should fall and crush you together? What is his purpose? Why comes that enemy of God hither to poison the air, which we breathe, with his horrid presence?" Such sentiments are received with great applause on the theatre of PARIS; but at LONDON the spectators would be full as much pleased to hear ACHILLES tell AGAMEMNON, that he was a dog in his forehead, and a deer in his heart, or JUPITER threaten JUNO with a sound drubbing, if she will not be quiet.

RELIGIOUS principles are also a blemish in any polite composition, when they rise up to superstition, and intrude themselves into every sentiment, however remote from any connection with religion. It is no excuse for the poet, that the customs of his country had burthened life with so many religious ceremonies and observances, that no part of it was exempt from that yoke. It must for ever be ridiculous in PETRARCH to compare his mistress, LAURA, to JESUS CHRIST. Nor is it less ridiculous in that agreeable libertine, BOCCACE, very seriously to give thanks to GOD ALMIGHTY and the ladies, for their assistance in defending him against his enemies.

Commentary on Hume

From the beginning of his essay up until $\boxed{a} \mapsto$ Hume is establishing what he calls the 'variety of taste'. People differ in the aesthetic judgements they make, in three ways: (1) within any given culture or circle of people, (2) across different cultures and times, (3) by agreeing on general features that are aesthetically good (elegance, simplicity) or bad (affectation, coldness, false brilliancy and fustian – the latter meaning roughly bombast), but finding no consensus as to which particular things their agreed terms apply to. At $\boxed{a} \mapsto$ Hume contrasts the wide lack of agreement in the case of aesthetic judgement with 'matters of opinion and science', and from $\boxed{b} \mapsto$ to $\boxed{c} \mapsto$ he makes a lengthy parallel with the case of ethics.

The essay really gets under way at $\boxed{c}\!\mapsto$, when Hume announces that it is natural to seek a standard of taste.

> **What would a standard of taste be? What function would it have?**

Hume's immediate words to describe a standard are 'a rule, by which the various sentiments of men may be reconciled; at least, a decision afforded, confirming one sentiment, and condemning another.' A sentiment is a feeling of some kind – presumably of pleasure or pain – which one has as a response to something experienced, in this case a work of art (note that Hume's examples are all literary). As regards these sentiments, Hume's sought-for standard might seem to have conflicting roles. It is one thing to have a way of deciding which response to a work of art is *correct* (or *more correct* than some others); another to reconciling people's responses, if that means getting them all to respond the same way. What Hume presumably means is that, even if one cannot change everyone's feelings so that they harmonize, one could at least stop open disagreement in judgements based upon differing feelings, if one had a rule that revealed one way of responding as the correct one.

The paragraphs labelled $\boxed{d}\!\mapsto$ and $\boxed{e}\!\mapsto$ are crucial in setting up the tension that governs the whole essay. Note especially the important 'But' at $\boxed{e}\!\mapsto$, which is the hinge around which the central problem turns.

> **What is the central problem presented in the paragraphs $\boxed{d}\!\mapsto$ and $\boxed{e}\!\mapsto$?**

Hume sets out two observations available to common sense, the first of which is also supported by a 'species of philosophy':

1   Taste seems irredeemably subjective: everyone has his or her own taste, and there can be no measure of rightness and wrongness in aesthetic judgements.
2   On the other hand, there are certain judgements of works of art which virtually everyone will accept as right, and others which they will accept as absurd. (Hume uses as an example someone preferring the work of John Ogilby, a verse translator of the day, to that of John Milton. Here is another: if I wrote a string quartet over the next few days, then, barring miracles, anyone who thought it better than a Mozart string quartet would be regarded as quite definitely wrong.)

Now there is perhaps a way of reading Hume's essay that makes the choice of solutions extreme: a choice between *relativism*, according to which there is no genuine right and wrong in matters of aesthetic judgement, and the view that there are *aesthetic rules* or *principles* which can be appealed to as setting the standard of taste.

Does Hume offer any encouragement to relativism? Does he appeal to aesthetic principles?

Hume opens with what look like some arguments for relativism. Here we need to look at the paragraph marked d⟶ and ask what are the reasons for thinking that there can be no measure of rightness and wrongness in aesthetic judgements.

The argument from d⟶ is clear. Sentiments cannot be wrong, all are 'right', because no sentiment 'represents what is really in the object', and each refers to 'nothing beyond itself'. I feel what I feel, and no one can correct me by pointing to any properties of the object. Since I judge an object beautiful solely on the grounds of the pleasure it brings about in me, an object may be beautiful to me and 'deformed' to another person; but to ask whether it is 'really' beautiful makes no sense.

But Hume does not rest with this out-and-out relativism. For although sentiments do not represent any properties really in objects, and although the feeling of a sentiment is in itself neither right nor wrong, nevertheless it is a fact (as Hume states convincingly from e⟶ onwards) that we regard some critical judgements as right and others as wrong.

Hume's problem is to avoid relativism without retracting the point that judgements of beauty rest upon sentiments, or the point that sentiments represent nothing in the object. His main attempt at a solution is to delineate conditions under which sentiments are ideally received, and to say that only sentiments felt by certain human minds in the right conditions count as authoritative regarding the beauty of objects. The stretch of text from j⟶ to w⟶ carries out this task, to which we shall return shortly.

But we posed a question above that we left unanswered.

Does Hume appeal to aesthetic principles?

At f⟶ Hume mentions 'rules of composition', suggesting principles to be followed by artists if they wish to produce aesthetically successful works. It is unclear exactly what role Hume expects these rules or principles to play. One recent commentator, Mary Mothersill, has argued that Hume equivocates over this question of principles: he repeatedly says they exist, but gives no examples, does not clearly rely on them in his central argument, and actually makes some points which suggest he does not really believe in them (see Mothersill, *Beauty Restored*, pp. 188–92).

The principles Hume talks of at f⟶ are supposed to be 'general observations, concerning what has been universally found to please in all countries and in all ages'. But there are problems with this. One is that, as Hume emphasized at the beginning, we might despair of thinking that anything pleases universally, given the observable variety of taste. Another problem is that when he later gives an example of something that has been generally liked and has aesthetically stood the test of time, it is the works of Homer that he chooses (see $\boxed{l} \mapsto$): a particular poem or poems, not general principles. (It is worth reflecting on why a general principle such as 'Poems composed like the *Iliad* are aesthetically good' would not be a satisfactory one for artists or critics to follow.)

A third problem that Hume raises for his own idea of rules of composition is that exceptions to any supposed rules may equally well be aesthetically pleasing in some contexts. At $\boxed{g} \mapsto$, $\boxed{h} \mapsto$, and $\boxed{i} \mapsto$ this thought emerges with some clarity. Exaggerations, falsehoods, and departures from standard meaning are violations of rules, yet they can all contribute to artistic success. If an artist makes 'faults' but these are the very features in virtue of which we take pleasure in the work, then they cannot really be counted as faults. And, finally, there are features such as clearness of expression or inventiveness which please us quite apart from the question of rules; and if we are pleased enough by these features, then we regard the breaking of rules as irrelevant.

At other times Hume talks not of rules of composition for artists to follow, but of generalizations about what *naturally* pleases human beings. For example, at $\boxed{j} \mapsto$ he mentions 'the common sentiments of human nature' and at $\boxed{k} \mapsto$ 'The relation which nature has placed between the form and the sentiment'. At $\boxed{p} \mapsto$ and $\boxed{r} \mapsto$ again we find that 'some objects, by the structure of the mind, [are] naturally calculated to give pleasure' and that 'there are certain qualities in objects, which are fitted by nature to produce [...] feelings' of beauty and deformity. (See also $\boxed{m} \mapsto$ and $\boxed{n} \mapsto$ for similar ideas.) This really gives the main thrust of Hume's argument. A natural propensity of qualities in objects to cause pleasure or displeasure in human minds determines which objects are aesthetically valuable and which are not.

> If there is a natural relation between qualities in objects and pleasurable responses, why do human beings not all feel the same way when they experience objects?

Allied to his notion of a natural relation between qualities and sentiments, Hume requires an account of how it is that some people are, to put it bluntly, better at responding naturally than others. From $\boxed{o} \mapsto$ onwards the essay is dominated by an account of the various ways in which the mind can be rendered imperfect in its reception of the sentiments that 'naturally' it would feel. Hume introduces the topic under the notion of 'defects of the internal organs', the most obvious of which for him is a lack of 'delicacy of imagination'. There follows a vivid tale taken from *Don Quixote*. This story sticks in the memory and is often repeated in detail by students in examinations. Less often are the following questions asked:

What point is illustrated by the tale of Sancho Panza's kinsmen in the paragraph beginning at $\boxed{\text{q}}\!\mapsto$? What is the analogy with the case of aesthetic judgement?

A simple answer to our question is that this story, in which Sancho's kinsmen are exceptionally good at detecting minute aspects of the taste of wine, simply gives an example of delicacy, or fineness of discrimination, showing that only a minority of people may have it.

But what is the parallel with the aesthetic case? The ability to perceive very fine features and to discriminate small differences in objects with exactitude is relevant to the ability to make aesthetic judgements. But Hume seems to want to make more of the parallel. In the story there is an independent check on the correctness of the sentiments, that is the sensations of metallic and leathery taste had by Sancho's kinsmen. Hume (at $\boxed{\text{s}}\!\mapsto$) says that discovering 'general rules or avowed patterns of composition' would be like finding the key with a leather thong that showed these sentiments to be justified. So knowing the general rule about what qualities in objects naturally gave rise to pleasurable sentiments of beauty would show my particular pleasurable sentiments to have been rightly felt.

Two problems with this are: (1) in most critical situations in the arts, the delicacy of someone's ability to discriminate very finely is confirmed by other people's fine discriminations – the story would be more of a proper parallel if it had other people tasting the wine and experiencing the leather or iron taste they could not discriminate before; (2) if only an exceptional subset of people are capable of fine enough discriminations to feel the right sentiments, then most people's responses will have to be discounted in order to find the correct general rule – as if only Sancho's kinsmen and a few others like them had the ability to discover the key in the wine.

Here we encounter an apparent circularity in Hume's argument. There is supposed to be a rule that shows certain responses to be correct, but the rule can be grasped only by people who have the correct responses. Before we address this, let us look at the different features that for Hume characterize the 'true judge', that is, the person who has an ideal receptivity to sentiments of beauty. Having discussed delicacy of imagination as one of these characteristics, Hume adds practice at experiencing and judging art works, comparison between many works, styles, and genres, freedom from prejudice, and what he calls 'good sense', a form of rational understanding, for example of the way the plot of a play or novel is structured, or the purposes with which it is constructed. At $\boxed{\text{v}}\!\mapsto$ we reach Hume's conception of a 'true judge': someone whose receptivity to sentiments is without any of the defects listed: 'Strong sense, united to delicate sentiment, improved by practice, perfected by comparison, and cleared of all prejudice, can alone entitle critics to this valuable character.'

There may be some problems concerning Hume's true judges: Where are they to be found? How are they to be recognized? But at $\boxed{w}\!\!\rightarrow$ Hume replies that all he wants to establish is the inequality of people's status as authoritative judges; exactly who are the true judges is difficult to resolve, but less important. One might ask whether his coolness over this issue is justified. Surely it could not be enough, if you and I disagree in our judgements, for us simply to know in general that some people are better at judging than others: that will scarcely resolve our sentiments or make one of us defer to the other. But Hume moves on quickly to say that in practice true judges rise to the top and are easily found. Here the circularity we commented on above might threaten again.

> Are true judges recognized by the superior judgements they make? Are judgements superior simply because true judges make them?

If the criterion of being a true judge were simply and solely that one made the 'right' judgements based upon the 'right' sentiments, then Hume would have a serious problem with circularity. However, it may be that some of the characteristics of true judges can be identified independently of the critical judgements they make. For example, there might be criteria for someone's being relatively free of prejudice and having good rational understanding that made no reference to their aesthetic judgements.

Another serious problem, however, concerns Hume's notion of the *joint* verdict of true judges. Suppose we are confident of there being two or three judges whose receptivity to sentiments of beauty is ideal in the ways described. Suppose further that each judge exactly equals the others in his or her degree (however measured) of delicacy of imagination, practice, comparison, good sense, and freedom from prejudice – what guarantees that they will all have the same sentiments? None of their shared qualities as judges necessitates their all *liking* the same things. So there might never be a consensus among true judges, and without such a consensus it is hard to see how Hume really has a genuine standard of taste of the universal kind he sought initially.

From $\boxed{x}\!\!\rightarrow$ onwards Hume ends his essay by pointing to some differences among people which he thinks provide unsurmountable barriers to reconciling their taste. People have different temperaments that lead them simply to like different things, especially when variation in age is taken into account. And (see $\boxed{y}\!\!\rightarrow$) people in different historical periods and in different cultures will inevitably like different things. We might wonder whether these are the only two unsurmountable factors. What about people's sex, sexual orientation, political inclinations, upbringing, genetic make-up, and other factors? Perhaps then the most realistic conclusion for Hume would be to abandon any notion of a universal taste?

Many issues are opened up by Hume's essay that there is no space to explore here. Let us end with one that commentators have sometimes addressed.

Does Hume's argument fail to distinguish fully between liking an object and evaluating it?

Most of Beethoven's music is clearly great – it has high value as music. But, in sincerely and knowledgably asserting this, I do not commit myself to liking Beethoven's music. Conversely, I may find myself irresistibly drawn to hear some ephemeral pop music in preference to Beethoven. My liking the pop music more does not commit me to evaluating it more highly as music.

Now Hume seems to want to give a purely causal account of aesthetic judgement, in the sense that his enquiry is driven by the questions:

- What sentiments are people caused to have by certain objects?
- In what sort of person would be the right sentiments be caused?

But, one might argue, the fact that most people would be caused to like X rather than Y does not yet tell us whether it would be right to judge X better than Y. And no more does it bear on the rightness of a comparative evaluation of X and Y that most, or even all, true judges would be caused to like X rather than Y. There is considerable debate about this question in the literature on Hume's essay. Questions that appear unresolved are: Is Hume's a causal account? If it is, could it ever explain the rightness and wrongness of evaluative judgements in the way that Hume wants?

Introduction to Kant

Immanuel Kant (1724–1804) has little competition for the title of greatest philosopher of the modern era. In his critical philosophy, beginning with the *Critique of Pure Reason* (1781) he revolutionized philosophical thinking in ways whose consequences philosophers are still coming to terms with. His contributions to epistemology, metaphysics, and ethics are monumental. In 1790 he published what he regarded as the completion of his philosophy, his third Critique, entitled *Critique of Judgement* (more literally *Critique of the Power of Judgement*). The first major part of this work concerns aesthetic judgement, and has often been regarded as foundational for the discipline of aesthetics as a whole.

Of all the extracts in this book this is likely to be the hardest to read. Kant is notorious for contortions of style and the introduction of technical vocabulary. I have chosen a short section from the middle of the book. Kant here recaps his previous argument succinctly in terms of the two 'peculiarities' of judgements of taste – that they claim universal assent and that there can be no proof of their correctness. He then proceeds in the so-called Deduction of Judgements of Taste to offer his solution to the problem of how these two peculiarities can co-exist. The aim is to take the reader relatively unfamiliar with Kant straight to the heart of the problem he raises for aesthetic judgement. If the style of writing in the extract seems difficult, it may help initially to focus on some of the examples Kant gives and work outwards from them to the more general points he is trying to illustrate.

Immanuel Kant, *Critique of the Power of Judgment* (extract)

§32   First Peculiarity of the Judgment of Taste

[a]→ The judgment of taste determines its object with regard to satisfaction (as beauty) with a claim to the assent of **everyone**, as if it were objective.

[b]→   To say "This flower is beautiful" is the same as merely to repeat its own claim to everyone's satisfaction. On account of the agreeableness of its smell it has no claims at all. For one person is enraptured by this smell, while another's head is dizzied by it. Now what should one infer from this except that the beauty must be held to be a property of the flower itself, which does not correspond to the difference of heads and so many senses, but to which instead the latter must correspond if [c]→ they would judge it? And yet this is not how it is. For the judgment of taste consists precisely in the fact that it calls a thing beautiful only in accordance with that quality in it by means of which it corresponds with our way of receiving it.

[d]→   Moreover, it is required of every judgment that is supposed to prove the taste of the subject that the subject judge for himself, without having to grope about by means of experience among the judgments of others and first inform himself about their satisfaction or dissatisfaction in the same object, and thus that he should pronounce his judgment not as imitation, because a thing really does please universally, but *a priori*. One would think, however, that an *a priori* judgment must contain a concept of the object, for the cognition of which [e]→ it contains the principle; the judgment of taste, however, is not grounded on concepts at all, and is above all not cognition, but only an aesthetic judgment.

[f]→   Hence a young poet does not let himself be dissuaded from his conviction that his poem is beautiful by the judgment of the public nor that of his friends, and, if he does give them a hearing, this is not because he now judges it differently, but rather because, even if (at least in his view) the entire public has a false taste, he nevertheless

(even against his judgment) finds cause to accommodate himself to the common delusion in his desire for approval. Only later, when his power of judgment has been made more acute by practice, does he depart from his previous judgment of his own free will, just as he does with those of his judgments that rest entirely on reason. Taste makes claim merely to autonomy. To make the judgments of others into the determining ground of one's own would be heteronomy.

g→ That the works of the ancients are rightly praised as models, and their authors called classical, like a sort of nobility among writers, who give laws to the people through their precedence, seems to indicate *a posteriori* sources of taste and to contradict the autonomy of taste in every subject. But one could just as well say that the ancient mathematicians, who have been regarded until now as nearly indispensable models of the greatest thoroughness and elegance of the synthetic method, also demonstrate an imitative reason on our part and its incapacity to produce from its own resources strict proofs, with the greatest intuitive evidence, by means of the construction of concepts. There is no use of our powers at all, however free it might be, and even of reason (which must draw all its judgments from the common source *a priori*), which, if every subject always had to begin entirely from the raw predisposition of his own nature, would not fall into mistaken attempts if others had not preceded him with their own, not in order to make their successors into mere imitators, but rather by means of their method to put others on the right path for seeking out the principles in themselves and thus for following their own, often better, course. Even in religion, where, certainly, each must derive the rule of his conduct from himself, because he also remains responsible for it himself and cannot shift the guilt for his transgressions onto others, whether as teachers or as predecessors, general precepts, which one may either have acquired from priests or philosophers or drawn from oneself, never accomplish as much as an example of virtue or holiness, which, established in history, does not make the autonomy of virtue out of one's own original idea of morality (*a priori*) dispensable or transform this into a mechanism of imitation. **Succession**, related to a precedent, not imitation, is the correct expression for any influence that the products of an exemplary author can have on others, which means no more than to create from the same sources from which the latter created, and to learn from one's predecessor only the manner of conducting oneself in so doing. But among all the faculties and talents, taste is precisely the one which, because its judgment is not determinable by means of concepts and precepts, is most in need of the examples of what in the progress of culture has longest enjoyed approval if it is not quickly to fall back into barbarism and sink back into the crudity of its first attempts.

§33   Second Peculiarity of the Judgment of Taste

[h]→   The judgment of taste is not determinable by grounds of proof at all, just as if it were merely **subjective**.

[i]→   If someone does not find a building, a view, or a poem beautiful, then, **first**, he does not allow approval to be internally imposed upon himself by a hundred voices who all praise it highly. He may of course behave as if it pleased him as well, in order not to be regarded as lacking in taste; he can even begin to doubt whether he has adequately formed his taste by acquaintance with a sufficient number of objects of a certain kind (just as one who believes himself to recognize something in the distance as a forest, which everyone else regards as a town, doubts the judgment of his own eyes). But what he does see clearly is this: that the approval of others provides no valid proof for the judging of beauty, that others may perhaps see and observe for him, and that what many have seen in one way what he believes himself to have seen otherwise, may serve him as a sufficient ground of proof for a theoretical, hence a logical judgment, but that what has pleased others can never serve as the ground of an aesthetic judgment. The judgment of others, when it is unfavorable to our own, can of course rightly give us reservations about our own, but can never convince us of its incorrectness. Thus there is no empirical **ground of proof** for forcing the judgment on anyone.

[j]→   **Second**, an *a priori* proof in accordance with determinate rules can determine the judgment on beauty even less. If someone reads me his poem or takes me to a play that in the end fails to please my taste, then he can adduce **Batteux** or **Lessing**, or even older and more famous critics of taste, and adduce all the rules they established as proofs that his poem is beautiful; certain passages, which are the very ones that displease me, may even agree with rules of beauty (as they have been given there and have been universally recognized): I will stop my ears, listen to no reasons and arguments, and would rather believe that those rules of the critics are false or at least that this is not a case for their application than allow that my judgment should be determined by means of *a priori* grounds of proof, since it is supposed to be a judgment of taste and not of the understanding or of reason.

It seems that this is one of the chief causes on account of which this faculty of aesthetic judging has been given the very name of "taste." For someone may list all the ingredients of a dish for me, and remark about each one that it is otherwise agreeable to me, and moreover even rightly praise the healthiness of this food; yet I am deaf to all these grounds, I try the dish with **my** tongue and my palate, and on that basis (not on the basis of general principles) do I make my judgment.

k→   In fact, the judgment of taste is always made as a singular judgment about the object. The understanding can make a universal judgment by comparing how satisfying the object is with the judgments of others, e.g., all tulips are beautiful; but in that case that is not a judgment of taste, but a logical judgment, which makes the relation of an object to taste into a predicate of things of a certain sort in general; but that by means of which I find a single given tulip beautiful, i.e., find my satisfaction in it universally valid, is the judgment of taste alone. Its peculiarity, however, consists in this: that although it has merely subjective validity, it nevertheless makes a claim on **all** subjects of a kind that could only be made if it were an objective judgment resting on cognitive grounds and capable of being compelled by means of a proof.

§34   No Objective Principle of Taste is Possible

By a principle of taste would be understood a fundamental proposition under the condition of which one could subsume the concept of an object and then by means of an inference conclude that it is beautiful. But that is absolutely impossible. For I must be sensitive of the pleasure immediately in the representation of it, and I cannot be talked into it by means of any proofs. Thus although critics, as Hume says, can reason more plausibly than cooks, they still suffer the same fate as them. They cannot expect a determining ground for their judgment from proofs, but only from the reflection of the subject on his own state (of pleasure or displeasure), rejecting all precepts and rules.

l→   However, what critics nonetheless can and should reason about, in a way that is useful for correcting and broadening our judgments of taste, is this: not the exposition of the determining ground of this sort of aesthetic judgments in a universally usable formula, which is impossible, but the investigation of the faculties of cognition and their functions in these judgments and laying out in examples the reciprocal subjective purposiveness, about which it has been shown above that its form in a given representation is the beauty of its object. Thus the critique of taste itself is only subjective, with regard to the representation by means of which an object is given to us: that is, it is the art or science of bringing under rules the reciprocal relation of the understanding and the imagination to each other in the given representation (without relation to an antecedent sensation or concept), and consequently their concord or discord, and of determining it with regard to its conditions. It is **art** if it shows this only in examples; it is **science** if it derives the possibility of such a judging from the nature of this faculty as a faculty of cognition in general. It is with the latter, as transcendental critique, that we are here alone concerned. It should develop and justify the subjective principle of taste as an *a priori* principle of the power of judgment. Criticism, as an art, merely seeks to apply the physiological (here psychological) and hence empirical rules, according to which taste actually proceeds to the judging of its objects (without reflecting on its possibility), and criticizes the products of fine art just as the **former** criticizes the faculty of judging them itself.

§35   The Principle of Taste is the Subjective Principle of the Power of Judgment in General

The judgment of taste differs from logical judgment in that the latter subsumes a representation under concepts of the object, but the former does not subsume under a concept at all, for otherwise the necessary universal approval could be compelled by proofs. All the same, however, it is similar to the latter in that it professes a universality and necessity, though not in accordance with concepts of the object, and hence a merely subjective one. Now since the concepts in a judgment constitute its content (that which pertains to the cognition of the object), but the judgment of taste is not determinable by means of concepts, it is grounded only on the subjective formal condition of a judgment in general. The subjective condition of all judgments is the faculty for judging itself, or the power of judgment. This, employed with regard to a representation by means of which an object is given, requires the agreement of two powers of representation: namely, the imagination (for the intuition and the composition of the manifold of intuition), and the understanding (for the concept as representation of the unity of this composition). Now since no concept of the object is here the ground of the judgment, it can consist only in the subsumption of the imagination itself (in the case of a representation by means of which an object is given) under the condition that the understanding in general advance from intuitions to concepts. I.e., since the freedom of the imagination consists precisely in the fact that it schematizes without a concept, the judgment of taste must rest on a mere sensation of the reciprocally animating imagination in its **freedom** and the understanding with its **lawfulness**, thus on a feeling that allows the object to be judged in accordance with the purposiveness of the representation (by means of which an object is given) for the promotion of the faculty of cognition in its free play; and taste, as a subjective power of judgment, contains a principle of subsumption, not of intuitions under **concepts**, but of the **faculty** of intuitions or presentations (i.e., of the imagination) under the **faculty** of concepts (i.e., the understanding), insofar as the former **in its freedom** is in harmony with the latter **in its lawfulness.**

Now in order to discover this justifying ground through a deduction of judgments of taste, only the formal peculiarities of this kind of judgments, that is, only insofar as it is merely their logical form that is considered, can serve as our guideline.

§36   On the Problem for a Deduction of Judgments of Taste

The perception of an object can be immediately combined with the concept of an object in general, for which the former contains the empirical predicates, for a judgment of cognition, and a judgment of experience can thereby be produced. Now this is grounded in *a priori* concepts of the synthetic unity of the manifold, in order to think it as the determination of an object; and these concepts (the categories) require a deduction, which, moreover, was given in the *Critique of Pure Reason*, by means of which the solution to the problem "How are synthetic *a priori* judgments of cognition possible?" was provided. This problem thus concerned the *a priori* principles of pure understanding and its theoretical judgments.

However, a perception can also be immediately combined with a feeling of pleasure (or displeasure) and a satisfaction that accompanies the representation of the object and serves it instead of a predicate, and an aesthetic judgment, which is not a cognitive judgment, can thus arise. Such a judgment, if it is not a mere judgment of sensation but a formal judgment of reflection, which requires this satisfaction of everyone as necessary, must be grounded in something as an *a priori* principle, even if only a merely subjective principle (if an objective principle for this kind of judgment would be impossible), but which, as such a principle, also requires a deduction, by means of which it may be comprehended how an aesthetic judgment could lay claim to necessity. This is the basis of the problem with which we are now concerned: How are judgments of taste possible? This problem thus concerns the *a priori* principles of the pure power of judgment in **aesthetic** judgments, i.e., in those where it does not (as in theoretical judgments) merely have to subsume under objective concepts of the

understanding and stands under a law, but where it is itself, subject-
ively, both object as well as law.

[o]→   This problem can also be represented thus: How is a judgment
possible which, merely from **one's own** feeling of pleasure in an
object, independent of its concept, judges this pleasure, as attached
to the representation of the same object **in every other subject**, *a
priori*, i.e., without having to wait for the assent of others?

That judgments of taste are synthetic is readily seen, because they
go beyond the concept and even the intuition of the object, and add to
that as a predicate something that is not even cognition at all, namely
the feeling of pleasure (or displeasure). However, that such judgments, even though the predicate (of **one's own** pleasure that is
combined with the representation) is empirical, are nevertheless, as
far as the requisite assent **of everyone** is concerned, *a priori* judgments, or would be taken as such, is already implicit in the expressions of their claim; and thus this problem of the critique of the power
of judgment belongs under the general problem of transcendental
philosophy: How are synthetic *a priori* judgments possible?

§37 What is Really Asserted *a priori* of an Object in a Judgment of Taste?

That the representation of an object is immediately combined with a
pleasure can be perceived only internally, and would, if one wanted to
indicate nothing more than this, yield a merely empirical judgment.
For I cannot combine a determinate feeling (of pleasure or displeasure) *a priori* with any representation, except where my ground is an *a
priori* principle of reason determining the will; for then the pleasure
(in the moral feeling) is the consequence of it, but precisely on that
account it cannot be compared with the pleasure in taste at all, since it
requires a determinate concept of a law, while the judgment of taste,
by contrast, is to be combined immediately with the mere judging,
prior to any concept. Hence all judgments of taste are also singular
judgments, since they combine their predicate of satisfaction not with
a concept but with a given singular empirical representation.

Thus it is not the pleasure but **the universal validity of this pleasure**
perceived in the mind as connected with the mere judging of an object
that is represented in a judgment of taste as a universal rule for the
power of judgment, valid for everyone. It is an empirical judgment
that I perceive and judge an object with pleasure. But it is an *a priori*
judgment that I find it beautiful, i.e., that I may require that satisfaction of everyone as necessary.

§38 Deduction of Judgments of Taste

If it is admitted that in a pure judgment of taste the satisfaction in the object is combined with the mere judging of its form, then it is nothing other than the subjective purposiveness of that form for the power of judgment that we sense as combined with the representation of the object in the mind. Now since the power of judgment in regard to the formal rules of judging, without any matter (neither sensation nor concept), can be directed only to the subjective conditions of the use of the power of judgment in general (which is restricted neither to the particular kind of sense nor to a particular concept of understanding), and thus to that subjective element that one can presuppose in all human beings (as requisite for possible cognitions in general), the correspondence of a representation with these conditions of the power of judgment must be able to be assumed to be valid for everyone *a priori*. I.e., the pleasure or subjective purposiveness of the representation for the relation of the cognitive faculties in the judging of a sensible object in general can rightly be expected of everyone.*

Remark

This deduction is so easy because it is not necessary for it to justify any objective reality of a concept; for beauty is not a concept of the object, and the judgment of taste is not a judgment of cognition. It asserts only that we are justified in presupposing universally in every human being the same subjective conditions of the power of judgment that we find in ourselves; and then only if we have correctly subsumed the given object under these conditions. Now although this latter has unavoidable difficulties that do not pertain to the logical power of judgment (because in the latter one subsumes under concepts, but in the aesthetic power of judgment one subsumes under a relation that is

---

* In order to be justified in laying claim to universal assent for judgments of the aesthetic power of judgment resting merely on subjective grounds, it is sufficient to admit: (1) In all human beings, the subjective conditions of this faculty, as far as the relation of the cognitive powers therein set into action to a cognition in general is concerned, are the same, which must be true, since otherwise human beings could not communicate their representations and even cognition itself. (2) The judgment has taken into consideration solely this relation (hence the **formal condition** of the power of judgment), and is pure, i.e., mixed with neither concepts of the object nor with sensations as determining grounds. If an error is made with regard to the latter, that concerns only the incorrect application to a particular case of the authority that a law gives us, by which the authority in general is not suspended.

merely a matter of sensation, that of the imagination and the understanding reciprocally attuned to each other in the represented form of the object, where the subsumption can easily be deceptive); yet nothing is thereby taken away from the legitimacy of the claim of the power of judgment in counting on universal assent, which only comes down to this: the correctness of the principle for validly judging for everyone on subjective grounds. For as far as the difficulty and the doubt about the correctness of the subsumption under that principle is concerned, it makes the legitimacy of the claim to this validity of an aesthetic judgment in general, and thus the principle itself, no more doubtful than the equally (although not as often and as easily) erroneous subsumption of the logical power of judgment under its principle can make the latter, which is objective, doubtful. But if the question were to be "How is it possible to assume nature as a sum of objects of taste *a priori*?," then this problem is related to teleology, because producing forms that are purposive for our power of judgment would have to be regarded as an end of nature that pertains to its concept essentially. But the correctness of this assumption is still very dubious, whereas the reality of the beauties of nature is open to experience.

Commentary on Kant

Kant's topic is what he calls judgements of taste. These are judgements such as 'This flower is beautiful' or 'My poem is beautiful'. Such judgements, for Kant, are always singular, never generalizations, and always pronounced upon an object of the judger's own experience. We may assume that 'is beautiful' here is equivalent to 'has aesthetic value': beauty for Kant is the most general term of aesthetic approbation. He does not himself use the term 'aesthetic' in this more recent sense. For him 'aesthetic' means, in this context, 'based upon feeling or sensation' (in line with the original Greek word *aisthesis*). Therefore it is not a tautology for Kant to say, as at $\boxed{e}{\mapsto}$, that a judgement of taste is an aesthetic judgement. He means that a judgement that something is beautiful is grounded on a subjective feeling of pleasure.

Some way through this extract, at $\boxed{o}{\mapsto}$, Kant states what he sees as the central problem to be solved. Leaving out a few technicalities, it is: How, merely from one's feeling of pleasure in an object, can one judge in advance that all other subjects should feel the same pleasure?

There are two main tasks for Kant here. One is to convince us that judgements of taste (or judgements of beauty) really are such that this problem arises. This he does predominantly in §§32–3 where he discusses the 'peculiarities' of the judgement of taste, and §34 where he reiterates the point that there are no objective principles of taste. The remaining sections are oriented towards the second task, that of showing a way out of the problem for judgements of taste. The way out, expressed by Kant in a compressed and technical manner, essentially involves the thought that there are ways in which the minds of all human beings work in common, indeed structural or formal conditions that all cognition must conform to. So, Kant hopes, the universality that I claim when judging an object beautiful can be grounded in the presupposition of a 'subjective element in all human beings' that gives me the right to expect of everyone the same pleasure in experiencing a given object.

How the problem arises

At a⟩→ and h⟩→ Kant states two 'peculiarities' of the judgement of taste. What about them raises a problem?

It would appear to be only the conjunction of two propositions that makes for a problem, namely (to paraphrase) *that judgements of beauty claim the assent of everyone* and that *judgements of beauty are not determinable by grounds of proof.*

On a closer look, Kant problematizes each of his statements internally by inserting an 'as if'. The judgement of taste behaves as if it were objective (implication: when it is not), and it behaves as if it were merely subjective (implication: when it is not). These judgements are peculiar indeed if they are neither objective nor subjective, but seem to be both. Let us address the two peculiarities in turn.

What grounds does Kant give for thinking that a judgement of taste (a) claims the assent of everyone, and (b) is not objective?

At b⟩→ Kant simply states that judging something beautiful 'is the same as' claiming that everyone should take satisfaction in it. In another passage, not included here, he says that no one would ever think of saying 'It is beautiful *for me*'. Thus it is built into this kind of judgement that it is universal in a way that is comparable to an ordinary judgement that ascribes an objective property to an object. Yet, says Kant, we cannot make the inference we might expect: to say that the flower is beautiful is not to ascribe an objective property to the flower itself (see c⟩→).

We might try to undo Kant's problem by moving in either of two directions, towards subjectivity or towards objectivity.

Should we agree with Kant that 'X is beautiful' is not a merely subjective judgement?

Sometimes when we make such evaluative judgements we may be prepared to retreat to a mere statement about what we like: 'it works for me', 'it's attractive to me', or whatever. But are all aesthetic judgements of that kind? Arguably, Kant is right that at least sometimes we make a judgement that we are prepared to assert on behalf of others too, the sort of judgement where I regard someone else as wrong if they do not find the object beautiful, or at least where I think that there is a genuine disagreement such that we cannot both be right. If one person says 'It works for me' whereas another person says 'It doesn't work for me', that is not a genuine disagreement. Kant's position remains intact provided we think that not all aesthetic judgements are of this latter type. The problem he is addressing concerns the remaining judgements where genuine disagreement is possible.

But how is genuine disagreement possible? What about the suggested move towards greater objectivity?

> **Should we agree with Kant that 'X is beautiful' ascribes no property to X itself?**

If we could think of 'X is beautiful' as ascribing a property to X itself, then it would be easier to see how genuine aesthetic disagreement could be possible. 'X is beautiful' would be true if X itself had the relevant property, false if it did not. Now Kant's alternative to this is that we 'call a thing beautiful only in accordance with that quality in it by means of which it corresponds with our way of receiving it' (see $\boxed{c}\mapsto$). So there is at least a relevant 'quality' in the object. However, the problem is that our only way of detecting whether the object is such as to be received with pleasure, is to feel the pleasure. And pleasure, to repeat Hume's point, does not represent what is really in the object. So all we can do in the case of judgements of taste is to attribute to the object the propensity to cause pleasure universally, on the basis of the pleasure we feel ourselves. That is why, as Kant puts it, the judgement of taste is not founded upon concepts (see $\boxed{e}\mapsto$). The object pleases me, but not because I can classify it as falling under any determinate concept, nor because it meets some specification or purpose. A flower could please me because it fell under some conceptual description (being a tulip, growing well in shady situations, being edible to humans, being resistant to slugs). But in the case of a judgement of taste there is no such concept in virtue of which I like it and judge it beautiful.

Kant's next major point (in the paragraphs marked $\boxed{d}\mapsto$ and $\boxed{f}\mapsto$) is that a judgement of taste cannot be based on the judgements of others. In making a judgement of taste I am not *reporting that* everyone finds the object pleasing. Even if no one else judges it beautiful, if it affects me with pleasure then I will judge it beautiful on behalf of everyone, thereby implying that everyone else has missed something I have seen in the object. Kant's example of the young poet illustrates this point. The young poet is right not to amend his judgement if he still feels the pleasure on which his judgement of taste is based. But he is right to change his mind when more mature, because now he does not feel the same pleasure on the basis of which to pronounce his poems beautiful.

The remainder of §32, from g→ onwards, addresses the objection that there are great classical works of art that function as models for judgement, so that there are some kind of empirical rules for what counts as beautiful, on the basis of which we may judge a new object. Kant's reply is that these works give examples of the creative process, not models to be imitated. These examples are needed so that there is some kind of progress and continuity in our cultural products. But the ability to make judgements of taste is still autonomous in each individual, not dictated by rules derived from past works.

Let us now turn to the points covered by Kant's discussion of the 'second peculiarity' in §33.

> What grounds does Kant give for thinking that a judgement of taste (a) is not determinable by grounds of proof, and (b) is not merely subjective?

In a way, much of this is a repetition of what went before. There can be no proof of a judgement of taste because it is not based on concepts or rules, only on each person's autonomous feeling of pleasure; but the judgement is not merely subjective because it claims the assent of everyone.

Kant argues here that there could in theory be two ways of giving a proof for a judgement of taste, empirically and *a priori*, but that neither can be done. Therefore there can be no proof of a judgement of taste.

The argument against empirical proof is at i→. Kant acknowledges that we might pause to re-examine our judgement if large numbers of people make judgements that go against it; also that we might have social reasons to agree verbally with the majority verdict. But all of this is different from counting or surveying others' contrary judgements to decide that we are wrong. If our judgement is genuinely aesthetic (that is, feeling-based), then only a change in our feeling should make us alter our judgement.

The argument against *a priori* proof is at j→. This again combats the once fashionable idea that there are rules for successful artistic composition that all works of art must meet on pain of failure, and to meet which is some kind of guarantee of aesthetic success. Established critics may have worked out such rules, and seek to apply them *a priori* to whatever works come their way. But a judgement of taste is simply not based on rules or authority, but is an autonomous judgement based upon one's own feeling of pleasure on confronting an object.

An important feature of judgements of taste is that they are always singular, not general (see k→). How could one make a judgement of taste that all tulips are beautiful unless one had seen them all? One could judge that all tulips are flowers, because then one is simply making a cognitive judgement, attaching, as Kant says, a predicate to things of a certain sort in general. Kant even allows that there could be a general judgement that 'all tulips are beautiful' – only then it would not be a judgement of taste.

In §34 Kant states that there could be no objective principle of taste to justify the claim of universality that a judgement of beauty makes. This is a plausible statement, given what has gone before, or in a sense just repeats what has gone before. One is not, in judging an object beautiful, subsuming it under a concept to make a cognitive judgement, and cannot use proofs to persuade someone that an object is such as to be experienced by them with pleasure. In the remainder of the section, from ⬚1⬚⊢→, Kant moves towards his solution to the problem of judgements of taste, when he mentions, in somewhat veiled fashion, 'the faculties of cognition' and a 'reciprocal subjective purposiveness' in experience. These notions will be addressed in the next section of the commentary.

Kant's solution

Kant's presentation of a solution in the 'Deduction of Judgements of Taste' retains a degree of impenetrability even for scholars who know Kant's works well. Let us first sketch some background in the briefest fashion.

In his *Critique of Pure Reason* Kant put forward a particular structure of the mind which he argued to be a necessary *a priori* requirement for cognition, or experience of a world of objects. He refers explicitly to this account at ⬚n⬚⊢→, and implicitly throughout the surrounding argument. Kant argued that for a mind to have experience of a world of objects, it must be able to make judgements, and that for it to make judgements, there must be reception of multiple data (or what he calls a manifold of intuitions), assembly or synthesis of the various data in the imagination, and an active capacity for unifying these data under concepts. In the present discussion he abbreviates this into the claim that the mind, in order to experience an objective world, must have both an imagination and an understanding. See ⬚m⬚⊢→ for a statement along these lines.

Now in ordinary experience the understanding *unifies* the data assembled by the imagination, and it does so by applying to them concepts. Because of the application of concepts, instead of experiencing merely a multiplicity of diverse data, I am able to experience a determinate object with a location in space and time and relations to other objects. By applying specific concepts I can then make objective judgements, judging the object to be a flower, the flower to be a lily, and so on.

Kant's model of the experience that leads me to judge an object beautiful is (roughly) that I experience the same kind of unity as occurs in objective judgements, but without any determinate concept or judgement issuing from it. So I feel simply a kind of purposiveness or rightness in the experience itself, and to feel this is fulfilling, without any determinate objective judgement having to be made.

The argument in §38 is designed to show that the claim to universal agreement we make in judgements of taste is a legitimate one: that we are entitled to
claim everyone's agreement, even on the sole basis of our own subjective
pleasure. 'Deduction' is here a term borrowed from the context of law, where
it means a proof of the legitimacy of something. Kant applies the term here to
his argument concerning the legitimacy of the claim made by a judgement of
taste.

In rough outline here is one way of construing the argument:

1   The same subjective conditions underlie the cognitive capacities of all
    judging subjects.
2   The subjective conditions underlying cognition are those required for
    aesthetic response.
3   Therefore, anyone capable of cognition is capable of aesthetic response –
    i.e. all judging subjects are capable of that response which founds aesthetic
    judgement.
4   Therefore, aesthetic judgements are justified in claiming the assent of all.

The idea is that, if my own pleasurable response to an object is occasioned by
the free play of my cognitive faculties, then I am experiencing the suitability of
the object to the cognitive faculties in general. This justifies me in claiming
that every subject capable of cognition ought to have the response I have, and
ought therefore to judge the object beautiful.

There are many difficulties raised by this argument, some of them relatively
technical points about how Kant envisages the mind working in ordinary
perception and how that relates to what happens in the experience of beauty.
One might think the working of the imagination and understanding that
grounds a judgement of beauty should be exceptional – otherwise why does
not every perceptual experience issue in a judgement that the perceived object
is beautiful? On the other hand, Kant needs the workings of the imagination
and understanding that ground judgements of taste to be guaranteed as
universal to all judging subjects, and to be found in the power of making
judgements quite generally.

Whatever Kant actually means by the 'subjective conditions' that are the same
in all judging subjects, can he really go so far as to say that for all of us perceiving
and judging must *feel* the same? It is hard to know what that amounts to as a
general thesis about all perception and judgement. And it would seem far-
fetched to claim that for some particular flower or poem, say, the experience
of it in perception must *feel* the same to all who can perceive and judge it.

It has been suggested that the most Kant is entitled to conclude from his
Deduction argument is that someone making a judgement of taste is justified
in assuming that all judging subjects *can* feel the same. This is less than he sets
out to show, but may be a good start towards establishing the kind of
community of taste that he is interested in.

Having seen the difficulties Kant has in proving that judgements of taste make a justified claim to universality, we might suggest a broader criticism, going back to Kant's initial assumptions. Why insist that a judgement of something's aesthetic value should be shared by *all* judging subjects? Hume seems wiser in his realization that individual temperament, age, and cultural background will always divide subjects' tastes from one another. If I judge a piece of music by Janáček to be beautiful, I mean that other listeners should agree in finding beauty in that piece of music, and not just that I like it. But as long as a few friends who are used to listening to twentieth-century orchestral music agree with me, and a handful of critics who are experienced in judging such things, then I am satisfied. I do not expect that literally everyone will agree.

Kant's philosophical project, embracing epistemology and ethics as well as aesthetics, gives him strong reason to hold out for universality in aesthetic judgements. However, an aesthetic theory closer to the ground, as it were, might be able to dispense with the demand for universality, without lapsing back into the idea that aesthetic judgements are nothing but subjective statements of preference.

4

The Nature of Art

Introduction to the Issues

An understandable preoccupation in the philosophy of art is the question 'What is art?' Some philosophers, as in the second reading in this chapter, undertake to find a definition of art. Others have tried to show what characterizes the best art and demarcates it from other similar activities that may even be called art, but which do not succeed as the best or most authentic art does. The first reading, from R. G. Collingwood, falls broadly into this category.

The question of defining art is, in fact, fraught with difficulties. First, the concept of art is commonly used both to describe and to evaluate. Often when someone pronounces of some gallery exhibit 'I wouldn't call that a work of art', they mean something to do with the thing's lack of value in their eyes. But in the descriptive sense the thing may still be a work of art, just a bad, dull, or disgusting one. So if we are offering a definition we have to decide whether to leave aside the question of value and simply specify the conditions for something being correctly classified as a work of art. This is the starting-point for the definition offered by George Dickie in the second reading.

Secondly, there may be no genuine definition to be had. 'Art' may be what followers of Wittgenstein have termed a 'family-resemblance' concept: some paintings might have some features in common with some sculptures, some pieces of music with some poems, some novels with some operas, and so on, but there may be no single set of features that all and only works of art have. The increasing variety of what is described as art has also fed the conviction that there is no essence to art, and that it is an open-ended, ever revisable category.

Thirdly, we may have to consider features of art works which may not be discernible on a simple perceptual encounter, perhaps features that they have in relation to other things. In different ways both of our authors light upon relational features of works as what marks them out as art. For Collingwood the work of art gains its status by being an expression of a state of emotion felt and articulated by its author. Dickie, rejecting the simple relation of work to author as inadequate, holds that what makes something art is a more complex relation in which it stands to an institutional setting and the actions of persons with roles that are constitutive of that setting, which he calls the artworld.

Introduction to Collingwood

R. G. Collingwood (1889–1943) was Professor of Philosophy at the University of Oxford. He was a historian as well as a philosopher, and did important work in the philosophy of history among other areas. His approach to philosophy was at odds with the nascent analytical philosophy of the day, which led to some of his work being comparatively neglected, but in aesthetics his book *The Principles of Art* (1938) has been widely respected as an original and clearly focused contribution. Collingwood is concerned to demarcate 'art proper' from art 'falsely so called'. He maintains that he is not redefining art, but trying to explicate what is contained in the term as it is already used. 'Art', when it means 'art proper', is an evaluative term for Collingwood: for something to be art is for it to succeed in doing something specific, namely to achieve the articulate expression of felt emotions. There is something of a crusading tone to Collingwood's powerful prose, for he believes that a different paradigm of art tends to be widely accepted, which he refers to as the 'technical theory' of art. Collingwood places this theory's origins in the writings of Plato and Aristotle, for whom the Greek word *techne* means skill, craft, or expert knowledge. According to this popular conception of art, the artist is a skilled producer, whose aim is to arouse certain specific emotions in an audience, and whose means is an art work in which he or she strives to represent the world, or some aspect of it. Art is representation designed to arouse emotions, according to the view Collingwood rejects. He insists that art is properly distinct from craft, having no true means–end or matter–form distinctions, and that the essential feature of art is not the arousal of emotions in others, but the expression of emotions that are felt by the artist and communicated through their articulation and embodiment in an artistic medium.

The rejection of the 'technical theory' is not just of theoretical importance for Collingwood. The idea that art is a skilled technique of representation to arouse emotions breeds art that actually operates in that fashion, and is either 'art as amusement' (bringing about emotions for their own sake) or 'art as magic' (bringing about emotions of a socially useful type, such as loyalty or religious conviction). For Collingwood these are inauthentic forms of art. When art proper arises, it is because someone has succeeded in making an emotion articulate, in a way not specifiable independently of the work itself in which the emotion is expressed.

R. G. Collingwood,
The Principles of Art (extracts)

VI   Art Proper: (1) As Expression

§1   *The new problem*

We have finished at last with the technical theory of art, and with the various kinds of art falsely so called to which it correctly applies. We shall return to it in the future only so far as it forces itself upon our notice and threatens to impede the development of our subject.

That subject is art proper. It is true that we have already been much concerned with this; but only in a negative way. We have been looking at it so far as was necessary in order to exclude from it the various things which falsely claimed inclusion in it. We must now turn to the positive side of this same business, and ask what kinds of things they are to which the name rightly belongs.

[a]⊢→ In doing this we are still dealing with what are called questions of fact, or what in the first chapter were called questions of usage, not with questions of theory. We shall not be trying to build up an argument which the reader is asked to examine and criticize, and accept if he finds no fatal flaw in it. We shall not be offering him information which he is asked to accept on the authority of witnesses. We shall be trying as best we can to remind ourselves of facts well known to us all: such facts as this, that on occasions of a certain kind we actually do use the word art or some kindred word to designate certain kinds of thing, and in the sense which we have now isolated as the proper sense of the word. Our business is to concentrate our attention on these usages until we can see them as consistent and systematic. This will be our work throughout this chapter and the next. The task of defining the usages thus systematized, and so constructing a theory of art proper, will come later.

[...]

[b]⊢→ An erroneous philosophical theory is based in the first instance not on ignorance but on knowledge. The person who constructs it begins by partially understanding the subject, and goes on to distort what he

knows by twisting it into conformity with some preconceived idea. A theory which has commended itself to a great many intelligent people invariably expresses a high degree of insight into the subject dealt with, and the distortion to which this has been subjected is invariably thoroughgoing and systematic. It therefore expresses many truths, but it cannot be dissected into true statements and false statements; every statement it contains has been falsified; if the truth which underlies it is to be separated out from the falsehood, a special method of analysis must be used. This consists in isolating the preconceived idea which has acted as the distorting agent, reconstructing the formula of the distortion, and re-applying it so as to correct the distortion and thus find out what it was that the people who invented or accepted the theory were trying to say. In proportion as the theory has been more widely accepted, and by more intelligent persons, the likelihood is greater that the results of this analysis will be found useful as a starting-point for further inquiries.

This method will now be applied to the technical theory of art. The formula for the distortion is known from our analysis of the notion of craft in Chapter 11, §1. Because the inventors of the theory were prejudiced in favour of that notion, they forced their own ideas about art into conformity with it. The central and primary characteristic of craft is the distinction it involves between means and end. If art is to be conceived as craft, it must likewise be divisible into means and end. We have seen that actually it is not so divisible; but we have now to ask why anybody ever thought it was. What is there in the case of art which these people misunderstood by assimilating it to the well-known distinction of means and end? If there is nothing, the technical theory of art was a gratuitous and baseless invention; those who have stated and accepted it have been and are nothing but a pack of fools; and we have been wasting our time thinking about it. These are hypotheses I do not propose to adopt.

[c]→ (1) This, then, is the first point we have learnt from our criticism: that there is in art proper a distinction resembling that between means and end, but not identical with it.

(2) The element which the technical theory calls the end is defined by it as the arousing of emotion. The idea of arousing (i.e. of bringing into existence, by determinate means, something whose existence is conceived in advance as possible and desirable) belongs to the philosophy of craft, and is obviously borrowed thence. But the same is not [d]→ true of emotion. This, then, is our second point. Art has something to do with emotion; what it does with it has a certain resemblance to arousing it, but is not arousing it.

(3) What the technical theory calls the means is defined by it as the making of an artifact called a work of art. The making of this artifact is described according to the terms of the philosophy of craft: i.e. as the transformation of a given raw material by imposing on it a form preconceived as a plan in the maker's mind. To get the distortion out of this we must remove all these characteristics of craft, and thus we reach the third point. Art has something to do with making things, but these things are not material things, made by imposing form on matter, and they are not made by skill. They are things of some other kind, and made in some other way.

We now have three riddles to answer. For the present, no attempt will be made to answer the first: we shall treat it merely as a hint that the second and third should be treated separately. In this chapter, accordingly, we shall inquire into the relation between art and emotion; in the next, the relation between art and making.

§2 Expressing emotion and arousing emotion

e→ Our first question is this. Since the artist proper has something to do with emotion, and what he does with it is not to arouse it, what is it that he does? It will be remembered that the kind of answer we expect to this question is an answer derived from what we all know and all habitually say; nothing original or recondite, but something entirely commonplace.

f→ Nothing could be more entirely commonplace than to say he expresses them. The idea is familiar to every artist, and to every one else who has any acquaintance with the arts. To state it is not to state a philosophical theory or definition of art; it is to state a fact or supposed fact about which, when we have sufficiently identified it, we shall have later to theorize philosophically. For the present it does not matter whether the fact that is alleged, when it is said that the artist expresses emotion, is really a fact or only supposed to be one. Whichever it is, we have to identify it, that is, to decide what it is that people are saying when they use the phrase. Later on, we shall have to see whether it will fit into a coherent theory.

g→ They are referring to a situation, real or supposed, of a definite kind. When a man is said to express emotion, what is being said about him comes to this. At first, he is conscious of having an emotion, but not conscious of what this emotion is. All he is conscious of is a perturbation or excitement, which he feels going on within him, but of whose nature he is ignorant. While in this state, all he can say about his emotion is: 'I feel... I don't know what I feel.' From this helpless and oppressed condition he extricates himself by doing something which we call expressing himself. This is an activity which has something to do with the thing we call language: he expresses himself by speaking. It has also something to do with consciousness: the emotion expressed is an emotion of whose nature the person who feels it is no longer unconscious. It has also something to do with the way in which he feels the emotion. As unexpressed, he feels it in what we have called a helpless and oppressed way; as expressed, he feels it in a way from which this sense of oppression has vanished. His mind is somehow lightened and eased.

This lightening of emotions which is somehow connected with the expression of them has a certain resemblance to the 'catharsis' by which emotions are earthed through being discharged into a make-believe situation; but the two things are not the same. Suppose the emotion is one of anger. If it is effectively earthed, for example by fancying oneself kicking some one down stairs, it is thereafter no longer present in the mind as anger at all: we have worked it off and are rid of it. If it is expressed, for example by putting it into hot and bitter words, it does not disappear from the mind; we remain angry; but instead of the sense of oppression which accompanies an emotion of anger not yet recognized as such, we have that sense of alleviation which comes when we are conscious of our own emotion as anger, instead of being conscious of it only as an unidentified perturbation. This is what we refer to when we say that it 'does us good' to express our emotions.

The expression of an emotion by speech may be addressed to some one; but if so it is not done with the intention of arousing a like emotion in him. If there is any effect which we wish to produce in the hearer, it is only the effect which we call making him understand how we feel. But, as we have already seen, this is just the effect which expressing our emotions has on ourselves. It makes us, as well as the people to whom we talk, understand how we feel. A person arousing emotion sets out to affect his audience in a way in which he himself is not necessarily affected. He and his audience stand in quite different relations to the act, very much as physician and patient stand in quite different relations towards a drug administered by the one and taken by the other. A person expressing emotion, on the contrary, is treating himself and his audience in the same kind of way; he is making his emotions clear to his audience, and that is what he is doing to himself.

It follows from this that the expression of emotion, simply as expression, is not addressed to any particular audience. It is addressed primarily to the speaker himself, and secondarily to any one who can understand. Here again, the speaker's attitude towards his audience is quite unlike that of a person desiring to arouse in his audience a certain emotion. If that is what he wishes to do, he must know the audience he is addressing. He must know what type of stimulus will produce the desired kind of reaction in people of that particular sort; and he must adapt his language to his audience in the sense of making sure that it contains stimuli appropriate to their peculiarities. If what he wishes to do is to express his emotions intelligibly, he has to express them in such a way as to be intelligible to himself; his audience is then in the position of persons who overhear him doing this. Thus the stimulus-and-reaction terminology has no applicability to the situation.

The means-and-end, or technique, terminology too is inapplicable. Until a man has expressed his emotion, he does not yet know what emotion it is. The act of expressing it is therefore an exploration of his own emotions. He is trying to find out what these emotions are. There is certainly here a directed process: an effort, that is, directed upon a certain end; but the end is not something foreseen and preconceived, to which appropriate means can be thought out in the light of our knowledge of its special character. Expression is an activity of which there can be no technique.

§3 Expression and individualization

Expressing an emotion is not the same thing as describing it. To say 'I am angry' is to describe one's emotion, not to express it. The words in which it is expressed need not contain any reference to anger as such at all. Indeed, so far as they simply and solely express it, they cannot contain any such reference. The curse of Ernulphus, as invoked by Dr. Slop on the unknown person who tied certain knots, is a classical and supreme expression of anger; but it does not contain a single word descriptive of the emotion it expresses.

This is why, as literary critics well know, the use of epithets in poetry, or even in prose where expressiveness is aimed at, is a danger. If you want to express the terror which something causes, you must not give it an epithet like 'dreadful'. For that describes the emotion instead of expressing it, and your language becomes frigid, that is inexpressive, at once. A genuine poet, in his moments of genuine poetry, never mentions by name the emotions he is expressing.

Some people have thought that a poet who wishes to express a great variety of subtly differentiated emotions might be hampered by the lack of a vocabulary rich in words referring to the distinctions between them; and that psychology, by working out such a vocabulary, might render a valuable service to poetry. This is the opposite of the truth. The poet needs no such words at all; the existence or non-existence of a scientific terminology describing the emotions he wishes to express is to him a matter of perfect indifference. If such a terminology, where it exists, is allowed to affect his own use of language, it affects it for the worse.

[j]→ The reason why description, so far from helping expression, actually damages it, is that description generalizes. To describe a thing is to call it a thing of such and such a kind: to bring it under a conception, to classify it. Expression, on the contrary, individualizes. The anger which I feel here and now, with a certain person, for a certain cause, is no doubt an instance of anger, and in describing it as anger one is telling truth about it; but it is much more than mere anger: it is a peculiar anger, not quite like any anger that I ever felt before, and probably not quite like any anger I shall ever feel again. To become fully conscious of it means becoming conscious of it not merely as an instance of anger, but as this quite peculiar anger. Expressing it, we saw, has something to do with becoming conscious of it; therefore, if being fully conscious of it means being conscious of all its peculiarities, fully expressing it means expressing all its peculiarities. The poet, therefore, in proportion as he understands his business, gets as far away as possible from merely labelling his emotions as instances of this or that general kind, and takes enormous pains to individualize them by expressing them in terms which reveal their difference from any other emotion of the same sort.

This is a point in which art proper, as the expression of emotion, differs sharply and obviously from any craft whose aim it is to arouse emotion. The end which a craft sets out to realize is always conceived in general terms, never individualized. However accurately defined it may be, it is always defined as the production of a thing having characteristics that could be shared by other things. A joiner, making a table out of these pieces of wood and no others, makes it to measurements and specifications which, even if actually shared by no other table, might in principle be shared by other tables. A physician treating a patient for a certain complaint is trying to produce in him a condition which might be, and probably has been, often produced in others, namely, the condition of recovering from that com-

[k]→ plaint. So an 'artist' setting out to produce a certain emotion in his audience is setting out to produce not an individual emotion, but an emotion of a certain kind. It follows that the means appropriate to its production will be not individual means but means of a certain kind: that is to say, means which are always in principle replaceable by other similar means. As every good craftsman insists, there is always a 'right way' of performing any operation. A 'way' of acting is a general

pattern to which various individual actions may conform. In order that the 'work of art' should produce its intended psychological effect, therefore, whether this effect be magical or merely amusing, what is necessary is that it should satisfy certain conditions, possess certain characteristics: in other words be, not this work and no other, but a work of this kind and of no other.

This explains the meaning of the generalization which Aristotle and others have ascribed to art. We have already seen that Aristotle's *Poetics* is concerned not with art proper but with representative art, and representative art of one definite kind. He is not analysing the religious drama of a hundred years before, he is analysing the amusement literature of the fourth century, and giving rules for its composition. The end being not individual but general (the production of an emotion of a certain kind) the means too are general (the portrayal, not of this individual act, but of an act of this sort; not, as he himself puts it, what Alcibiades did, but what anybody of a certain kind would do). Sir Joshua Reynold's idea of generalization is in principle the same; he expounds it in connexion with what he calls 'the grand style', which means a style intended to produce emotions of a certain type. He is quite right; if you want to produce a typical case of a certain emotion, the way to do it is to put before your audience a representation of the typical features belonging to the kind of thing that produces it: make your kings very royal, your soldiers very soldierly, your women very feminine, your cottages very cottagesque, your oak-trees very oakish, and so on.

Art proper, as expression of emotion, has nothing to do with all this. The artist proper is a person who, grappling with the problem of expressing a certain emotion, says, 'I want to get this clear.' It is no use to him to get something else clear, however like it this other thing may be. Nothing will serve as a substitute. He does not want a thing of a certain kind, he wants a certain thing. This is why the kind of person who takes his literature as psychology, saying 'How admirably this writer depicts the feelings of women, or bus-drivers, or homosexuals...', necessarily misunderstands every real work of art with which he comes into contact, and takes for good art, with infallible precision, what is not art at all.

§4   *Selection and aesthetic emotion*

It has sometimes been asked whether emotions can be divided into those suitable for expression by artists and those unsuitable. If by art one means art proper, and identifies this with expression, the only possible answer is that there can be no such distinction. Whatever is expressible is expressible. There may be ulterior motives in special cases which make it desirable to express some emotions and not others; but only if by 'express' one means express publicly, that is, allow people to overhear one expressing oneself. This is because one cannot possibly decide that a certain emotion is one which for some reason it would be undesirable to express thus publicly, unless one first becomes conscious of it; and doing this, as we saw, is somehow bound up with expressing it. If art means the expression of emotion, the artist as such must be absolutely candid; his speech must be absolutely free. This is not a precept, it is a statement. It does not mean that the artist ought to be candid, it means that he is an artist only in so far as he is candid. Any kind of selection, any decision to express this emotion and not that, is inartistic not in the sense that it damages the perfect sincerity which distinguishes good art from bad, but in the sense that it represents a further process of a non-artistic kind, carried out when the work of expression proper is already complete. For until that work is complete one does not know what emotions one feels; and is therefore not in a position to pick and choose, and give one of them preferential treatment.

From these considerations a certain corollary follows about the division of art into distinct arts. Two such divisions are current: one according to the medium in which the artist works, into painting, poetry, music, and the like; the other according to the kind of emotion he expresses, into tragic, comic, and so forth. We are concerned with the second. If the difference between tragedy and comedy is a difference between the emotions they express, it is not a difference that can be present to the artist's mind when he is beginning his work; if it were, he would know what emotion he was going to express before he had expressed it. No artist, therefore, so far as he is an artist proper, can set out to write a comedy, a tragedy, an elegy, or the like. So far as he is an artist proper, he is just as likely to write any one of these as any other; which is the truth that Socrates was heard expounding towards the dawn, among the sleeping figures in Agathon's dining-room.[1] These distinctions, therefore, have only a very limited value. They can be properly used in two ways. (1) When a work of art is

---

[1] Plato, *Symposium*, 223D. But if Aristodemus heard him correctly, Socrates was saying the right thing for the wrong reason. He is reported as arguing, not that a tragic writer as such is also a comic one, but that ὁ τέχνῃ τραγῳδοποιός is also a comic writer. Emphasis on the word τέχνῃ is obviously implied; and this, with a reference to the doctrine (*Republic*, 333E–334A) that craft is what Aristotle was to call a potentiality of opposites, i.e. enables its possessor to do not one kind of thing only, but that kind and the opposite kind too, shows that what Socrates was doing was to assume the technical theory of art and draw from it the above conclusion.

complete, it can be labelled *ex post facto* as tragic, comic, or the like, according to the character of the emotions chiefly expressed in it. But understood in that sense the distinction is of no real importance. (2) If we are talking about representational art, the case is very different. Here the so-called artist knows in advance what kind of emotion he wishes to excite, and will construct works of different kinds according to the different kinds of effect they are to produce. In the case of representational art, therefore, distinctions of this kind are not only admissible as an *ex post facto* classification of things to which in their origin it is alien; they are present from the beginning as a determining factor in the so-called artist's plan of work.

The same considerations provide an answer to the question whether there is such a thing as a specific 'aesthetic emotion'. If it is said that there is such an emotion independently of its expression in art, and that the business of artists is to express it, we must answer that such a view is nonsense. It implies, first, that artists have emotions of various kinds, among which is this peculiar aesthetic emotion; secondly, that they select this aesthetic emotion for expression. If the first proposition were true, the second would have to be false. If artists only find out what their emotions are in the course of finding out how to express them, they cannot begin the work of expression by deciding what emotion to express.

In a different sense, however, it is true that there is a specific aesthetic emotion. As we have seen, an unexpressed emotion is accompanied by a feeling of oppression; when it is expressed and thus comes into consciousness the same emotion is accompanied by a new feeling of alleviation or easement, the sense that this oppression is removed. It resembles the feeling of relief that comes when a burdensome intellectual or moral problem has been solved. We may call it, if we like, the specific feeling of having successfully expressed ourselves; and there is no reason why it should not be called a specific aesthetic emotion. But it is not a specific kind of emotion pre-existing to the expression of it, and having the peculiarity that when it comes to be expressed it is expressed artistically. It is an emotional colouring which attends the expression of any emotion whatever.

[. . .]

§7 *Expressing emotion and betraying emotion*

Finally, the expressing of emotion must not be confused with what may be called the betraying of it, that is, exhibiting symptoms of it. When it is said that the artist in the proper sense of that word is a person who expresses his emotions, this does not mean that if he is afraid he turns pale and stammers; if he is angry he turns red and bellows; and so forth. These things are no doubt called expressions; but just as we distinguish proper and improper senses of the word 'art', so we must distinguish proper and improper senses of the word 'expression', and in the context of a discussion about art this sense of expression is an improper sense. The characteristic mark of expression proper is lucidity or intelligibility; a person who expresses something thereby becomes conscious of what it is that he is express-ing, and enables others to become conscious of it in himself and in them. Turning pale and stammering is a natural accompaniment of fear, but a person who in addition to being afraid also turns pale and stammers does not thereby become conscious of the precise quality of his emotion. About that he is as much in the dark as he would be if (were that possible) he could feel fear without also exhibiting these symptoms of it.

Confusion between these two senses of the word 'expression' may easily lead to false critical estimates, and so to false aesthetic theory. It is sometimes thought a merit in an actress that when she is acting a pathetic scene she can work herself up to such an extent as to weep real tears. There may be some ground for that opinion if acting is not an art but a craft, and if the actress's object in that scene is to produce grief in her audience; and even then the conclusion would follow only if it were true that grief cannot be produced in the audience unless symptoms of grief are exhibited by the performer. And no doubt this is how most people think of the actor's work. But if his business is not amusement but art, the object at which he is aiming is not to produce a preconceived emotional effect on his audience but by means of a system of expressions, or language, composed partly of speech and partly of gesture, to explore his own emotions: to discover emotions in himself of which he was unaware, and, by permitting the audience to witness the discovery, enable them to make a similar discovery about themselves. In that case it is not her ability to weep real tears that would mark out a good actress; it is her ability to make it clear to herself and her audience what the tears are about.

This applies to every kind of art. The artist never rants. A person who writes or paints or the like in order to blow off steam, using the traditional materials of art as means for exhibiting the symptoms of emotion, may deserve praise as an exhibitionist, but loses for the moment all claim to the title of artist. Exhibitionists have their uses; they may serve as an amusement, or they may be doing magic. The second category will contain, for example, those young men who, learning in the torment of their own bodies and minds what war is like, have stammered their indignation in verses, and published them in the hope of infecting others and causing them to abolish it. But these verses have nothing to do with poetry.

[...]

VII Art Proper: (2) As Imagination

[...]

§2 Making and creating

[...]

To create something means to make it non-technically, but yet consciously and voluntarily. Originally, *creare* means to generate, or make offspring, for which we still use its compound 'procreate,' and the Spaniards have *criatura*, for a child. The act of procreation is a voluntary act, and those who do it are responsible for what they are doing; but it is not done by any specialized form of skill. It need not be done (as it may be in the case of a royal marriage) as a means to any preconceived end. It need not be done (as it was by Mr. Shandy senior) according to any preconceived plan. It cannot be done (whatever Aristotle may say) by imposing a new form on any pre-existing matter. It is in this sense that we speak of creating a disturbance or a demand or a political system. The person who makes these things is acting voluntarily; he is acting responsibly; but he need not be acting in order to achieve any ulterior end; he need not be following a preconceived plan; and he is certainly not transforming anything that can properly be called a raw material. It is in the same sense that Christians asserted, and neo-Platonists denied, that God created the world.

This being the established meaning of the word, it should be clear that when we speak of an artist as making a poem, or a play, or a painting, or a piece of music, the kind of making to which we refer is the kind we call creating. For, as we already know, these things, in so far as they are works of art proper, are not made as means to an end; they are not made according to any preconceived plan; and they are not made by imposing a new form upon a given matter. Yet they are made deliberately and responsibly, by people who know what they are doing, even though they do not know in advance what is going to come of it.

[...]

§3 *Creation and imagination*

We must proceed to a further distinction. All the things taken above
as examples of things created are what we ordinarily call real things.
A work of art need not be what we should call a real thing. It may be
what we call an imaginary thing. A disturbance, or a nuisance, or a
navy, or the like, is not created at all until it is created as a thing
having its place in the real world. But a work of art may be completely
created when it has been created as a thing whose only place is in the
artist's mind.

Here, I am afraid, it is the metaphysician who will take offence. He
will remind me that the distinction between real things and things that
exist only in our minds is one to which he and his fellows have given a
great deal of attention. They have thought about it so long and so
intently that it has lost all meaning. Some of them have decided that
the things we call real are only in our minds; others that the things we
describe as being in our minds are thereby implied to be just as real as
anything else. These two sects, it appears, are engaged in a truceless
war, and any one who butts in by using the words about which they
are fighting will be set upon by both sides and torn to pieces.

I do not hope to placate these gentlemen. I can only cheer myself up
by reflecting that even if I go on with what I was saying they cannot
eat me. If an engineer has decided how to build a bridge, but has not
made any drawings or specifications for it on paper, and has not
discussed his plan with any one or taken any steps towards carrying
it out, we are in the habit of saying that the bridge exists only in his
mind, or (as we also say) in his head. When the bridge is built, we say
that it exists not only in his head but in the real world. A bridge which
'exists only in the engineer's head' we also call an imaginary bridge;
one which 'exists in the real world' we call a real bridge.

This may be a silly way of speaking; or it may be an unkind way of
speaking, because of the agony it gives to metaphysicians; but it is a
way in which ordinary people do speak, and ordinary people who
speak in that way know quite well what kind of things they are
referring to. The metaphysicians are right in thinking that difficult
problems arise from talking in that way; and I shall spend the greater
part of Book II in discussing these problems. Meanwhile, I shall go on
'speaking with the vulgar'; if metaphysicians do not like it they need
not read it.

The same distinction applies to such things as music. If a man has
made up a tune but has not written it down or sung it or played it or
done anything which could make it public property, we say that the
tune exists only in his mind, or only in his head, or is an imaginary

tune. If he sings or plays it, thus making a series of audible noises, we call this series of noises a real tune as distinct from an imaginary one. [...]

When a man makes up a tune, he may and very often does at the same time hum it or sing it or play it on an instrument. He may do none of these things, but write it on paper. Or he may both hum it or the like, and also write it on paper at the same time or afterwards. Also he may do these things in public, so that the tune at its very birth becomes public property, like the disturbance we have just considered. But all these are accessories of the real work, though some of them are very likely useful accessories. The actual making of the tune is something that goes on in his head, and nowhere else.

I have already said that a thing which 'exists in a person's head' and nowhere else is alternatively called an imaginary thing. The actual making of the tune is therefore alternatively called the making of an imaginary tune. This is a case of creation, just as much as the making of a plan or a disturbance, and for the same reasons, which it would be tedious to repeat. Hence the making of a tune is an instance of imaginative creation. The same applies to the making of a poem, or a picture, or any other work of art.

The engineer, as we saw, when he made his plan in his own head, may proceed to do something else which we call 'making his plans'. His 'plans', here, are drawings and specifications on paper, and these are artifacts made to serve a certain purpose, namely to inform others or remind himself of the plan. The making of them is accordingly not imaginative creation; indeed, it is not creation at all. It is fabrication, and the ability to do it is a specialized form of skill, the craft of engineer's draughtsmanship.

The artist, when he has made his tune, may go on to do something else which at first sight seems to resemble this: he may do what is called publishing it. He may sing or play it aloud, or write it down, and thus make it possible for others to get into their heads the same thing which he has in his. But what is written or printed on music-paper is not the tune. It is only something which when studied intelligently will enable others (or himself, when he has forgotten it) to construct the tune for themselves in their own heads.

The relation between making the tune in his head and putting it down on paper is thus quite different from the relation, in the case of the engineer, between making a plan for a bridge and executing that plan. The engineer's plan is embodied in the bridge: it is essentially a form that can be imposed on certain matter, and when the bridge is built the form is there, in the bridge, as the way in which the matter composing it is arranged. But the musician's tune is not there on the

paper at all. What is on the paper is not music, it is only musical notation. The relation of the tune to the notation is not like the relation of the plan to the bridge; it is like the relation of the plan to the specifications and drawings; for these, too, do not embody the plan as the bridge embodies it, they are only a notation from which the abstract or as yet unembodied plan can be reconstructed in the mind of a person who studies them.
[…]

§5   The work of art as imaginary object

If the making of a tune is an instance of imaginative creation, a tune is an imaginary thing. And the same applies to a poem or a painting or any other work of art. This seems paradoxical; we are apt to think that a tune is not an imaginary thing but a real thing, a real collection of noises; that a painting is a real piece of canvas covered with real colours; and so on. I hope to show, if the reader will have patience, that there is no paradox here; that both these propositions express what we do as a matter of fact say about works of art; and that they do not contradict one another, because they are concerned with different things.

When, speaking of a work of art (tune, picture, etc.), we mean by art a specific craft, intended as a stimulus for producing specific emotional effects in an audience, we certainly mean to designate by the term 'work of art' something that we should call real. The artist as magician or purveyor of amusement is necessarily a craftsman making real things, and making them out of some material according to some plan. His works are as real as the works of an engineer, and for the same reason.

But it does not at all follow that the same is true of an artist proper. His business is not to produce an emotional effect in an audience, but, for example, to make a tune. This tune is already complete and perfect when it exists merely as a tune in his head, that is, an imaginary tune. Next, he may arrange for the tune to be played before an audience. Now there comes into existence a real tune, a collection of noises. But which of these two things is the work of art? Which of them is the music? The answer is implied in what we have already said: the music, the work of art, is not the collection of noises, it is the tune in the composer's head. The noises made by the performers, and heard by the audience, are not the music at all; they are only means by which the audience, if they listen intelligently (not otherwise), can reconstruct for themselves the imaginary tune that existed in the composer's head.

This is not a paradox. It is not something παρὰ Δόξαν, contrary to what we ordinarily believe and express in our ordinary speech. We all know perfectly well, and remind each other often enough, that a person who hears the noises the instruments make is not thereby possessing himself of the music. Perhaps no one can do that unless he does hear the noises; but there is something else which he must do as well. Our ordinary word for this other thing is listening; and the listening which we have to do when we hear the noises made by musicians is in a way rather like the thinking we have to do when we hear the noises made, for example, by a person lecturing on a scientific subject. We hear the sound of his voice; but what he is doing is not simply to make noises, but to develop a scientific thesis. The noises are meant to assist us in achieving what he assumes to be our purpose in coming to hear him lecture, that is, thinking this same scientific thesis for ourselves. The lecture, therefore, is not a collection of noises made by the lecturer with his organs of speech; it is a collection of scientific thoughts related to those noises in such a way that a person who not only hears but thinks as well becomes able to think these thoughts for himself. We may call this the communication of thought by means of speech, if we like; but if we do, we must think of communication not as an 'imparting' of thought by the speaker to the hearer, the speaker somehow planting his thought in the hearer's receptive mind, but as a 'reproduction' of the speaker's thought by the hearer, in virtue of his own active thinking.

The parallel with listening to music is not complete. The two cases are similar at one point, dissimilar at another. They are dissimilar in that a concert and a scientific lecture are different things, and what we are trying to 'get out of' the concert is a thing of a different kind from the scientific thoughts we are trying to 'get out of' the lecture. But they are similar in this: that just as what we get out of the lecture is something other than the noises we hear proceeding from the lecturer's mouth, so what we get out of the concert is something other than the noises made by the performers. In each case, what we get out of it is something which we have to reconstruct in our own minds, and by our own efforts; something which remains for ever inaccessible to a person who cannot or will not make efforts of the right kind, however completely he hears the sounds that fill the room in which he is sitting.

Commentary on Collingwood

Our passage begins with the central contrast between 'art proper' and 'art falsely so-called'. The latter is art conceived as a craft or technique for producing emotions (what Collingwood calls the 'technical' theory), while the former will be explained as the expression of emotion (see [f]↦ onwards).

The central characteristics of a craft can be gleaned from the points set out at [c]↦. Art conceived as a craft would have a distinction between means and end, be concerned with arousing emotion and make a material artefact. Collingwood denies that any of these conditions hold of art proper. He indicates that his chapter VI will explore the connection of art and emotion, and the following chapter the relation of art and making.

Before looking at these topics, let us consider Collingwood's strategy.

> Collingwood claims at the outset (see [a]↦) to be simply reminding us of 'facts' which we already know. How credible is this claim?

Until we have followed Collingwood's train of thought further, we do not know what alleged facts are at issue, but a couple of sceptical observations might be in order. First, if so many people have been in error and have falsely called various things art which are not, how can the reader, who is to be saved from such errors, already be trusted to know facts about what art properly is?

Secondly, since 'art' is a term very widely and loosely applied, which of the facts about its use are we to discount as improper, and by what criterion? There is, it would seem, a greater element of stipulation or persuasion in Collingwood's account than he admits. Still, he may succeed in locating one factual use of the term 'art' for special attention, and may yet persuade us of its salience.

Art and emotion

> How does Collingwood support the ideas (a) that the artist 'has something to do with' emotions, and (b) that the artist 'expresses' emotions?

The first idea is supported by the thought that so many people would not have allied themselves with the theory of the arousal of emotions by art, if there were not *some* connection between art and emotion. The second is supported by its sounding natural to say that an artist expresses emotions (see [b]↦, [d]↦, [e]↦, and [f]↦ for the arguments).

We may continue to wonder whether the feature Collingwood highlights will be just one possible feature of artistic production rather than the central feature of all art.

> For Collingwood, what is expressing an emotion? Is his account plausible?

The crucial passage here is from [g]↦ until [h]↦. Among the more notable features of Collingwood's account are the impossibility he alleges of specify-

ing the emotion prior to its expression, the corollary impossibility of the same
emotion being expressed by another utterance or in another medium, and the
continuity he asserts between artistic expression and self-expression in language. The latter point suggests some questions tangential to Collingwood's
main account: Are we all artists in a minor sense when we succeed in
articulating our emotions in words? Should we then assume that the same
form of articulation of emotion into conscious form can be attained in non-
linguistic art forms such as music, sculpture, or painting?

The aspects of Collingwood's theory of expression we mentioned above
arguably contain great insight. Imagine the process of writing a poem. Before
the poem takes shape is it possible to state, except in the very vaguest terms,
what it is that the finished piece will express? Collingwood seems correct in
saying that the final recognition of the rightness of a certain word or line is
itself the process of crystallizing the emotion felt, rather than the finding of a
vehicle for something pre-formed. By the same token you could not take just
what you have expressed in this poem and express it in other words – let alone
in paint or in musical notes.

Collingwood further illuminates his notion of expression by contrasting it
with other ways in which we may think of emotions being dealt with by
artists. In §2 he distinguishes expressing from arousing emotion, then in
subsequent sections from describing, selecting and betraying emotions.
These are vital distinctions, and Collingwood's basic treatment of them is
admirably clear.

> What distinguishes expressing an emotion from arousing, describing,
> selecting, or betraying it?

The asymmetry between expressing and arousing is obvious enough. If A
arouses an emotion in B, B feels it, but A need not; if A expresses an emotion,
A must feel it, but B, to whom the expression is communicated, need not.

Describing an emotion by applying literal language to report its presence is
also different from expressing it. See Collingwood's clear example at $\boxed{\text{i}}\mapsto$.
And Collingwood seems right in saying that there is something inartistic in the
mere description of emotions. But what of the further philosophical points he
wishes to make about the difference between expression and description? At
$\boxed{\text{j}}\mapsto$ Collingwood claims that description generalizes, while expression individualizes.

> Is Collingwood right to align the distinction between expression and de-
> scription with that between individualization and generalization?

It might be instructive to try to think of an example. Suppose a writer who is
intent upon arousing pity in the audience (in the manner suggested by Aristotle to be characteristic of tragedians and criticized by Collingwood), and

who writes a description of the emotional states felt by a central character in the story. Cannot the emotions described be those of that particular (albeit fictional) man or woman at that moment in the narrative in response to very specific objects? Why must the description generalize?

Collingwood then returns to the distinction between expressing and arousing, and suggests (at $\boxed{k}\!\rightarrow$) that someone setting out to arouse emotions can only do so as a generality. Again, we may wonder whether this is right: surely if I try to arouse an emotion in you, it will usually be a specific emotion, directed towards the specific object that I want you to feel something about. It is only in peculiar circumstances that I would wish to arouse a generalized emotion. If I wanted to see what happened when you got angry as such, I could pick any old enraging thing to tell you about; but if I tell you that someone is in the process of vandalizing my new car, it is surely a very particular anger, motivating particular attitudes and actions, that I want you to feel. If Shakespeare's aim in writing the scene of Gloucester's torture in *King Lear* had been just to make us horrified, this scene would have been interchangeable with any number of other events. But presumably the aim was to horrify us about just this sequence of events carried out by just these agents in the particular context of the story.

> Is it right to deny artistic value to works which bring general psychological insights? See $\boxed{l}\!\rightarrow$ and $\boxed{n}\!\rightarrow$.

Even if Collingwood is right in his point about generalization, do we agree with him that 'how admirably this writer depicts the feelings of women, or bus-drivers or homosexuals' is a consideration irrelevant to the value of something as art? Is this not too narrow a ruling about what has artistic value?

Collingwood wants to supplant both *representation* and *arousal of emotion* as definitive features of art. In offering expression as the definitive feature he is combating both, and the contrast with description is part of the same strategy.

> Is 'representative art' always a matter of craftlike arousal of emotions?

This is implied by passages at $\boxed{m}\!\rightarrow$ and $\boxed{p}\!\rightarrow$ (as well as being more explicitly stated in earlier parts of Collingwood's book not reprinted here). He in effect assumes there is a theory (which he attacks) that holds:

(i)   art essentially represents reality;
(ii) art essentially seeks to arouse specified emotions.

He then proceeds as if (i) entails (ii), as if a representation of X simply aimed to bring about in us the feelings we would have towards X in reality. This is highly questionable as a blanket view of all artistic representation. Also, clearly, not everything that aims to arouse emotion need be a representation. For instance, 'pure' music or architecture could be used to entertain or inspire patriotism or some other feelings, without needing to represent anything.

Now to what Collingwood refers to as 'selection' of emotions. He presents artistic activity as a spontaneous activity of self-discovery which must remain unsullied by any prior conception of what is to be expressed.

> How plausible is Collingwood's claim at $\boxed{\text{o}}\mapsto$ about setting out to write a tragedy or comedy?

This is where many readers will feel Collingwood has gone too far, and unnecessarily so. From the good point that no specification of the emotion expressed can be given in advance of the achievement of its expression, it does not follow that one cannot set out to write a piece of a certain mood or overall plot structure. Of course, to set out to write a tragedy is no guarantee that one will write one, and whether one has succeeded in writing a good tragedy, or even a tragedy at all, must await the final result. But a great many art works are written for specific audiences and occasions, to commissions, for competitions, in deliberate use of genres and traditions that pre-exist their creation – all of which facts Collingwood can acknowledge only as something extraneous and essentially inartistic.

> What distinguishes expressing emotion from betraying emotion?

An emotion is betrayed, for Collingwood, when there are manifest effects of it that allow the inference that the emotion has occurred. So we might be able to infer from the brushstrokes on a painting that the artist was angry, just as we could from a dent in a car door or a bruise on a cat belonging to the artist. For Collingwood this is an extra-artistic phenomenon: we should be interested in understanding the artist's emotion as it is articulated in the work, not in making inferences about his or her state of mind from symptoms incidentally left in it.

The distinctions Collingwood makes in this chapter are without doubt illuminating and essential to bear in mind when thinking about expression in art. We have often asked, however, whether in his zeal to establish the importance of expression Collingwood has not given a one-sided or exaggerated picture of what goes in artistic creation. Here is a further question.

> Is Collingwood right to deny artistic value to all cases of arousing or betraying of emotions?

Consider (at $\boxed{\text{q}}\mapsto$) Collingwood's derogatory assessment of war poets, whose verses 'have nothing to do with poetry'. The implication of this passage is that if a piece of writing betrays indignation at the effects of war and by design arouses such indignation, then it is inartistic, or is not poetry. Even by Collingwood's own lights this seems incautious, for until we know whether the verses in question also successfully express felt emotions in authentic and articulate form, we have not settled whether they are artistic or not. It would seem wrong to prejudge that anything that aroused or betrayed emotions must fail to express emotions artistically.

Art and making

In his chapter VII Collingwood proposes to make good on his claim that although the artist makes something, it is not an artefact as the 'technical theory' would have it.

What, according to Collingwood, does the artist make?

The first, short answer is that the artist creates something by deliberate activity, and that this creation is imaginative creation, otherwise creation of something imaginary (see $\boxed{r} \mapsto$ and $\boxed{v} \mapsto$). But what does Collingwood mean by all this? It is common in aesthetics textbooks to see attributed to Collingwood something called the Ideal Theory, a view which holds that works of art have a particular ontological status, and are ideal as opposed to material. Some of Collingwood's pronouncements are very striking. See especially $\boxed{s} \mapsto$, $\boxed{u} \mapsto$, and $\boxed{w} \mapsto$, where he hammers home his message that a piece of music exists 'only in the artist's head' and then generalizes this to all the art forms.

Can Collingwood really mean that no material thing is an art work, that we do not see, hear, and touch art works, that they are available only to the artist in a private medium, in short that they exist only 'ideally'? If so, this would be an unfortunate theory for two reasons. Firstly, much artistic creation (or production, if we are squeamish about the supernatural-sounding 'creation' despite Collingwood's bluff rejection of that squeamishness) cannot be conceived without an involvement with a physical medium in which one expresses oneself. One is not really doing sculpture without modifying some physical stuff, and though one may compose a dance prior to any actual bodily movement, one's composition must make detailed and essential reference to possible movements, otherwise it is not dance that one has composed – and so on.

Secondly, the existence of art works as private, ideal entities would go against much that Collingwood wants to say himself. A consequence of his expression theory should be that the medium in which the clarification of one's emotion is achieved is essential to the emotion's being what it is. In some cases, at least, the medium is physical. But here there are difficulties which may need probing a little further.

Can *some* works of art exist only 'in the artist's head'? Can *all* works of art so exist?

Collingwood chooses as his examples here a *poem* and a *piece of music*. He is arguably right that these are not particular collections of physical things or events, and that they can exist when invented in someone's mind and manifested in no other way. The poem does not seem to be identical with any one physical copy, or with the totality of copies. The music is not the printed score, or the composer's autograph score, nor one particular performance, nor the totality of all performances. But from the fact that these works can in a sense exist 'in the mind' it would be extravagant to conclude that music and poetry are purely mental or ideal things.

Even more strange would be to argue that what applies in these cases applies to all art forms. Our intuition says that a painting is a physical object, which would not exist without the paint and canvas that constitute it. Only a very few paintings could be preconceived in sufficient detail to have a claim to exist solely 'in the artist's head', and the making of a painting involves the handling of the physical medium: precisely how it will need to be handled at every turn cannot (arguably) be preconceived in the artist's mind.

There are signs that Collingwood does not mean such a drastic confinement of art to a single mind as the Ideal Theory attributes to him. The making and reception of art is clearly collaborative: the audience can reconstruct the work (see $\boxed{x} \rightarrow$) by attending to it intelligently, for which its physical embodiments are necessary. And Collingwood does not conceive this as the audience guessing or detecting the nature of something hidden inside the artist: rather, they participate in the work directly in their activity of understanding it (see $\boxed{y} \rightarrow$). There is also something we 'get out of music', and here we may find a positive point to his otherwise odd-sounding dismissal of the heard sounds as not containing the music. As Aaron Ridley has recently put it,

> Collingwood's point, essentially, is that to experience a work of art with understanding is to engage in a certain sort of activity with respect to it; it is to make a certain sort of effort. [...] The crucial distinction Collingwood is making, then, is between a brute series of noises (as might be perceived by a cat, say) and the piece of music heard by a person who understands these notes *as* music (cats don't hear music). (Ridley, *R. G. Collingwood: A Philosophy of Art*, p. 22)

Art's existence, on this reading, depends on the intelligent interpretation of its physical embodiments as expressive of states of mind, and, in having access to the states of mind thus expressed, the audience experiences the art work as much as the artist does. It is unfortunate that Collingwood chose to convey that point in an overstated and misleading way.

Introduction to Dickie

George Dickie is Professor Emeritus of Philosophy at the University of Illinois, Chicago. He has written extensively on aesthetics, and his books include *Art and the Aesthetic* (1974) and *The Art Circle* (1984). The present extract is taken from *Introduction to Aesthetics: An Analytic Approach* (1997), in which Dickie defends an institutional definition of art which he had developed in his earlier work. His enterprise arose in the context of a commonly expressed scepticism about the possibility of defining art. Certain prominent definitions or theories of the essence of art had been tried, but found to be too narrow to cover what most people would like to encompass within the term 'art'. The notion of art as mimesis, claiming Plato as one of its originators, was popular in the eighteenth century when, for example, the French thinker Batteux suggested that what united the 'fine arts' was 'the imitation of beautiful nature'. A definition of art as imitation or representation in this manner seems to apply well to dominant trends in classical Greek visual art, epic and dramatic poetry, European art from Renaissance into the early twentieth century – but not to abstract art, architecture, or music.

Accounts of art from the first part of the twentieth century tended to abandon representation as a defining feature, Collingwood's conception of art as expression being one example, another being Clive Bell's formalist definition of art. In 1913 Bell wrote: 'Significant form is the one quality common to all visual works of art.... When I speak of significant form, I mean a combination of lines and colours (counting white and black as colours) that moves me aesthetically' (from 'Significant Form' (1913), reprinted in J. Hospers (ed.), *Introductory Readings in Aesthetics*, pp. 88–91). The problem with these accounts is that they fail to capture everything called art; and indeed they might also apply to things no one wants to call art.

In response to the failure of such accounts, some philosophers began to question whether it was desirable or even possible to give a definition of art. Firstly, one might point to the heterogeneity of things called 'art' at one time or another (short poems, improvised music, ten-hour long religious dramas, an Ingmar Bergman film, a watercolour, a ballet, a shark in a tank by Damien Hirst, and so on) and not find it surprising if they had no one feature in common other than their being *called* art.

A theoretical stimulus to this anti-essentialism came from Wittgenstein's remarks about 'family resemblance', that is, the loose way in which the various instances of a concept may hang together, without there being any one single characteristic or set of characteristics that they all have in common. Anti-essentialists (such as Morris Weitz, to whom Dickie refers in the extract) say that art is an 'open' concept, that there are no necessary or sufficient conditions for its application, and in principle no limits to what could be subsumed under it.

Dickie wants to argue against such anti-essentialism, while avoiding the faults of the more traditional definitions. He distinguishes between 'art' used as an evaluative term and 'art' used to classify things, and sets out to define art in the purely classificatory sense, so that whether something is art or not is, within his theory, never a question about whether it is good or not. Secondly, his definition relies not on features intrinsic to or manifest in an art work itself, but on particular relations that it stands in to the activities of human beings. Art's being art consists in its being embedded in certain specific institutions populated by artists, critics, and audiences.

Finally, the definition Dickie offers can be called procedural rather than functional, in the following sense: what matters in defining an artist's product as art is not what result he or she succeeds in bringing about – such as arousing emotions, representing things accurately, or giving aesthetic pleasure. Rather, what makes an artist's work art is his or her being an artist and acting in certain ways in certain settings provided by the institution that Dickie calls the artworld.

George Dickie, 'The Institutional Theory of Art'

Guided by the ideas in Mandelbaum's article and Danto's earliest article, beginning in 1969 with "Defining Art"[1] and culminating in 1974 with *Art and the Aesthetic*,[2] I worked out the earlier of two versions of the institutional theory of art. In response to a variety of criticisms of the earlier version, I presented a greatly revised, and I think improved, version of the institutional theory in my 1984 book, *The Art Circle*.[3] I will give accounts of both versions.

Traditional theories of art place works of art within simple and narrowly focused networks of relations. The imitation theory, for example, suspends the work of art in a three-place network between artist and subject matter, and the expression theory places the work of art in a two-place network of artist and work. Both versions of the institutional theory attempt to place the work of art within a multi-placed network of greater complexity than anything envisaged by the various traditional theories. The networks or contexts of the traditional theories are too "thin" to be sufficient. Both versions of the institutional theory attempt to provide a context that is "thick" enough

---

[1] George Dickie, "Defining Art," *The American Philosophical Quarterly* (1969), pp. 253–6.
[2] George Dickie, *Art and the Aesthetic* (Ithaca, NY: Cornell University Press, 1974), p. 204.
[3] George Dickie, *The Art Circle* (New York: Haven Publications, 1984), p. 116.

to do the job. The network of relations or context within which a theory places works of art I will call "the framework" of that theory.

All the traditional theories assume that works of art are artifacts, although they differ about the nature of the artifacts. There is, then, a sense in which the institutional approach is a return to the traditional way of theorizing about art, for in both of its versions I maintain that works of art are artifacts. By "artifact" I mean the ordinary dictionary definition: "an object made by man, especially with a view to subsequent use." Furthermore, although many are, an artifact need not be a physical object: for example, a poem is not a physical object, but it is, nevertheless, an artifact. Still further, things such as performances (for example, improvised dances) are also "made by man" and are, therefore, artifacts.

On the surface anyway, there is no mystery about the making of the great bulk of artifactual art; they are crafted in various traditional ways – painted, sculpted, and the like. There is, however, a puzzle about the artifactuality of some relatively recent works of art: Duchamp's readymades, found art, and the like. Some deny that such things are art because, they claim, they are not artifacts made by artists. It can, I think, be shown that they are the artifacts of artists. The two versions diverge over how artifactuality is achieved in the cases of Duchamp's readymades and their like.

The Earlier Version

The earlier version of the institutional theory of art can be summed up in the following definition from my 1974 book, *Art and the Aesthetic*.

A work of art in the classificatory sense is (1) an artifact, (2) a set of the aspects of which has had conferred upon it the status of candidate for appreciation by some person or persons acting on behalf of a certain social institution (the artworld).[4]

The notion of conferring status is the central notion in this earlier version. The most obvious and clear-cut examples of the conferring of status are certain actions of the state in which legal status is involved. A king's conferring of knighthood or a judge pronouncing a couple husband and wife are examples in which a person acting on behalf of an institution (the state) confers *legal* status. The conferring of a PhD degree on someone by a university or the election of someone as

---

[4] *Art and the Aesthetic*, p. 34.

president of the Rotary are examples in which a person or persons confer nonlegal status. What the earlier institutional definition of "work of art" suggests is that just as two persons can acquire the status of being married within a legal system and as a person can acquire the nonlegal status of being president of the Rotary, an artifact can acquire the status of candidate for appreciation within the cultural system called "the artworld."

How, according to the earlier version, is the status of candidate for appreciation conferred? An artifact's hanging in an art museum as part of a show or a performance at a theater are sure signs that the status has been conferred. These two examples seem to suggest that a number of people are required for the actual conferring of the status in question. A number of people are required to make up the cultural institution of the artworld, but only one person is required to act on behalf of or as an agent of the artworld and to confer the status of candidate for appreciation. The status in question is typically acquired by *a single person's treating an artifact as a candidate for appreciation.* Of course nothing prevents a group of persons conferring the status, that is, acting as an artist, but it is usually conferred by a single person, the artist who creates the artifact. In fact, many works of art are never seen by anyone but the persons who create them, but they are still works of art.

It may be felt that the notion of conferring status within the artworld, as conceived in the earlier version, is excessively vague. Certainly this notion is not as clear-cut as the conferring of status within the legal system, where procedures and lines of authority are explicitly defined and incorporated into law. The counterparts in the artworld to specified procedures and lines of authority are nowhere codified, and the artworld carries on its business at the level of customary practice. Still there is a practice and this defines a cultural institution. Such an institution need not have a formally established constitution, officers, and bylaws in order to exist and have the capacity to confer status. Some institutions are formal and some are informal.

Consider now the notion of appreciation. In the earlier version, the definition of "work of art" speaks of conferring the status of *candidate* for appreciation. Nothing is said about actual appreciation, and this allows for the possibility of works of art that are not appreciated. It is important not to build into the definition of the *classificatory* sense of "work of art" value properties such as actual appreciation; to do so would make it impossible to speak of unappreciated works of art and difficult to speak of bad works of art, and this is clearly undesirable. Any theory of art must preserve certain central features of the way in which we talk about art, and we do find it necessary sometimes to speak of unappreciated art and bad art. It should also be noted that not every aspect of a work of art is included in the candidacy for appreciation. For example, the color of the back of a painting is not ordinarily an object of appreciation. The reader will recognize that the question of which aspects of a work of art are to be included within the candidacy for appreciation has already been dealt with in Part I.

c → The earlier version of the institutional theory does not involve a special kind of *aesthetic* appreciation. In Part I it was argued that there is no special kind of aesthetic perception and there is no reason to think there is a special kind of aesthetic appreciation. All that is meant by "appreciation" in the earlier definition is something like "in experiencing the qualities of a thing one finds them worthy or valuable."

d → Both versions of the institutional theory of art have quite consciously been worked out with the practices of the artworld in mind – especially developments of the last hundred years or so, such as dadaism, pop art, found art, and happenings. The institutional theory and these developments raise a number of questions, and a few of these will be dealt with here.

e → First, if Duchamp can convert a urinal, a snowshovel, and a hatrack into works of art, can't natural objects such as driftwood also become works of art? Such natural objects can become works of art if any one of a number of things is done to them. One thing that would do the trick would be to pick a natural object up, take it home, and hang it on the wall. Another would be to pick it up and enter it in an exhibition. It was being assumed earlier that Weitz's sentence about the driftwood referred to a piece of driftwood in its ordinary situation on a beach and untouched by human hand. Please keep in mind that for something to be a work of art in the classificatory sense does not mean that it has any actual value. Natural objects which become works of art in the way being discussed are, according to the earlier version, artifactualized without the use of tools – the artifactuality is conferred on the object rather than worked on it. Of course, even if this is true, in the cases of the great majority of artworks, artifactuality is achieved by being crafted in some way. Thus, according to the earlier version, artifactuality can be achieved in two quite different ways: by being worked and being conferred. In the cases of things like Duchamp's readymades such as *Fountain*, a plumbing artifact has artistic artifactuality conferred on it and is a double artifact.

f → Note that according to the earlier version, two quite different kind of things can supposedly be conferred: artifactuality and candidacy for appreciation.

g→   Second, a question that frequently arises in connection with discussions of the concept of art and which seems especially relevant in the context of institutional theory is, "How are we to conceive of paintings done by individuals such as Betsy the chimpanzee from the Baltimore Zoo?" Calling Betsy's products "paintings" here is not meant to prejudge that they are works of art; it is just that some word is needed to refer to them. The question of whether or not Betsy's paintings are art depends on what is done with them. For example, The Field Museum of Natural History in Chicago once exhibited some chimpanzee and gorilla paintings. In the case of these paintings we must say that they are not works of art. However, if they had been exhibited a few miles away at the Chicago Art Institute they *could* have been works of art – the paintings *could* have been art if someone at the Art Institute had, so to speak, gone out on a limb. It all depends on the institutional setting – the one setting is congenial for the creation of art and the other is not. (In speaking of institutional setting, I am not referring to the Art Institute as such but to an institutional practice.) According to the earlier version, what would make Betsy's paintings works of art would be some agent's conferring artifactuality and the status of candidacy for appreciation on them on behalf of the artworld. Despite the fact that Betsy did the painting, the resulting works of art would not be Betsy's but the work of the person who does the conferring. Betsy cannot do the conferring because she cannot see herself as an agent of the artworld – she is unable to participate (fully) in our culture.

Weitz charged that the defining of art or its subconcepts forecloses creativity. Some of the traditional definitions of art may have and some of the traditional definitions of its subconcepts probably did foreclose creativity, but neither version of the institutional account of art would. The requirement of artifactuality can scarcely prevent creativity, since artifactuality is a necessary condition of creativity. How could there be an instance of creativity without an artifact of some kind being produced? The other requirement of the earlier version involving the conferring of the status of candidate for appreciation could not inhibit creativity; in fact, it encourages it. Since it is possible for almost anything whatever to be used to make art, the definition imposes no restraints on creativity. Weitz is probably right that the definition of some of the subconcepts of art have foreclosed creativity, but this danger is now a thing of the past. With the well-established disregard for established genres and the clamor for novelty in art, this obstacle to creativity probably no longer exists. Today, if a new and unusual work is created and it is fairly similar to some members of an established type, then it will usually be accommodated within that type, or if the new work is very unlike any existing works, then a new subconcept will probably be created. Artists today are not easily intimidated, and they regard art genres as loose guidelines rather than rigid specifications.

The earlier version of the institutional theory of art may sound like saying, "A work of art is an object of which someone has said, 'I christen this object a work of art.'" And it is rather like that; although this does not mean that becoming art, as conceived by the earlier version, is a simple matter. Just as christening a child has as its background the history and structure of the Church, becoming art has as its background the Byzantine complexity of the artworld. Some people may find it strange that in the nonart cases discussed it appears that there are ways in which the conferring can go wrong, while there does not appear to be a way in which the conferring involved in producing art can be invalid. For example, an indictment might have been improperly drawn up, and the person charged would not actually be indicted. But nothing parallel seems possible in the case of art. This fact reflects the differences between the artworld and legal institutions. The legal system deals with matters of grave personal consequences and its procedures must reflect this; the artworld deals with important matters also, but they are of a different sort entirely. The artworld does not require rigid procedures; it admits and even encourages frivolity and caprice without losing its serious purpose. However, if it is not possible to make a mistake in the conferring involved in producing art, it is possible to make a mistake by conferring candidacy for appreciation. In conferring such status on an object, one assumes a certain kind of responsibility for the object in its new status; presenting a candidate for appreciation always faces the possibility that no one will appreciate it and that the person who did the conferring will thereby lose face. One *can* make a work of art out of a sow's ear, but that does not necessarily make it a silk purse.

The Later Version

The earlier version of the institutional theory is, I believe, defective in several respects, but the institutional approach is, I think, still viable. In the earlier version, I claimed, I now think mistakenly, that artifactuality is conferred on things such as Duchamp's *Fountain* and found art. I now believe that artifactuality is not the sort of thing that can be conferred.

Typically an artifact is produced by altering some pre-existing material: by joining two pieces of material, by cutting some material, by sharpening some material, and so on. This is usually done so that the altered material can be used to do something. When materials are so altered, one has clear cases that neatly fit the dictionary definition of "artifact" – "An object made by man, especially with a view to subsequent use." Other cases are less clear-cut. Suppose one picks up a piece of driftwood and without altering it in any way digs a hole or brandishes it at a threatening dog. The unaltered driftwood has been *made* into a digging tool or a weapon by the use to which it is put. These two cases do not conform to the nonnecessary clause of the definition "especially with a view to subsequent use" because they are pressed into service on the spot. There does seem to be a sense in which something is made in these cases. What, however, has been made if the driftwood is unaltered? In the clear cases in which material is altered, a complex object is produced: the original material is for present purposes a simple object and its being altered produces the complex object – altered material. In the two less clear-cut cases, complex objects have also been made – the wood used as a digging tool and the wood used as a weapon. In neither of the two less clear-cut cases is the driftwood alone the artifact; the artifact in both cases is the driftwood manipulated and used in a certain way. The two cases in question are exactly like the sort of thing that anthropologists have in mind when they speak of unaltered stones found in conjunction with human or human-like fossils as artifacts. The anthropologists conclude that the stones were used in some way because of, say, certain marks of the stones that they take to be traces left on the stones by that use. The anthropologists have in mind the same notion of a complex object made by the use of a simple (i.e., unaltered) object.

A piece of driftwood may be used in a similar way within the context of the artworld, that is, picked up and displayed in the way that a painting or a sculpture is displayed. Such a piece of driftwood would be being used as an artistic medium and thereby would become part of the more complex object – the-driftwood-used-as-an-artistic-medium. This complex object would be an artifact of an artworld system. Duchamp's *Fountain* can be understood along the same lines. The urinal (the simple object) is being used as an artistic medium to make *Fountain* (the complex object), which is an artifact within the artworld – Duchamp's artifact. The driftwood would be being used and the urinal was used as an artistic medium in the way that pigments, marble, and the like are used to make more conventional works of art. The driftwood used as a weapon and the urinal used as an artistic medium are artifacts of the most minimal sort. Duchamp did not confer artifactuality; he made a minimal artifact.

A second difficulty with the earlier account was pointed out by Monroe Beardsley. He observed that in the discussion surrounding the definition in the earlier version of the theory, I characterized the artworld as an "established practice," an informal kind of activity. He then goes on to point out that the quoted definition makes use of such phrases as "conferred status" and "acting on behalf of." Such phrases typically have application within formal institutions such as states, corporations, universities, and the like. Beardsley correctly notes that it is a mistake to use the language of formal institutions to try to describe an informal institution as I conceive the artworld to be. Beardsley queries, "does it make sense to speak of acting on behalf of a practice? Status-awarding authority can center in [a formal institution], but practices, as such, seem to lack the requisite source of authority."[5]

k→ Accepting Beardsley's criticism, I have abandoned as too formal the notions of *status conferral* and *acting on behalf of* as well as those aspects of the earlier version that connect up with these notions. Being a work of art is a status all right, that is, it is the occupying of a position within the human activity of the artworld. Being a work of art does not, however, involve a status that is conferred but is rather a status that is achieved as the result of creating an artifact within or against the background of the artworld.

The later version claims (as does the earlier version) that works of art are art as the result of the position or place they occupy within an established practice, namely, the artworld. There are two crucial questions about the claim: is the claim true and if the claim is true, how is the artworld to be described?

This is a claim about the existence of a human institution, and the test of its truth is the same as for any other claim about human organization – the test of observation. "Seeing" the artworld and the works of art embedded in its structures, however, is not as easy as "seeing" some of the other human institutions we are more accustomed to thinking about.

Danto's visually indistinguishable-objects argument shows that works of art exist within a context or framework, but it does not reveal the nature of the elements making up the framework. Moreover, many different frameworks are possible. Each of the traditional theories of art, for example, implies its own particular framework. For one example, Susanne Langer's view that "Art is the creation of forms symbolic of human feeling" implies a framework of artist (one

---

[5] "Is Art Essentially Institutional?," in: *Culture and Art*, ed. Lars Aagaard-Mogensen (Atlantic Highlands, NJ: Humanities Press, 1976), p. 202.

who creates) and a specific kind of subject matter (human feeling). Langer's theory and the other traditional theories, however, fall easy prey to counterexamples, and, consequently, none of the frameworks they imply can be the right one. The reason that the traditional theories are easy prey for counterexamples is that the frameworks implied by the theories are too narrowly focused on the artist and the more obvious characteristics works of art may have rather than on *all* the framework elements that surround works of art. The result is that it is all too easy to find works of art that lack the properties seized on by a particular traditional theory as universal and defining.

The frameworks of the traditional theories do lead in the right direction in one respect. Each of the traditional theories conceives of the making of art as a human practice, as an established way of behaving. Consequently, the framework of each of these theories is conceived of as a cultural phenomenon that persists through time and is repeatable. The persistence of a framework as a cultural practice is enough, I think, to make the traditional theories themselves quasi-institutional. In every one of the traditional theories, however, there is only one established role envisioned and that is the role of the artist or the maker of artifacts. And, in every case, the artist is seen as the creator of an artifact with a property such as being representative, being symbolic, or being an expression. For the traditional theories the artist role is envisaged as simply that of producing representations, producing symbolic forms, producing expressions, or some such thing. This narrow conception of the artist role is responsible for the ease with which counterexamples can be produced. Since the traditional theories are inadequate, there must be more to the artist role than the producing of any, or even all, of these kinds of things that the traditional theories envisage. What an artist understands and does when he or she creates a work of art far exceeds the simple understanding and doing entailed by the traditional theories.

1→ Whenever an artist creates art, it is always created for a *public*. Consequently, the framework must include a role for a *public* to whom art is presented. Of course, for a variety of reasons many works of art are never in fact presented to any public. Some works just never reach their publics although their makers intended for them to do so. Some works are withheld from their publics by their creators because they judge them to be in some way inferior and unworthy of presentation. The fact that artists withhold some of their works because they judge them unworthy of presentation shows that the works are things of a *kind* to be presented, otherwise it would be pointless to judge them unworthy of presentation. Thus, even art not intended for public presentation presupposes a public, for not only is it possible to present it to a public (as sometimes happens), it is a thing of a type that has as a goal presentation to a public. The notion of a public hovers always in the background, even when a given artist refuses to present his or her work. In those cases in which works of art are withheld from a public, there is what might be called a "double intention" – there is an intention to create a thing of a kind that is presented, but there is also an intention not to actually present it.

What is an artworld public? It is not just a collection of people. The members of an artworld public know how to fulfill a role that requires knowledge and understanding similar in many respects to that required of an artist. There are as many different publics as there are different arts, and the knowledge required for one public is different from that required by another public. An example of one bit of knowledge required of the public of stage plays is the understanding of what it is for someone to act a part. Any given member of a public would have a great many such bits of information.

m→ The artist and public roles are the minimum framework for the creation of art, and the two roles in relation may be called "the presentation group." The role of artist has two central aspects: first, a general aspect characteristic of all artists, namely, the awareness that what is created for presentation is art, and, second, the ability to use one or more of a wide variety of art techniques that enable one to create art of a particular kind. Likewise, the role of a public has two central aspects: first, a general aspect characteristic of all publics, namely, the awareness that what is presented to it is art and, second, the abilities and sensitivities which enable one to perceive and understand the particular kind of art with which one is presented.

n→ In almost every actual society that has an institution of art-making, in addition to the roles of artist and public, there will be a number of supplementary artworld roles such as those of critic, art teacher, director, curator, conductor, and many more. The presentation group, that is, the roles of artist and public in relation, however, constitutes the essential framework for art-making.

Among the more frequent criticisms of the earlier version was that it failed to show that art-making is institutional because it failed to show that art-making is rule-governed. The underlying assumption of the criticism is that it is rule-governedness that distinguishes institutional practices such as, say, promising from noninstitutional ones such as, say, dog-walking. And it is true that the earlier version did not bring out the rule-governedness of art-making and this requires correcting. There are rules implicit in the theory developed in the earlier book, but unfortunately I failed to make them explicit. There is no point in discussing the rules governing art-making implicit in the earlier theory, but those of the present revised theory can be stated. Earlier I argued that actifactuality is a necessary condition for being a work of art. This claim of necessity implies one rule of art-making: if one wishes to make a work of art, one must do so by creating an artifact. I also claimed that being a thing of a kind that is presented to an artworld public is a necessary condition for being a work of art. This claim of necessity implies another rule of art-making: if one wishes to create a work of art, one must do so by creating a thing of a kind which is presented to an artworld public. These two rules are jointly sufficient for making works of art.

The question naturally arises as to why the framework described as the institutional one is the correct essential framework rather than some other framework. The frameworks of the traditional theories are clearly inadequate, but their inadequacy does not prove the correctness of the framework of the present version of the institutional theory. Proving that a theory is true is notoriously difficult, although proving that a theory is false is sometimes easy to do. It can be said of the present version of the institutional theory that it is a conception of a framework in which works of art are clearly embedded and that no other plausible framework is in the offing. For lack of a more conclusive argument that the institutional theory's framework is the right one, I will have to rely on the description of it I have given to function as an argument as to its rightness. If the description is correct, or approximately so, then it should evoke a "that's right" experience in the listener.

In the earlier version, I talked a great deal about conventions and how they are involved in the institution of art. I tried to distinguish between what I called "the primary convention" and other "secondary conventions" that are involved in the creation and presentation of art. One example of the so-called secondary conventions discussed there is the Western theatrical convention of concealing stagehands behind the scenery. This Western convention was there contrasted with that of classical Chinese theater in which the stagehand (called the property man) appears on stage during the action of the play and rearranges props and scenery. These two different theatrical solutions for the same task, namely, the employment of stagehands, brings out an essential feature of conventions. Any conventional way of doing something could have been done in a different way.

The failure to realize that things of the kind just discussed are conventions can result in confused theory. For example, it is another convention of Western theater that spectators do not participate in the action of a play. Certain aesthetic-attitude theorists failed to realize that this particular convention is a convention and concluded that the nonparticipation of spectators is a rule derived from aesthetic consciousness and that the rule must not be violated. Such theorists are horrified by Peter Pan's request for the members of the audience to applaud to save Tinkerbell's life. The request, however, merely amounts to the introduction of a new convention that small children, but not some aestheticians, catch on to right away.

There are innumerable conventions involved in the creation and presentation of art, but there is not, as I claimed in the earlier version, *a primary* convention to which all the other conventions are secondary. In effect, in the earlier version, I claimed that not only are there many conventions involved in the creation and presentation of art, but that at bottom the whole activity is completely conventional. But theater, painting, sculpting, and the like, are not ways of doing something that could be done in another way, and, therefore, they are not conventional. If, however, there is no *primary* convention, there is a primary *something* within which the innumerable conventions that there are have a place. What is primary is the understanding shared by all involved that they are engaged in an established activity or practice within which there is a variety of roles: artist roles, public roles, critic roles, director roles, curator roles, and so on. Our artworld consists of the totality of such roles with the roles of artist and public at its core. Described in a somewhat more structured way, the artworld consists of a set of individual artworld systems, each of which contains its own specific artist and public roles plus other roles. For example, painting is one artworld system, theater is another, and so on.

The institution of art, then, involves rules of very different kinds. There are conventional rules that derive from the various conventions employed in presenting and creating art. These rules are subject to change. There are more basic rules that govern the engaging in an activity, and these rules are not conventional. The artifact rule – if one wishes to make a work of art, one must do so by creating an artifact – is not a conventional rule, it states a condition for engaging in a certain kind of practice.

As I remarked earlier, the artifact rule and the other nonconventional rule are sufficient for the creating of art. And, as each rule is necessary, they can be used to formulate a definition of "work of art."

o⟶   A work of art is an artifact of a kind created to be presented to an artworld public.

This definition explicitly contains the terms "artworld" and "public" and it also involves the notions of *artist* and *artworld system*. I now define these four as follows:

An artist is a person who participates with understanding in the making of a work of art.

A public is a set of persons the members of which are prepared in some degree to understand an object which is presented to them.

The artworld is the totality of all artworld systems.

An artworld system is a framework for the presentation of a work of art by an artist to an artworld public.[6]

These five definitions provide the leanest possible description of the institution of art and thus the leanest possible account of the institutional theory of art.

⟦p⟧→ To forestall an objection to the definition of "work of art," let me acknowledge that there are artifacts that are created for presentation to the artworld publics that are not works of art: for example, playbills. Such things are, however, parasitic on or secondary to works of art. Works of art are artifacts of a primary kind in this domain, and playbills and the like that are dependent on works of art are artifacts of a secondary kind within this domain. The word "artifact" in the definition should be understood to be referring to artifacts of the primary kind.

The definition of "work of art" given in the earlier version was, as I acknowledged, circular, although not viciously so. The definition of "work of art" just given is also circular, although again not viciously so. In fact, the definitions of the five central terms constitute a logically circular set of terms.

There is an ideal of noncircular definition that assumes that the meaning of terms used in a definition ought not to lead back to the term originally defined, but rather ought to be or lead to terms that are more basic. The ideal of noncircular definition also assumes that we ought to be able to arrive at terms that are primitive in the sense that they can be known in some nondefinitional way, say, by direct sensory experience or rational intuition. There may be some sets of definitions that satisfy this ideal, but the definitions of the five central terms of the institutional theory do not. Does this mean that the institutional theory involves a vicious circularity? The circularity of the definitions shows the interdependency of the central notions. These central notions are *inflected*, that is, they bend in on, presuppose, and support one another. What the definitions reveal is that

<hr>

[6] *The Art Circle*, pp. 80–2.

art-making involves an intricate, co-relative structure that cannot be described in the straightforward, linear way envisaged by the ideal of noncircular definition. The inflected nature of art is reflected in the way that we learn about art. This learning is sometimes approached through being taught how to be an artist – learning how to draw pictures that can be displayed, for example. This learning is sometimes approached through being taught how to be a member of an artworld public – learning how to look at pictures that are presented as the intentional products of artists. Both approaches teach us about artists, works, and publics all at the same time, for these notions are not independent of one another. I suspect that many areas within the cultural domain also have the same kind of inflected nature that the institution of art has – for example, the area involving the notions of *law, legislature, executive,* and *judiciary.*

The ideal of noncircular definition holds also that sets of circular definitions cannot be informative. This may be true of some sets of definitions, but it is not, I think, true of the definitions of the institutional theory. For these definitions just mirror the mutually dependent items that constitute the art enterprise, and, thereby, informs us of its inflected nature.

In recent years Jerrold Levinson,[7] Noël Carroll,[8] Stephen Davies,[9] and others have published theories of art or drawn theoretical conclusions about art that relate in one way or another to the institutional theory of art.

Commentary on Dickie

The present piece by Dickie is retrospective: it describes two versions of his institutional theory of art, and some reflections on what led him to modify his views. It is best to start by locating the two versions of the institutional theory, at $\boxed{b}\!\mapsto$ and $\boxed{o}\!\mapsto$. Differences between the two will emerge as the commentary proceeds. The initial definition has two clauses, and it may be profitable to consider them separately.

---

[7] Jerrold Levinson, "Defining Art Historically," *The British Journal of Aesthetics,* 19 (1979), pp. 232–50; and "Extending Art Historically," *The Journal of Aesthetics and Art Criticism,* 51 (1993), pp. 421–2.
[8] Noël Carroll, "Art, Practice, and Narrative," *The Monist,* 71 (1988), pp. 140–56; "Historical Narratives and the Philosophy of Art," *The Journal of Aesthetics and Art Criticism,* 51 (1993), pp. 313–26; and "Identifying Art," in *Institutions of Art,* ed. Robert J. Yanal (University Park, PA: The Pennsylvania State University Press, 1994), pp. 3–38.
[9] Stephen Davies, *Definitions of Art* (Ithaca, NY: Cornell University Press, 1991), p. 243.

Artefactuality

First, there is the claim that a work of art is an artefact – Dickie takes 'artefact' to mean 'an object made by man, especially with a view to subsequent use' (see $\boxed{a} \mapsto$). Collingwood denied that the artist makes an artefact, because he wanted to deny that the artwork had a purely material existence and that the process of making it was craftlike. Dickie takes the notion of an artefact in a different direction, but for him too an artwork is not necessarily physically made or 'worked'.

One motivation of Dickie's account is to allow the concept of art to stretch from covering more traditional art forms to include also 'developments of the last hundred years or so, such as dadaism, pop art, found art, and happenings' (see $\boxed{d} \mapsto$). A question worth raising is whether these deliberately challenging recent developments in the history of art should be made central to our understanding of what art is. A hard line (exemplified above in chapter 2 by the proponents of the aesthetic theory of art attacked by Carroll) would say that such things are not art because they do not provide the requisite experience. In response to this, Dickie would point out that he is not defining art in the evaluative sense, and that he does not make the completion of any particular function essential to something's being an art work. A less hard-line but still sceptical approach would be to point out that these many movements from Dada onwards have expressly attacked, problematized, or made fun of the notion of art, of art's separateness from other commodities, of artistic creation as opposed to production, of the privileged status of the artist and the art object, and so on. True, the artworld has welcomed this kind of self-critique into its heart; but does that mean that philosophers must take practices that confuse and challenge us about the nature of art as paradigmatic of art itself?

In both versions of his theory Dickie holds that all art works are artefacts. See the stretch of text from $\boxed{e} \mapsto$ to $\boxed{f} \mapsto$ for the discussion of this issue in the earlier version, and $\boxed{h} \mapsto$ to $\boxed{j} \mapsto$ for discussion in the later version. A larger question can be posed:

Is Dickie right to say that all works of art are artefacts?

The problem cases for Dickie are: (1) the natural object that is found rather than worked upon (for example, a piece of driftwood), but which is admired for its sculptural properties and placed in an art gallery to be viewed, and (2) the readymade, an object that is made by human effort, but is taken by an artist and somehow becomes an art work. Duchamp, who coined the term 'readymade', provides the standard examples, such as the work that consists of a manufactured porcelain urinal transported to a gallery and exhibited under the title *Fountain*. Dickie wants both the driftwood (which is not made at all) and the readymade (which is not made by the artist) to be classed as artefacts (see especially $\boxed{i}\!\!\rightarrow$). Is either of his accounts persuasive on this score?

In the first version of his theory he says that an artist (or other person acting on behalf of the institution, the artworld) can confer artefact-status upon the driftwood or the manufactured urinal. Dickie abandons this talk (see $\boxed{h}\!\!\rightarrow$), and one might think that he does so wisely. For the parallels with other institutional conferrals seem to break down here. Someone becomes married, or becomes president, by a process in which a person with the right authority confers that status upon them. But it is hard to grasp how a thing can become *something that someone made* by any similar process.

In his second version Dickie says (see $\boxed{h}\!\!\rightarrow$) that an artist can bring into existence a new object 'the-driftwood-used-as-an-artistic-medium' or 'the-urinal-used-as-artistic-medium'. But are there really such objects as these? And do we bring new objects into existence every time we give something a new use? By walking on the carpet do I make the complex object 'carpet-used-as-walking-surface', and if I sit down on it do I make a 'carpet-used-as-sitting-surface', and so on? If not, why should we say that new objects of this sort can crop up in the artistic cases?

If both his versions of the claim that art works are artefacts fail, Dickie is faced with a dilemma: either drop the claim that all art works must be artefacts, or drop the claim that *Fountain* and the exhibited driftwood are art works. There might be some debate as to which of these claims it is better to drop, but that one of them should go seems more plausible than Dickie's compromise.

A work's relation to the artworld

Every part of Dickie's first definition (at $\boxed{b}\!\!\rightarrow$) can be (and indeed has been) subjected to scrutiny. What is 'conferring' here? What is it to act 'on behalf of' the artworld? What kind of 'appreciation' do people seek when they put a work forward? What kind of 'institution' is the artworld?

Dickie himself questions parts of his earlier definition. At $\boxed{k}\!\!\rightarrow$ he rejects the notions of *status conferral* and *acting on behalf of*, as suggesting a kind of institution which is too formal.

What sorts of roles might count as participating in the artworld?

Dickie mentions artist and public as the two absolutely essential roles without which there would be no artwork (see $\boxed{l}\!\!\rightarrow$ and $\boxed{m}\!\!\rightarrow$). He lists other roles at $\boxed{n}\!\!\rightarrow$. The boundaries of the artworld and of the roles that compose it are not to be formally defined, so presumably there are activities at the margins which may or may not count as artworld roles: what of, for instance, painting a classmate's portrait at primary school, or watching a television documentary on the music of Benjamin Britten, or taking a book of poetry out of the public library?

Another troublesome notion is that of *appreciation*.

Is Dickie's notion of appreciation illuminating about the nature of art?

At [c]→ Dickie distances himself from the notion of aesthetic appreciation, whose existence he doubts. Instead (at least in the earlier version) what he calls appreciating occurs simply when 'in experiencing the qualities of a thing one finds them worthy or valuable'. But this is vague, and the experience of many kinds of thing could be appreciated in this sense, such as an efficient functional object, an enticing advertising image or a piece of pornography. Dickie abandons the notion of appreciation in his later version, where a work of art is now something that is just 'presented' to an artworld public.

In fact Dickie adds two qualifications. Consider:

(a)   an artefact presented to an artworld public;
(b)   an artefact created to be presented to an artworld public;
(c)   an artefact of a kind created to be presented to an artworld public.

Why does Dickie prefer to define an art work as (c) rather than as (a) or (b)?

The first point is that not all works of art are presented to a public. It seems wrong to say that if Brahms had secretly hid a complete fifth symphony in his drawer and destroyed it shortly before he died, it would not have been a work of art, but if he had presented it to the public it would have been a work of art; or that if it had lain undiscovered and was presented to the public for the first time in 2004, it would have become a work of art only in 2004.

But what about compositions that an artist makes but never intends to present? There are many subtle and uncertain points here. For example, some preliminary sketches by painters can be works in their own right, others remain mere sketches or tests. With some poems, the unpublished first version discovered later becomes the definitive work, in other cases it remains a separate but related poem. Most importantly, much artistic activity results in products that the artist would never dream of releasing to the public, even though they are to all intents and purposes finished works.

Dickie has made the artist–public relation constitutive of art, and so is open to the objection that withheld works would not count as works of art on his theory. In putting forward (c) Dickie hopes to fend off this objection and save art status for products that are withheld from any public. Is it clear, however, which artefacts are *of a kind* created to be presented to an artworld public? If the only available answer to the question 'What kinds of thing are created to be presented to an artworld public' is 'the kind that are works of art', this definition becomes circular and uninformative.

The issue of circularity arises on a larger scale too.

Dickie acknowledges that his definition is circular. Should we regard this as more problematic than he does?

Both versions of the definition are circular, 'although [he says] not viciously so'; they merely show the interdependency of the concepts used, and so illuminate the nature of the institution. The second version of the definition of a work of art, with its subsidiary definitions of 'artist', 'public', 'artworld' and 'artworld system', makes this conceptual circle both wider and more explicit. We may object that the definition is uninformative in the following way: anyone wishing to know what an artist is or does needs some prior understanding of 'work of art' to understand anything by the definition given; someone asking to have 'work of art' explained is thrown back onto the notion of an artworld public, and so on. Dickie's reply would be that this is the only way to understand what an artist is or a work of art is. Submersion in the practice is the way in which we learn about it – rather like the rules of chess, for example – and from outside the practice there can be no truly intelligible definition.

A related worry, though, is the extent to which the theory carries any information that addresses our characteristic concerns with art. Theorizing about art has often been concerned to explain the place of art within human lives, to respond implicitly or explicitly to Plato's challenge and give reasons why art is beneficial or essential to a good human life. The traditional theories of art we referred to earlier attempt to do this, but Dickie's theory offers no answer to Plato at all. We have no idea from his theory why the whole practice called the artworld is worth having, any more than the world of chess or basketball or stamp collecting. Even if it captured within its terms all and everything that is art – which would be quite an achievement – would it remain unsatisfying because it does nothing to justify or explain the importance of the artworld?

In fact, we may wonder whether the theory does succeed in capturing all and only those things we wish to call art.

Does Dickie's theory of art apply to everything that we would want to call art? Does it allow in other objects and practices that we would not wish to call art?

A few examples only can be discussed here. One is used by Dickie himself, namely Betsy the chimpanzee (see [g]→). Some marks are made on paper by this animal, and are exhibited to the public. Dickie maintains that if these paintings were exhibited in an art gallery, then they could be art. This may seem counter-intuitive to some readers, especially given the fact that in Dickie's description 'someone at the Art Institute' decides to exhibit the chimpanzee's products, and thereby they become works *of that person*. Having removed any notion of appreciation and made the artworld a very informal institution, has not Dickie allowed too many potential acts of 'presentation' to a public to count as art?

Another query is one that Dickie also mentions when talking of things like playbills: these are made to be presented to an artworld public, but do not count as art in the ordinary run of things. Dickie comments that he assumes art works will be 'primary' artefacts, while playbills are secondary ($\boxed{\text{p}}\!\rightarrow$). But how satisfactory is this distinction? The set and costume designs are secondary to most theatre productions, but might well claim art status.

Could someone in total isolation from the artworld make a work of art?

A consequence of the institutional theory is that a human being working in some part of the world that has no conception of art and no art institutions *could not* produce a work of art. Whatever ingenuity or skill he or she applied, however beautiful or expressive the result, however intriguing and open to interpretive play, it could not be an art work. It could become one, of course, if someone from 'our' artworld presented it as such to the right public. But there is perhaps something suspiciously unsatisfying about this.

In the case of the readymade considered earlier, the act of presentation of the object to a public was itself of some interest, rather than the object. But with an object appropriated from another culture and 'converted' into an art work by the act of presentation to an artworld public, we are prone to imagine an object that itself has some intrinsic interest. We might suspect that such an object deserved to be art because of its formal, technical, expressive, or interpretive qualities. We started from the thought that none of these kinds of quality was comprehensive enough to be definitive of art. But if we intuitively seek such features as a reason for presenting something as art, then the institutional theory has not accounted for some of our intuitions about what may matter in an art work.

Writing about the institutional theory, Richard Wollheim posed a pointed question: 'Is it to be presumed that those who confer status upon some artefact do so for good reasons, or is there no such presumption?' (*Art and its Objects*, p. 160). If there is no such presumption, then being a work of art seems an arbitrary status; but if there can be good reason for some things to become art and not others – such as their beauty, expressiveness, or richness of meaning – then the taking up of things into the artworld cannot be the only factor in their being art. Dickie may reply that this lets evaluative considerations in by the back door, since the concept of a reason for art status suggests that of deserving art status, which is already an evaluative notion. Dickie's starting point was to exclude questions of evaluation from his definition of art. Some of the considerations we have raised may throw doubt on the possibility or desirability of doing so.

5

Authors and Works

Introduction to the Issues

Questions about the interpretation of art are many. Is there one privileged or correct interpretation for an art work? If there may be multiple legitimate interpretations for a work, what makes some legitimate and others not? If we incline to think of a single correct interpretation, is it fixed by what the author actually intended or wanted, or by the best construal that could hypothetically be placed upon the author's product by a well-informed audience? Finally, what influence upon interpretation, if any, should be granted to mere biographical information about authors, or to authors' direct claims about the meaning of their works?

The question that dominates this chapter is: When we are interpreting a work of art, what role is played by our knowledge of its author? The passages selected here give substantially different answers, though admittedly they approach the question in very different ways and neither states it in just this form. On the one hand we have the claim, extremely influential in recent literary and cultural theory, that the 'author' or 'subject' is a historical construct, a concept that arose in the modern period – interestingly, round about the same time as the concepts of art and the aesthetic – but which in the artistic practice and theory of today can be discarded. Literary texts, according to this view, confront a reader who brings any interpretive strategies to bear upon them, and it is the reader who places significance and unity in them – the mind or intentions of the author should, in this view, be abandoned as a kind of fiction that is not helpful in the task of reading and producing criticism.

On the other hand, we have the idea that even to identify a work of art we have to take into account its history of production and be aware of the interpretations that it can bear, given the way it came about and where it is situated in history and in the artworld. That suggests that the identity, thoughts, and intentions of the author in part constitute what the work is. According to this view there is a certain creativity in interpretation, in that a new interpretation brings about a new work, but interpretation can genuinely assign a meaning to a work only if it locates the work in the context of its history of production. Given different histories, the same sequence of words or array of brushstrokes could belong to quite different works, or to something that was not an art work at all.

In the English-speaking philosophical tradition, a well-known paper by Wimsatt and Beardsley from the 1940s argued that it was a fallacy to interpret a work in the light of its author's intentions, if those intentions were conceived as 'external' to the work itself. Only what was 'internal' to the work in front of the reader or spectator could or should count towards interpreting it. This claim is sometimes assimilated to that of Barthes' in 'The Death of the Author', though the latter is usually seen as a progenitor of Postmodernism, whereas Wimsatt and Beardsley belong to the earlier movement known as New Criticism. One crucial difference, symptomatic of a far-reaching change in the practice of art criticism, is that Wimsatt and Beardsley wanted to concentrate attention on the *work* as opposed to the author, whereas Barthes wants to valorize the creative role of the *reader*, in abstraction from whom the work cannot really have discrete existence or integrity.

The piece by Arthur Danto enters the philosophy of art from a different angle, posing questions about how an object comes to be a work of art, and what makes one work of art distinct from another. But his answer is that a work of art exists only when a certain kind of interpretation is available, and that different interpretations breed different works of art, even when they are interpretations of indistinguishable objects. For Danto, 'internal' interpretation of a work can never be sufficient, because without a theory about the work's history we cannot even be clear what work we have before us.

Introduction to Barthes

The French thinker Roland Barthes (1915–80) was an influential essayist and critic of culture. His philosophical background was in structuralism, a movement influenced by Ferdinand de Saussure, whose notions of 'signifier' and 'signified' Barthes uses in the piece reproduced here. Barthes came to influence the later movement in philosophy and art theory known as Postmodernism, especially through this short essay, which was first published in 1968.

The issue here could be seen as one of power or authority. When we are interpreting a piece of writing, we tend, Barthes alleges, to invest the figure of the author with a supreme, singular kind of authority over what the text means. One strand to this conception of authority is the idea of ownership or rights: the belonging of a text or literary work to the human being who originated it. Barthes claims that this proprietorial conception of the author is a relatively recent development, and thinks that it exerts a distorting influence over interpretation and criticism. It is as if the author, conceived as a kind of owner of the text, had rights also over what it means.

Another strand is that of desiring a single meaning or correct way of reading for a text. Quite independently of the notion of ownership, we might think that one reading was the authoritative and final one, if only we could arrive at it; and criticism might then be viewed as a quest for the single right reading. Where would the certification of this reading come from? An available answer might seem to be: from discovering or reconstructing what was in the author's mind prior to the work's existing. Barthes makes a number of suggestions against this conception of criticism.

There is a kind of political metaphor underlying the discussion, as if the author, or at least the conception of criticism which makes use of the author in a supposedly authoritarian way, is an oppression from which the text and its readers need to be liberated. One question is whether that way of regarding the philosophy of criticism is appropriate. Another problem is the apparent amalgamation of two distinct theses: that the allegedly oppressive conception of the author ought to be abandoned, and that it has already been abandoned. The author should die; but the author is already dead. A more sophisticated reading of this dichotomy might assimilate it to Nietzsche's famous dictum that God is dead (a parallel Barthes might endorse since he refers to the rejected conception of the author as 'theological'). Nietzsche thinks that the most advanced thought of his day has abandoned belief in God, but that the values that underlay that belief have yet to be truly questioned. Barthes may, likewise, think that while progressive writers and critics have revised their theory about the nature of criticism so as to remove crude notions about the authority of the artist, they have not yet started to live by the true consequence of that theoretical change.

Roland Barthes, 'The Death of the Author'

In his story *Sarrasine* Balzac, describing a castrato disguised as a woman, writes the following sentence: '*This was woman herself, with her sudden fears, her irrational whims, her instinctive worries, her impetuous boldness, her fussings, and her delicious sensibility.*' Who is speaking thus? Is it the hero of the story bent on remaining ignorant of the castrato hidden beneath the woman? Is it Balzac the individual, furnished by his personal experience with a philosophy of Woman? Is it Balzac the author professing 'literary' ideas on femininity? Is it universal wisdom? Romantic psychology? We shall never know, for the good reason that writing is the destruction of every voice, of every point of origin. Writing is that neutral, composite, oblique space where our subject slips away, the negative where all identity is lost, starting with the very identity of the body writing.

[a]→ No doubt it has always been that way. As soon as a fact is *narrated* no longer with a view to acting directly on reality but intransitively, that is to say, finally outside of any function other than that of the very practice of the symbol itself, this disconnection occurs, the voice loses its origin, the author enters into his own death, writing begins. The sense of this phenomenon, however, has varied; in ethnographic societies the responsibility for a narrative is never assumed by a person but by a mediator, shaman or relator whose 'performance' – the mastery of the narrative code – may possibly be admired but never

[b]→ his 'genius'. The author is a modern figure, a product of our society insofar as, emerging from the Middle Ages with English empiricism, French rationalism and the personal faith of the Reformation, it discovered the prestige of the individual, of, as it is more nobly put, the 'human person'. It is thus logical that in literature it should be this positivism, the epitome and culmination of capitalist ideology, which has attached the greatest importance to the 'person' of the author. The *author* still reigns in histories of literature, biographies of writers, interviews, magazines, as in the very consciousness of men of letters anxious to unite their person and their work through diaries and

[c]→ memoirs. The image of literature to be found in ordinary culture is tyrannically centred on the author, his person, his life, his tastes, his passions, while criticism still consists for the most part in saying that Baudelaire's work is the failure of Baudelaire the man, Van Gogh's his madness, Tchaikovsky's his vice. The *explanation* of a work is always sought in the man or woman who produced it, as if it were always in the end, through the more or less transparent allegory of the fiction, the voice of a single person, the *author* 'confiding' in us.

[d]→ Though the sway of the Author remains powerful (the new criticism has often done no more than consolidate it), it goes without saying that certain writers have long since attempted to loosen it. In France, Mallarmé was doubtless the first to see and to foresee in its full extent the necessity to substitute language itself for the person who until then had been supposed to be its owner. For him, for us too, it is language which speaks, not the author; to write is, through a prerequisite impersonality (not at all to be confused with the

castrating objectivity of the realist novelist), to reach that point where only language acts, 'performs', and not 'me'. Mallarmé's entire poetics consists in suppressing the author in the interests of writing (which is, as will be seen, to restore the place of the reader). Valéry, encumbered by a psychology of the Ego, considerably diluted Mallarmé's theory but, his taste for classicism leading him to turn to the lessons of rhetoric, he never stopped calling into question and deriding the Author; he stressed the linguistic and, as it were, 'hazardous' nature of his activity, and throughout his prose works he militated in favour of the essentially verbal condition of literature, in the face of which all recourse to the writer's interiority seemed to him pure superstition. Proust himself, despite the apparently psychological character of what are called his *analyses*, was visibly concerned with the task of inexorably blurring, by an extreme subtilization, the relation between the writer and his characters; by making of the narrator not he who has seen and felt nor even he who is writing, but he who *is going to write* (the young man in the novel – but, in fact, how old is he and who is he? – wants to write but cannot; the novel ends when writing at last becomes possible), Proust gave modern writing its epic. By a radical reversal, instead of putting his life into his novel, as is so often maintained, he made of his very life a work for which his own book was the model; so that it is clear to us that Charlus does not imitate Montesquiou but that Montesquiou – in his anecdotal, historical reality – is no more than a secondary fragment, derived from Charlus. Lastly, to go no further than this prehistory of modernity, Surrealism, though unable to accord language a supreme place (language being system and the aim of the movement being, romantically, a direct subversion of codes – itself moreover illusory: a code cannot be destroyed, only 'played off'), contributed to the desacrilization of the image of the Author by ceaselessly recommending the abrupt disappointment of expectations of meaning (the famous surrealist 'jolt'), by entrusting the hand with the task of writing as quickly as possible what the head itself is unaware of (automatic writing), by accepting the principle and the experience of several people writing together. Leaving aside literature itself (such distinctions really becoming invalid), linguistics has recently provided the destruction of the Author with a valuable analytical tool by showing that the whole of the enunciation is an empty process, functioning perfectly without there being any need for it to be filled with the person of the interlocutors. Linguistically, the author is never more than the instance writing, just as *I* is nothing other than the instance saying *I*: language knows a 'subject', not a 'person', and this subject, empty outside of the very enunciation which defines it, suffices to make language 'hold together', suffices, that is to say, to exhaust it.

The removal of the Author (one could talk here with Brecht of a veritable 'distancing', the Author diminishing like a figurine at the far end of the literary stage) is not merely an historical fact or an act of writing; it utterly transforms the modern text (or – which is the same thing – the text is henceforth made and read in such a way that at all its levels the author is absent). The temporality is different. The Author, when believed in, is always conceived of as the past of his own book: book and author stand automatically on a single line divided into a *before* and an *after*. The Author is thought to *nourish* the book, which is to say that he exists before it, thinks, suffers, lives for it, is in the same relation of antecedence to his work as a father to his child. In complete contrast, the modern scriptor is born simultan-eously with the text, is in no way equipped with a being preceding or exceeding the writing, is not the subject with the book as predicate; there is no other time than that of the enunciation and every text is eternally written *here and now*. The fact is (or, it follows) that *writing* can no longer designate an operation of recording, notation, repre-sentation, 'depiction' (as the Classics would say); rather, it designates exactly what linguists, referring to Oxford philosophy, call a per-formative, a rare verbal form (exclusively given in the first person and in the present tense) in which the enunciation has no other content (contains no other proposition) than the act by which it is uttered – something like the *I declare* of kings or the *I sing* of very ancient poets. Having buried the Author, the modern scriptor can thus no longer believe, as according to the pathetic view of his predeces-sors, that this hand is too slow for his thought or passion and that consequently, making a law of necessity, he must emphasize this delay and indefinitely 'polish' his form. For him, on the contrary, the hand, cut off from any voice, borne by a pure gesture of inscription (and not of expression), traces a field without origin – or which, at least, has no other origin than language itself, language which ceaselessly calls into question all origins.

We know now that a text is not a line of words releasing a single 'theological' meaning (the 'message' of the Author–God) but a multi-dimensional space in which a variety of writings, none of them original, blend and clash. The text is a tissue of quotations drawn from the innumerable centres of culture. Similar to Bouvard and Pécuchet, those eternal copyists, at once sublime and comic and whose profound ridiculousness indicates precisely the truth of writ-ing, the writer can only imitate a gesture that is always anterior, never original. His only power is to mix writings, to counter the ones with the others, in such a way as never to rest on any one of them. Did he wish to *express himself*, he ought at least to know that the inner 'thing' he thinks to 'translate' is itself only a ready-formed dictionary, its words only explainable through other words, and so on indefinitely; something experienced in exemplary fashion by the young Thomas de Quincey, he who was so good at Greek that in order to translate absolutely modern ideas and images into that dead language, he had, so Baudelaire tells us (in *Paradis Artificiels*), 'created for himself an unfailing dictionary, vastly more extensive and complex than those resulting from the ordinary patience of purely literary themes'. Succeeding the Author, the scriptor no longer bears within him passions, humours, feelings, impressions, but rather this immense dictionary from which he draws a writing that can know no halt: life never does more than imitate the book, and the book itself is only a tissue of signs, an imitation that is lost, infinitely deferred.

Once the Author is removed, the claim to decipher a text becomes quite futile. To give a text an Author is to impose a limit on that text, to furnish it with a final signified, to close the writing. Such a conception suits criticism very well, the latter then allotting itself the important task of discovering the Author (or its hypostases: society, history, psyché, liberty) beneath the work: when the Author has been found, the text is 'explained' – victory to the critic. Hence there is no surprise in the fact that, historically, the reign of the Author has also been that of the Critic, nor again in the fact that criticism (be it new) is today undermined along with the Author. In the multiplicity of writing, everything is to be *disentangled*, nothing *deciphered*; the structure can be followed, 'run' (like the thread of a stocking) at every point and at every level, but there is nothing beneath: the space of writing is to be ranged over, not pierced; writing ceaselessly posits meaning ceaselessly to evaporate it, carrying out a systematic exemption of meaning. In precisely this way literature (it would be better from now on to say *writing*), by refusing to assign a 'secret', an ultimate meaning, to the text (and to the world as text), liberates what may be called an anti-theological activity, an activity that is truly revolutionary since to refuse to fix meaning is, in the end, to refuse God and his hypostases – reason, science, law.

Let us come back to the Balzac sentence. No one, no 'person', says it: its source, its voice, is not the true place of the writing, which is reading. Another – very precise – example will help to make this clear: recent research (J.-P. Vernant[1]) has demonstrated the constitutively

---

[1]   Cf. Jean-Pierre Vernant (with Pierre Vidal-Naquet), *Mythe et tragédie en Grèce ancienne* (Paris, 1972), esp. pp. 19–40, 99–131.

ambiguous nature of Greek tragedy, its texts being woven from words with double meanings that each character understands unilaterally (this perpetual misunderstanding is exactly the 'tragic'); there is, however, someone who understands each word in its duplicity and who, in addition, hears the very deafness of the characters speaking in front of him – this someone being precisely the reader (or here, the listener). Thus is revealed the total existence of writing: a text is made of multiple writings, drawn from many cultures and entering into mutual relations of dialogue, parody, contestation, but there is one place where this multiplicity is focused and that place is the reader, not, as was hitherto said, the author. The reader is the space on which all the quotations that make up a writing are inscribed without any of them being lost; a text's unity lies not in its origin but in its destination. Yet this destination cannot any longer be personal: the reader is without history, biography, psychology; he is simply that *someone* who holds together in a single field all the traces by which the written text is constituted. Which is why it is derisory to condemn the new writing in the name of a humanism hypocritically turned champion of the reader's rights. Classic criticism has never paid any attention to the reader; for it, the writer is the only person in literature. We are now beginning to let ourselves be fooled no longer by the arrogant antiphrastical recriminations of good society in favour of the very thing it sets aside, ignores, smothers, or destroys; we know that to give writing its future, it is necessary to overthrow the myth: the birth of the reader must be at the cost of the death of the Author.

Commentary on Barthes

Barthes' essay is short, and appears to make essentially one point, elaborated upon in various terms and with various examples. The title announces the central point metaphorically: a task for the reader is to state literally what is meant by the death of the author.

Note here in passing that if we ask 'what Barthes means' by the metaphor of the death of the author, we may risk falling into the kind of author-based enquiry that the piece asks us to avoid. But we have various choices here. One is not to take talk of 'what Barthes means' in too heavy a fashion, leaving open that it may be equivalent to 'what we interpret the text to mean'. Another is to reserve judgement as to whether there is any problem in referring to the author as an anchor-point for interpretation (since we cannot assume from the outset that Barthes, or his text, is going to convince us).

What point or points are being made under the metaphorical heading of 'the death of the author'?

Barthes makes points chiefly of two related kinds. One is historical: that in the practice of modern writing a certain conception of the author *has already* become obsolete. The second is normative: our practice of reading and criticism *ought* to dispense with this same conception of the author.

Thus we have a number of lines to pursue. First, what is the conception of the author in question? Secondly, what reasons does Barthes give us to believe his claims about this conception?

What conception of the author is, or should be, dead?

To answer this question we need to read actively and pick up clues scattered through the essay. $\boxed{b}\rightarrow$ and $\boxed{c}\rightarrow$ may start us off. Here Barthes talks of a particular modern conception of the author that dovetails with that of the individual or human person, which he calls the 'culmination of capitalist ideology'. The idea that there was no conception of the person or individual before early modern times is too exaggerated to be taken seriously as a historical claim. We may allow that notions of the individual as a locus of rights and responsibilities, of the individual as the subject of philosophical enquiry, or of the person as a legal entity, came into prominence over a certain period of history. But Barthes surely cannot be objecting to the simple idea that individual human beings produce literary texts – so what is he objecting to?

The passage starting at $\boxed{c}\rightarrow$ shows that his target is a certain conception of the significance of the relation between the author, as human individual or person, and the work. Both in ordinary culture and (more culpably) in criticism, much attention is paid to explaining the work in terms of the author's life, including his or her mental states, character traits, and moral failings, and to exploring diaries, memoirs, and the like. Artists try to present themselves as objects of interest, as if 'their person and their work' were united.

Is Barthes right in his implication that this kind of biographical preoccupation with the artist is inappropriate in criticism?

Writing recently on the topic, Peter Lamarque has said: 'there does seem to be a general consensus that concentration on purely biographical factors – or the so-called personality of the author – is not integral to a serious critical discipline' ('The Death of the Author: an Analytical Autopsy', p. 324). As we shall see, Barthes is not concerned to combat only this biographical conception of criticism. But then the question is whether his opposition to it advances his case for the more radical claims he wishes to make.

The conception of the author that Barthes wants to remove also includes the notion of 'interiority' (see especially $\boxed{e}\mapsto$, $\boxed{j}\mapsto$, $\boxed{1}\mapsto$). This is the notion that the author's mental states, such as passions, feelings, and impressions are both (a) private or 'secret' to the author, and (b) the single definitive source of meaning for texts. This conjunction of views would give credence to a conception of criticism as the attempt to discover a single correct interpretation of what was in the artist's mind, a question over which the artist has absolute privilege.

Should we conceive of criticism as concerned with the artist's 'interiority'?

It seems right to oppose this conjunction of views. It is unnecessary to conceive the mental states that may bear upon interpretation of a literary text as being private: we interpret the mental states of human beings in the light of their manifest actions, including their production of linguistic texts. And it is wrong to think that anyone, authors included, has absolute privilege over the meaning of their linguistic acts or the interpretation of their own mental states.

The driving force of Barthes' attack on the author comes from his alternative conception of writing and criticism, which has two main strands: (1) a claim that writing, properly understood, is in a sense authorless, and (2) a claim that an endless proliferation of meanings is more desirable in interpretation than establishing fixed meanings. (These points are presumably what has been realized by the authors that Barthes discusses from $\boxed{d}\mapsto$ to $\boxed{f}\mapsto$ in his sketch of the historical loosening of the sway of the author.)

Let us examine the set of claims about writing as authorless (see especially $\boxed{a}\mapsto$ and $\boxed{g}\mapsto$). Barthes claims that writing as such – or at least a certain kind of narrative, which we may for convenience label 'literary' – is without ulterior purpose, and is the mere production of symbols. A literary text is not a case of someone using language to persuade, inform, warn, or record. From this Barthes argues that a literary text is not really a case of someone using language at all, but is just a case of language, pure and simple, disconnected from any origin (see $\boxed{h}\mapsto$). This seems implicitly to buy into the 'pure aesthetic' or 'art's for art's sake' mode of thinking which we have already seen questioned in other chapters. In response we might say that literary texts may often have purposes: to entertain, arouse emotions, or acquaint with aspects of reality. But even if a text were a genuinely purposeless linguistic phenomenon, it would not follow that we should not interpret it in the light of its origin.

Barthes advances an alternative conception of the writer, or 'scriptor', as not an origin of the text, but as its product, something 'born simultaneously with the text'. Here $\boxed{g}\mapsto$ is the crucial passage. The 'scriptor' is not conceived as having priority in time or in interpretive weight over the text. The 'scriptor' is the voice enunciating the text, but this voice is constructed in the act of reading the text. If there is any authority over what meaning is to be found enunciated in the text, it rests with the reader

Before asking further questions about the conception of the 'scriptor', let us consider Barthes' assumption that generating a plurality of interpretations is *per se* a desirable feature of criticism. The passage from $\boxed{k}\mapsto$ onwards presents this view in powerful fashion: writing 'ceaselessly posits meaning ceaselessly to evaporate it', literature 'liberates...an activity that is truly revolutionary', because it 'refuses to fix meaning'. This seems an extreme view of interpretation. What grounds are we given for thinking it is the right one?

Some support for this view comes ostensibly from a claim (see $\boxed{i}\mapsto$ and $\boxed{m}\mapsto$) that any text is always only a mixture of existing linguistic elements, a set of quotations, borrowings or parodies newly blended together. Barthes presents this as something we 'know', but gives no apparent reason why we should believe it. So the idea of critical interpretation as an endless proliferation of meanings is either an unsupported predilection for the extreme, or must be supported via the conception of the writer as 'scriptor' or authorial voice that emerges from the text. Let us return to this conception.

> Do we have reason to prefer Barthes' conception of the 'modern scriptor' to the conception of the author he rejects?

We can interpret works where we know little or nothing of the individual's life and character. Perhaps the most famous example of this is Shakespeare. It has often been disputed who wrote the Shakespeare plays, and of the standard candidate from Stratford very little is actually known, and nothing about his 'interiority'. When we say 'Shakespeare meant such-and-such here' we mean, in effect, 'This passage from the corpus of Shakespeare plays is best interpreted to mean such-and-such.' This agrees, though without the same rhetoric, with Barthes' conception of the scriptor who arises with the text and has no prior existence.

Two positions in contemporary philosophical discussions of interpretation are known as 'actual intentionalism' and 'hypothetical intentionalism'. The first says that there is a correct interpretation of an art work which is correct because it identifies the intention of the artist expressed in the work. The second says that the criterion of adequacy for an interpretation is what an audience should or would understand to be intended in certain specifiable conditions. Thus one might ask what a speaker of English would understand by a certain sentence, or what an educated Elizabethan or Jacobean would understand, what someone acquainted with the other Shakespearean plays would understand, and so on.

Actual intentionalism falls foul of Barthes' predilection for multiplicity in interpretations, because it regards all other extant interpretations of a work as inferior to the correct one. Hypothetical intentionalism can allow for a multiplicity of interpretations, because of the flexibility in defining the audience, and because a single audience could well understand the same work in different ways. But neither of these forms of intentionalism needs to posit the author as sole authority on the interpretation of a text, or hold that one is any way concerned with the personality or life of the author in criticism.

We might take Barthes' text itself as a case in point. For example, it has an explicitly revolutionary agenda, positing as valuable in itself the overturning of established hierarchies and the empowerment of a plurality of views as against a monolithic authority. To read this in the light of the intellectual life of 1960s Paris might be to gain a more appropriate understanding of how to interpret the text, than to read it without such information. This is not a matter of indulging in biographical criticism, nor of exploring the supposed 'interiority' of the author, nor of investing the human being Roland Barthes with the single ultimate say-so about the meaning of his text. Yet it is in a sense to think of illuminating the text before us by the light of intentions that were possibly or plausibly those of the author, and which allow us to interpret it in a certain way.

The extracts that follow are from Arthur Danto. Here we encounter a distinction between a text and a work (or more generally between a work and a 'mere thing', Danto's primary focus being on works of visual art). From Barthes's point of view we might say that Danto demonstrates how easily and creatively meanings for a single object may proliferate. But for Danto each new interpretation generates a *work*, because it must always include a hypothesis or theory about what statement or gesture the artist was making against the background of certain sets of assumptions about art and its history.

Introduction to Danto

Arthur C. Danto (b. 1924) is Emeritus Professor of Philosophy at Columbia University, and has been an influential philosopher of art and art critic for several decades. Danto first used the notion of 'the artworld' in aesthetics in an article of the same name in 1964. His central idea was that to know that something is art, one must know something of the history of art, what conceptions of art an artist is likely to have, what aspects of the previous practice of art he or she might be drawing attention to, what innovations he or she may make as against established styles, and so on.

There is a difference, for Danto, between a thing which is art and something which is 'a mere real thing'. Consequently, any theory of art must show how art objects are distinguished from qualitatively identical real things. For example, what is the difference between the work Duchamp made by choosing that urinal and the ordinary functional urinal that we can imagine was sitting next to it in the warehouse, or between Andy Warhol's art work *Brillo Boxes* and a pile of real Brillo boxes that look just the same?

Our extract comes from what is probably the best known of Danto's books, *The Transfiguration of the Commonplace*, published in 1981. Some readers might be prone to say that two objects which they could in no way distinguish perceptually could not differ aesthetically, or that one of them could not be a work of art without the other also being a work of art, or that if two painted canvasses looked exactly the same they would to all intents and purposes be the same work of art. By the repeated use of thought experiments, some based on real works, some wholly imaginary, Danto persuades us that these assumptions are false. In the extracts reproduced here he introduces his theory about what differentiates works of art from one another and from mere real things, making a particular use of the notion of interpretation.

Arthur C. Danto, *The Transfiguration of the Commonplace* (extracts)

5   Interpretation and Identification

A companion and I are admiring Breugel's *Landscape with the Fall of Icarus*, in Antwerp. Suppose we have not yet noticed the title or that, because we are purists and believe the painting should "speak for itself," we have refused to examine the title. My companion says, pointing to a dab of white paint over to the lower right, "That must be someone's legs, sticking out of the water." Remarks like that are not uncommon in front of paintings, once the eye has executed its routine saccades, for one wants to make sure one has not overlooked something. Thus one says: "What do you make of the extra arm in the *Rondanini Pietà*?" Or: "Does it strike you that the woman in Degas's *The Tub* seems to have three legs?" In art as in life it is easy enough to overlook things that do not fit the spontaneous hypotheses that guide perception. In life, where perception is geared to survival and guided by experience, we structure the visual field in such a way as to relegate to inessential background whatever does not fit our schemata, and such habits of looking are carried over into the gallery, much in the way that the habit of scanning, which is essential to reading, is brought with us into the study, where we may find ourselves reading texts, until we deliberately intervene, somewhat as we would read a newspaper article. I have met people who have seen the *Rondanini* without having noticed that extra arm, largely I suppose because there is no room in their preformed concept of a statue for detached and disembodied arms, and hence no room in their constitution of the work for what, if noticed at all, is read out as a perceptual excrescence under inductive habit. Michelangelo could have cut it out, had he wished to, as he cut out the left leg – a loss also not often noticed – from the *Duomo Pietà with Saint Nicodemus*, and the assumption is that he left it there for some reason deeper than indifference to its presence. Perhaps it plays a role analogous to the lines left on the paper by an artist seeking for a form, where the sketch remains as much a record of the search for form as the presentation of the form itself, and where often the form is lost in the effort at finding it (which is the quality of a sketch). And perhaps the *Rondanini*'s arm is left there for something like that that reason, a stage in the process of discovering the form finally liberated from the marble column in which it lay imprisoned (we know what Michelangelo had to say about such things). There are, as a guard once said at the Uffizi, no unfinished Michelangelos – "Si Michelangelo è finito, è finito!" – so perhaps everything matters in some way, and certainly anything as obdurate as an arm has to be worked in somehow. But it is difficult to work it into an image of the *Mater Doloroso* and her stony son who fades into the rock he comes from, as she and he fade into one another, which is what most people no doubt see. Similarly, someone may not see the third appendage as an extra leg in the Degas, there being again no room for three-legged women in one's conceptual scheme; and one has almost to see it as an arm unless brought up short by the suggestion that perhaps Degas is reinventing the female body in a way which our familiarity with Picasso enables us to understand, and rearranging parts to suit some inner feeling about the bodies of women, toward whom it is known that Degas had complicated misogynist feelings. In any case, we seem to be on the subject of detached or reattached limbs, and here we are, noticing those limbs in the Breugel.

The third leg in Degas, the extra arm in the *Rondanini*: these are unusual and call for explanation once they are pointed out. It would be weird to point out the two legs in Botticelli's *Venus*, since there is nothing to pay attention to there beyond whatever interest the legs as such may have; but there being two legs is of no interest whatever. A detached arm in the painting of a battle would again call for no special explanation: it serves as an indicator that it is a battlescene; you expect limbs in battlescenes as you expect trees in landscapes or bottles in a still life. The legs in Breugel's landscape need call for no special explanation, not if, as the title of the picture indicates, it is a landscape. But with the further identification of the legs as belonging to Icarus, the whole work changes. The work will have a different structure than it would have had were you not to have noticed the legs at all, or not to have known they were Icarus' legs, and hence have believed something else central to the painting than what actually is: these legs are the focus of the whole work, not in the sense that the legs are the subject and the rest background, but in the sense that the whole structure of the painting is a function of these being Icarus' legs, the rest not being background at all; or, though there is some background, a decision has to be made as to what belongs to it and what does not. Take, for instance, the orange sun, which could just give the information that it is a sunny day if you did not know that it is causally related to the boy in the water who made the mistake of flying too close to it at the cost of melting the wax that held the feathers in place: if the *sun* were not *there*, the boy would not be *here*. But let us proceed step by step.

b→ To begin with, it plainly has to have been part of what Breugel had in mind that the legs should be easy to overlook, and his title, telling us that here is the fall of Icarus, sends us on a search that comes to an end when someone points to the legs, which are really pretty insignificant in themselves, and says, this must be Icarus. It was after all a Mannerist painting, and one of the features of Mannerism is just this: the subject is important inversely to its scale. Mannerism is said to have begun with Raphael's *Fire in the Borgo*, where the prominent figures are some large, muscular athletes in postures of panic, seeking to climb over walls, which themselves recede in orderly perspective into the background of the painting where the Pope stands, tiny by contrast with the foreground athletes. He is holding his hands up, and by so doing has extinguished the fire that caused the panic in the first place. The painting is about him and about that act, but you could not tell that by conventions of ordinary scale, which might lead you to believe it was a painting of athletes with, as it happens, a pope in the background, perhaps as spectator. It is an art-historical problem to identify the bridegroom in Breugel's *Peasant Wedding*, just as it takes a lot of looking in a modern Mannerist work to locate the Christ in the *Triumphal Entry of Christ into Brussels* by Ensor, as if these paintings were literal embodiments of the thesis that the first shall be last and the last shall be first. In any case, once we know those are Icarus' legs, as well as information about Icarus himself, we can begin to put the painting together in a way impossible if we lacked that information. You cannot say, for instance, as an interesting fact about the work, that the plowman is not looking at the boy, if the boy is not someone like Icarus in point of tragedy. There are, after all, many things the plowman is not looking at in the picture, and none of these negative facts is especially interesting and certainly none is compositionally relevant. It is not just that the plowman is not paying any attention, but that Icarus has fallen, and life goes on, indifferent to this tragedy. Think of the deep significance of this indifference, and hence of the relationship between the compositionally dominant and the cognitively dominant figures, in the light of Auden's remarkable poem on the painting.

Think now of how differently the picture must be read if it is titled simply *Plowman by the Sea*, a bucolic painting or a piece of early proletarian art. Or, for the matter, if it were called *Landscape # 12*, and someone noticing the legs might see them as a mere Flemish detail, like the shepherd's dog or figures winding along some distant path. If it were so painted that everyone were looking at the legs and their bodies were deployed in intense Baroque gestures, it might be a drowning boy (and *Landscape # 12* would be a cruel title). But since they are not turned that way, they are not turned any way so far as the structure of the picture is concerned; that is, they are no more turned away from the legs than from the ship or from the castle. They are not turned, merely placed where they are with the orientation they have, narratively and hermeneutically independent of one another. Giacometti sometimes succeeded in placing figures in a space where they could have nothing to do with one another, and this becomes an interpretive fact about the work, and perhaps a metaphor for loneliness and crowds. Or the painting could be called *Industry on Land and Sea* and the legs would belong to a pearl diver or an oysterman; there is nothing about the legs which tells you they belong to someone fallen from the sky or, for the matter, that they even belong to a boy. My children thought it was someone swimming. The picture could then be *Works and Pleasures*; the plowman would contrast with the boy; the relationship would be different; there would not be the tension there is "now." What tells us the boy is or is not swimming? Suppose Breugel had done the whole painting with no legs. Then, titled as it is, it would be mystifying, unless someone were to say: the boy has fallen in the waters and they have closed over him, calm is restored, life goes on (as in *The Israelites Crossing the Red Sea*). Or they might say: Icarus is plummeting down, has not yet entered the space of the picture. If Icarus were shown falling through space, the picture would be an illustration and would have many of the formal features it now has, but it would not make a comment: there would only be an odd object hurtling down the sky. Or it would make a different statement, and a more banal one.

The plowman must be read together with the boy. It is hard to read the plowman together with the ship, though they both connect via the boy in Auden's poem. If the picture were entitled *The Departure of the Armada*, the boy would relate to the plowman differently, and each would relate to one another via their contrasting connection with the boat. The boy would only add to the ordinariness of the summer day upon which the Armada sailed away. He would be a detail that might be regarded simply as a cluttering of the landscape. You might point to the legs as evidence for the Flemish propensity to crowd pictures with details. You might, indeed, point it out as an obtrusive and gratuitous element: nothing depends upon it, the purist would say; it should be eliminated in the interests of pure design. Or we could, finally, imagine someone looking in a puzzled way at the legs and wondering whether they were meant to be there at all; perhaps they should have been painted out, and would have been but for an oversight – like the extra arm in the *Rondanini*.

One may regard Auden's interpretation of the painting as literary, but something fairly literary was clearly intended by the artist, given the Mannerist dislocations already remarked on; apart from this, it is an interpretation that is not visually inert, where the painting merely illustrates a moral text. To see the painting in these terms, if one had not so seen it before, works to transform the entire composition, to pull it into a different shape and hence to constitute it a different work than it would have been without benefit of interpretation. The painting suddenly becomes organized around Icarus, and classes of relationships spring up which simply could not have existed before the identification. True, there may be inert elements in the painting in the respect that it makes no difference whether the legs belong to Icarus – there may be elements in a painting like the fixed stars in the cosmos – but in any event the very concept of "inert element" presupposes the analyses I have been seeking to sketch. Enough has been said, then, to underwrite what may seem a consolation prize to the inartistic, that responding to a painting complements the making of one, and spectator stands to artist as reader to writer in a kind of spontaneous collaboration. In terms of the logic of artistic identification, simply to identify one element imposes a whole set of other identifications which stand or fall with it. *The whole thing moves at once.*

It is instructive to speculate on how we would see the painting not only if we did not know the story of Icarus, but if we knew it but did not know the pertinence of the story to the work, say because the title was lost or no title was ever given. In a way, to identify the painting's parts as I have done is to imply what its title might be. Veronese's painting of Hercules with Omphale, which shows him transvestite, could be taken by someone unfamiliar with the story as a painting of a bearded lady, but then it could not be Hercules and Omphale. A title in any case is more than a name or a label; it is a *direction* for interpretation. Giving works neutral titles or calling them "Untitled" does not precisely destroy, only distorts the sort of connection here.

And, as we saw, "Untitled" at least implies it is an artwork, which it leaves us to find our way about in. As a final implication of the practice, since the title itself is given by a painter, it presumably implies what he intends by way of structuring of the work. And this is ipso facto to admit the possibility of different structurings. If it is an artwork, there is no neutral way of seeing it; or, to see it neutrally is not to see it as an artwork.

e → To interpret a work is to offer a theory as to what the work is about, what its subject is. This must, however, be justified through identifications of the sort we have been canvassing. To interpret Breugel's painting as simply about Icarus involves at best identifying the legs and the relationship between their owner and the sun, implying a narrative structure, a story the painting not so much tells as presupposes in order to integrate the elements. This interpretation then leaves much idle incidental depiction that interacts in no particular way with the central elements of the work. To interpret it with Auden as about suffering – about "the meaning of suffering," rather, since it is not a depiction of suffering as a painting of the martyrdom of St. Laurence would be – brings into the structure many more elements that must be redescribed as indifferent to what transpires. Breugel's painting of the conversion of Paul is not just of that particular crucial moment, though to be sure, as much as Caravaggio, he shows a man fallen off his horse. It is also about how such momentous events are seen and is a pictorial essay in, so to speak, moral optics: what we see almost immediately is the prominent feature of the work, the rear end of a horse. Then we may notice people in the painting noticing something, which carries us, almost as if we were there, to the cause of their excitement. The indifference of some and the excitement of others are registered as part of the structure of the work. *Not* to interpret the work is not to be able to speak of the structure of the work, which is what I meant by saying that to see it neutrally, say as what I have spoken of as the material counterpart of an artwork, is not to see it as art. And the structure of the work, the system of artistic identifications, undergoes transformation, in accordance with differences in interpretation. We saw this work with reference to relationship within *The Fall of Icarus*, but it can go far deeper than that. Let

f → me elucidate this with a contrived example.

Consider two paintings we may imagine commissioned by a library of science to be executed on facing walls, these to be in an appropriate contemporary manner, as suited after all to science, but to be about some famous laws in science, perhaps to celebrate the fact that science has a history of discovery. The laws chosen by the artistic commissioner are the first and third laws of motion from Isaac Newton's

Principia. Two artists, one of whom is J and the other his arch rival K, are commissioned and because of their mutual contempt, great efforts are taken on the part of either not to reveal the work in execution to the other; it is all carried out with the greatest secrecy. When all veils fall on the day of revelation, the works of J and K look like this:

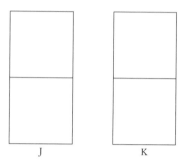

Inevitably there are charges and countercharges of theft and plagiarism, controversies over who had the idea first, and so on. But in truth these are distinct, enormously different works, however visually indiscernible: as much different, once interpreted, as *The Israelites Crossing the Red Sea* is from *Kierkegaard's Mood*.

J's painting is of Newton's third law, on which he did some research. The law, as J understands it, says that every action has an equal and opposite reaction, a physical gloss on *F* is equal to *ma*. There are, J tells us, two masses shown in the painting. The upper mass is pressing down with a force proportional to its acceleration and the lower mass is pressing up in just the same way in reaction to its counterpart's force. They have to be equal – hence of the same size – and opposite – hence one up and the other down (though J concedes that one could be left and the other right, which he avoided in order not to confuse things with the principle of conservation of parity, which he read had been overthrown). And after all one needs masses to show force, for how can there be a force of this sort without a mass? Newton's first law, turning now to K's work, holds that a body at rest will remain so forever, since a body in motion will move uniformly in a straight line, unless acted upon by impinging forces. That, K says, pointing to what, had it been J's painting, would have been where the two masses meet, "is the path of an isolated particle." Once in motion, always in motion: hence the line goes from edge to edge and could be protracted indefinitely. Were it to have begun in the middle of the painting, it would still be about the first law, since it implies dislocation from the state of rest; but then, K explains, he would have needed to show the force impinging, and the whole thing

would have become complicated where *he* was seeking radical sim-
plicities, "like Newton," he adds, modestly. Of course the line is
straight, but its being equidistant from top and bottom has an ingenious explanation: if it were closer to one than to the other, that would
require an explanation; but since no force is pulling it in either
direction, it bisects the painting, inclining neither way. Thus the
painting shows the absence of forces. How extraordinary, were one
to hear these explanations, to discover the indiscernibility of the
works. And at the level of visual discrimination, they cannot rele-
vantly be told apart. They are constituted as different works through
identifications that themselves are justified by an interpretation of
their subjects. In J's work there are masses, in K's work none. In K
there is movement, in J there is none. If J's work is dynamic, K's is
static. Aesthetically, it is widely agreed that K's is a success while J's is
a failure. Too weak by far for the subject, writes the critic for the
avant-garde journal *Artworks and Real Things*, who, while praising
K, wonders if J was the right person for the task, even whether J is not
beginning to "lose his touch."

   Let us ponder just what, in an effort at descriptive neutrality,
we shall designate as the "middle horizontal element." Shall we
identify it as an edge? If we do so, we are logically constrained to
regard it as belonging to a shape, since there are no unowned edges.
Edges are the boundaries of forms. Does the edge belong then to
the bottom rectangle or to the top one? As it happens, in J's painting
it has a richer description than "edge": it is a *join*, which entails
two edges and hence two forms. But there could be just one in a
visually similar painting: imagine the bottom form thrust up in empty
space. The point only is that if the element in question is an edge,
the whole surface must be made up of two forms, or at least one
form and one nonform. But then the element need not be an edge,
much less a join; it could be, as in K's work, a line. To be sure, K
describes it as a path, and a path divides, as it were, some pre-existing
space without defining, as an edge, a boundary of the space. But then
it certainly requires another sort of decision, namely what is the
relationship of the path to the space it sections, for a line or even
a path can be on or through or above or under. K's commentary
enables us to know that the path is through absolute space, but
whichever way we identify it, some complex further matters must
be resolved. Imagine that we are looking at a projected plane *at right
angles* to the plane depicted by K, seeing a line head on, so that it may
be represented by a dot. Then there are these four possibilities to
chose from:

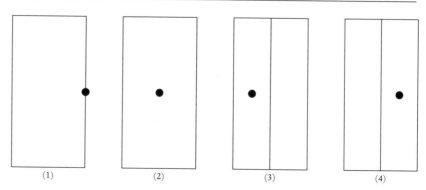

In (1), a painting indiscernible from K's depicts a plane with, as it happens, a line on it; it could be an aerial photograph of a road through a desert. K is actually represented by (2): a path through space, there being no plane depicted at all. In (3) the plane must be transparent enough to see the path through it; it could be the surface of the sea, and the path that of a swimmer. In (4) the plane could be transparent or opaque, but the path is at least above it, like that of a plane over the surface of the sea. Of course there is another possibility: where the surface of the painting is the plane in question (but then it is not depicted) and the dot the endview of a line inscribed on it, by a horizontalist follower of Barnett Newman.

Save with respect first to an "interpretation" and hence some artistic identification of the relevant element, no sensible or possible answer can be given to the question of how many elements the work contains. Are there two only, a line and a plane? Or maybe only one, in which case we have a portrait of a line with no more relationship to the surrounding pictorial space than the green paint around a portrait has to the head: it is simply painterly space, no more interpretatively relevant to the head than the paper is when one draws a head on a sheet of it. Or perhaps there are two elements, namely two rectangles, as in J's work. The middle element is not really an element at all, only part of one, and it is not clear that parts of an element are elements in their own right. But then there are always questions as to whether something is part of an element, hence belonging to the work or not. Are the edges of the surface on which the work is painted in any way part of the work? There are certainly paintings, as we saw, in which edges matter. In Poussin, for instance, respect for the edges is a compositional datum, in the respect that composition is defined with regard to the integrity of those edges. But the edges cannot be part of the work, since the interpretation of most of those works excludes them; they function, so to speak, like the boundaries of the

visual field which, Wittgenstein marvelously observes, are not themselves seen (they are not because then they would have to be included
in the visual field), much in the way that death is not part of life, since
it is not something we live through (which is a definition of "an event
in one's life").

There are, by contrast, paintings where the edges do not much
matter, where composition is a great deal less a dominating concern,
so that the painting itself could go on and on, past the edges; the
painting simply happens to stop there, in contrast with the painting
being resolved by means of them, just as there are accounts that simply
stop without in any structural sense coming to an end. I think of
Bonnard, or the Impressionists by and large, as producing works of
this somewhat *décousu* order. In J's work, the edges could be part of the
work, in that the boundaries of the canvas are the boundaries of the
masses that the canvas shows. They are edges brought into the work in
the manner of a painting by Picasso in which a frame is painted outside
a scene, so that the edges of the canvas and the edges of the frame are
one. But when this happens, the work itself undergoes a transformation of genre: it becomes, as it were, a three-dimensional work, a
sculpture in very flat relief. In this respect, we bring the object into *our
own* space, to the extent that the space we live in includes the edges of
Poussin's paintings but not the spaces included in those paintings; we
are not and cannot ever be co-occupants of the space in which the rape
of the Sabine women transpires as an event. Moreover, if the edges are
part of our space, so is the surface, which belongs to the masses in a way
in which the surface of the Poussin is never coincident with the surfaces
of anything he ever shows. It is, as it were, untouched by the surfaces of
the men and women or the buildings which are logically submerged
and cannot come up for air. The surface belongs to us, not to them.
Thus there is no geometry that contains us both, nor for the matter is
there a time scale. But this is generally true of art. There is no answer to
the question of how far away are Anna and Vronsky; the bedroom in
which they consummate their passion is certainly not included in the
bedroom in which you read about it, though the book may indeed be
there. And what about the corners? J's work can have real corners,
coincident with the corners of the masses (four "real" vertices, he tells
us, and four illusory ones, the painting occupying two worlds at once).
But K's painting can have no corners at all, or edges, given the constraints on the concept of absolute space, which has neither surface nor
boundaries. K's work, if you will, is more "classic," and in the manner
after all of Poussin.

A chapter back I cited the slogan in the philosophy of science,
which holds that there is no observation without interpretation and

that the observation terms of science are, in consequence, theory-laden to such a degree that to seek after a neutral description in favor of some account of science as ideally unprejudiced is exactly to forswear the possibility of doing science at all. My analysis of the works of J and K – not to mention the Elder Breugel – suggests that
i ⟶ something of the same order is true in art. To seek a neutral description is to see the work *as a thing* and hence not as an artwork: it is analytical to the concept of an artwork that there has to be an interpretation. To see an artwork without knowing it is an artwork is comparable in a way to what one's experience of print is, before one learns to read; and to see it as an artwork then is like going from the realm of mere things to a realm of meaning. But to go from J's work to K's is like exchanging one world or another inasmuch as these have, so to speak, disjoint sets of identifications, with almost no overlap. It is, in a way, like living through one of the great transformations in the history of the sciences, say from the Ptolemaic to the Copernican system. Nothing in the world will have undergone change, but *you*, through a vertiginous transformation of theoretical parallax, are thrust out into the heavens from having hugged the center; the earth itself is between planets (which would never have made sense before); and the sun does not move relative to us on the other planets – and all this is true even if (speaking anachronistically) a camera pointed at the sky would show the same configurations whether the revolution had
j ⟶ occurred or not. In art, every new interpretation is a Copernican revolution, in the sense that each interpretation constitutes a new work, even if the object differently interpreted remains, as the skies, invariant under transformation. An object o is then an artwork only under an interpretation I, where I is a sort of function that transfigures o *into a work*: $I(o) = W$. Then even if o is a perceptual constant, variations in I constitute different works. Now o may be looked at, but the work has to be achieved, even if the achievement is immediate and without any conscious effort on the observer's part. Charles Lamb, in writing of the engravings of Hogarth, says that they, in contrast with pictures we merely look at, must be read. So they have the power of texts. But so has any pictorial or for the matter artistic work which we may in fact think we are looking at rather than reading. In such cases, we read as we look because we interpret as we see.

It should not be automatic to assimilate the distinction between interpretation and object to the traditional distinction between content and form, but in a rough way the form of the work may be that gerrymandered portion of the object the interpretation picks out. Without the interpretation, that portion lapses invisibly back into the object, or simply disappears, for it is given existence by the

interpretation. But that gerrymandered portion is pretty much what I
mean by the work, whose *esse* is *interpretari*. That it should disappear
without the interpretation is on the other hand somewhat less start-
ling than Bishop Berkeley's thought that objects disappear when
unperceived, since their *esse* is *percipi*. One may be a realist about
objects and an idealist about artworks; this is the germ of truth in
saying without the artworld there is no art.

[. . .]

6 Works of Art and Mere Representations

In a quite respectable book called *Cezanne's Composition*, the critic
Erle Loran worked out some of the deeper formal structures of the
master's paintings, and the book itself is illustrated with some helpful
diagrams. One in particular has become notorious. It diagrams a
painting of Cezanne's wife, itself a celebrated portrait. It is just what
a diagram should be, with arrows, dotted lines, labeled areas; and it
reveals just the variations in direction and proportion it was Loran's
intention to make explicit. The notoriety of the diagram is due to the
fact that some years after the book appeared, Roy Lichtenstein produced a canvas, entitled *Portrait of Madame Cezanne* (1963), differing in scale and substance from Loran's diagram, but so like it by
criteria of optical indiscrimability as between, say, photographs of the
two, that Loran brought charges of plagiarism and a minor controversy swept the art journals of the time. Now, of course, at that period
Lichtenstein was "plagiarizing" from all over: a picture of a bathing
beauty from an advertisement that still appears for a resort in the
Catskills; various Picassos; and a number of things often so familiar
that the charge of plagiarism is almost laughably irrelevant. The Campbell Soup can, to cite an artifact that has a parallel artistic correlate, is
simply incapable of being plagiarized in the relevant way; an irrelevant
way is that in which a soupmaker pastes Campbell labels on his
product, exploiting familiarity and induction to save the expense of
marketing his own mulligatawny under an unknown name. Moreover,
Loran's book was so widely discussed in the artworld of the
fifties that the possibility of plagiarism could hardly arise. The issues,
however, are really not interestingly moral, but concern the serious
philosophical difference between the diagram of an artwork and an
artwork that consists in what looks like a diagram, and in at least
these cases the point is pretty clear. Loran's diagram is about a
specific painting and concerns the volumes and vectors of it. Lichtenstein's painting is about the way Cezanne painted his wife: it is *about*

the wife, as seen by Cezanne. It is fitting and interesting to show the world as it appeared to Cezanne as so many labeled areas, as so many arrows, rectangles, and dotted lines: we have the famous conversations with Emile Bernard, in which Cezanne speaks of nature as so many cubes, cones, and spheres, a kind of Pythagorean vision of the ultimate forms of reality, never mind what the senses say and conventional paintings show. Not many years after these geometrical speculations, the Cubists were painting the world in much those terms. But then how singularly apt to apply this geometrizing vision to Cezanne's *wife*, treated as though she were a Euclidean problem! For we know the sexual side of this man, in whom prude and satyr warred, and we know the passion and violence of his relationship with this woman, with whom he lived out of wedlock and by whom he had a son. And if the source and focus of all this feeling should be reduced to a kind of formula, how much this must tell us of the final triumph of the artistic impulse in his soul, even if it entailed a certain dehumanizing transfiguration of the subject; as if the person were so many planes, treated with no more and no less intensity and analytical subversion than a wax apple. One is reminded of Monet's anguished discovery that, sitting by the body of his late wife Camille, his model, love, support, angel, he had, instead of grieving, been studying the purple on her eyelids. He wondered what manner of monster he had become. Lichtenstein shows us the sort of monster Cezanne had become, if the parallel is allowed, but his in any case is a work of depth and wit, concerned with the way the world was perceived by the greatest painter of modern times. Loran's is not a work of art at all, but just, after all, the diagram of a painting. The issue of plagiarism is silly, inasmuch as the objects belong to disjoint categories, though both may be allowed to stand classification as vehicles of representation.

Yet this hardly can be said to have been proved, and the fact that the one has been accepted as an artwork and the other regarded merely as a diagram may all by itself only *seem* to have established a case that in philosophical honesty we must recognize remains to be made. For all that the analysis up to this point has established is that the two representations have different contents: the one concerns a painting by Cezanne and the other the vision and attitude someone who painted in that way may be conjectured to have had. One content may then be deeper than the other, without this difference in depth amounting to the sort of difference we are seeking. And we have known from the beginning that it is possible to have two works of art with different contents and which do nevertheless look perfectly alike. So unless we wished to claim that artworks have some special content, or some special kind of content, which sets them off from other representations altogether, the appeal to content would get us nowhere. And then we would have to demonstrate that Lichtenstein's work had that special kind of content and Loran's work did not (note the ambiguity on the word "work"). But I would hesitate to suppose even then that something having the same content as Lichtenstein's painting would *ipso facto* be an artwork (think of my own description of Cezanne's way of seeing). But if not in content, and not again in what meets the eye, wherein is the difference to be found? The example, interesting enough no doubt, only reproduces the problem it was to illuminate.

The failure of the example to reveal the differences we are seeking nevertheless suggests a reasonable next move. Suppose we can find a pair of things which not only resemble one another outwardly to whatever required degree, and have moreover the identical content, but where one of them is a work of art and the other not. Then the differences between works of art and mere representations should be discernible in whatever makes the difference in the pair. Of course, we may be unable to come up with the required example, in which case the arbitrariness of the concept of art is going to appear remarkably tantamount to mere injustice, just as J supposes at the beginning, where the relevant principle of justice requires that equals be treated equally. Either both or neither of such a pair will have to be art in virtue of congruity of shape and identity of content. But beyond that, it is going to seem hardly less arbitrary to call one of a pair of things which differs in content while retaining congruity of shape an artwork. And so on: we will systematically be forced into the worst caricatured formulations of the Institutional Theory of Art; that is art which is so designated by the effete snobs of the artworld. So a great deal turns, it seems to me, on whether or not the required example can be located.

Happily, the opening discussion in this chapter lends us license to draw our examples from whichever artistic genre is most convenient. So let us this time consider a text. Let us, for the matter, reflect upon the animating motive of Truman Capote's *In Cold Blood*, a text proclaimed when it appeared some years back as the first nonfiction novel: a philosophically innovative creation in that it demonstrated by counterexample that "All novels are fiction" is nonanalytical. The writer, apart from this stunning piece of philosophical imagination, invented nothing, or at least intended to invent nothing, in contrast with the typical novelist who invents characters, episodes, situations, and plots. Capote used the technologies of what today is called investigative journalism, and by constant digging came to know everything he could find out about the murder that was the subject of the book. It had the content of a very thorough forensic report written by someone in the district attorney's office. Or a newspaper article where the reporter had been as enterprising as Capote. Certainly, Capote could have made mistakes, but the appearance of these in his account would not make it a work of fiction, for then errors in the forensic report or in the newspaper article would constitute their authors as creative writers. What sets fiction apart from nonfiction is as subtle as what sets prose apart from poetry, and as there can be historical truth in fiction, there can be historical falsehood in nonfiction, without these transforming the texts into their opposites in either case. However, I am not interested in doing more than pointing out what may be left to the enterprising reader to elaborate. What counts is that we have three texts which, let us suppose, represent all and only the same facts. As they nevertheless differ in the manner in which they are written, they fail to satisfy one main condition for the example we need. They have only their content in common. Thereafter they diverge, as suits their differing purposes. Capote's book reads like a novel, as would be expected, given his mastery of the literary skills and his Edwardian Gothic sensibility, which is his cachet. But need a nonfiction novel in fact read that way? Is there any special way a novel, fiction or nonfiction, must read?

p→ Imagine, now that the possibility is before us, a nonfiction story, where the term "story" is meant to carry the connotation of a work of literary art. The imagined writer is considerably in advance of Capote as an artistic experimenter and, like many of the artists who have darkened these pages, is ideologically antiart. Call him M. Now M eschews anything one might identify as literary. He despises Capote, whom he grudgingly allows to have had a good idea, which he spoiled. M prizes texts of a sort beneath the scrutiny of literati and hardly ever used as such by writers pretending to art: telegrams, stock-market printouts, want ads, newspaper boiler plate, laundry lists, and the like. One of his major achievements is a Marilyn Monroe calendar. However, in the present instance he has chosen the format of a newspaper story, with place, date, byline, headline, subheadings, columns, and the rest. Well, let him investigate, in the manner of his predecessor, the suicide of a man in Patchogue after he killed the owner of a service station and several other customers. And now we have the form and the content of his nonfiction story – which differs, let us suppose, in no particular from a newspaper account of the same *fait divers* written by the provincial crime reporter for *Newsday*, whose name might as well also be M, to assure congruity of bylines. He is just doing his job. But M says he too is just doing his job, which is "to make art." The products of course match utterly. More elaborate and less credible examples could be furnished, but this one has the advantages of possibility. The question before us is fairly put: wherein do they differ, and what makes one a work of art if the other is not?

It seems to me now not difficult to see where they may differ. The nonfiction story uses the form of a newspaper story to make a point. The newspaper story, by contrast, uses that form because that is the way newspaper stories are; the writer is not making any special point by using that form. The newspaper story contrasts globally with literary stories, not being literature. The nonfiction story that happens to use the form of the newspaper story is a species of the class the newspaper story is excluded from. The author M's reasoning, as we may reconstruct it, is not without interest. He wants to make the point that the format of the newspaper story is the proper way facts of this sordid sort are commonly presented to a world steeped in media. So there is a nice relationship between content and form, twisted in the event by Capote in the interests of decadence. So M has repudiated the usual form of fictional presentation because this is, he says, nonfiction. It is nonfiction, but by no means nonliterature (like the newspaper story itself). We have already noted the way in which the Pop artist has pre-empted the screens and rasters of mass communication to present the charged images of our history and to underscore the violence of the times: chiaroscuro, scumbling, the glazing technique of the Old Masters, would be at odds with the depiction of the Kennedy assassinations, the Watergate confessionals, Vietnam (the wire-service photo suits these as the newsreel clip renders World War II, rotogravure the soggy realities of World War I, and the woodengraving the events of the Franco-Prussian War). The medium is not the message, but the form in which the message is given, and this is taken as a stylistic device by the artists who have become conscious of the structure of the media. The form of the newspaper story, which we pay little attention to because it is so commonplace in our culture, is chosen because of its commonplaceness by M – it is not commonplace in literature (yet).

There may be a question whether this difference makes the difference we want it to make. But it is a difference beyond visual congruity and identity of content. And the principle by which the example was generated may be extended and generalized. Any representation not an artwork can be matched by one that is one, the difference lying in the fact that the artwork uses the way the nonartwork presents its content to make a point about how that content is presented. Of course not all artworks take their flight from matching nonartworks, and those that do may almost be defined as modernist. Nevertheless, if the way the content is presented in relationship to the content itself is something that must always be taken into consideration in analyzing a work of art, we may be on the threshold of having our definition. One observes, meanwhile, that this may serve to show in what way a copy of an artwork may not be an artwork in its own right: the copy merely shows the way the artwork presents its content, without itself especially presenting this in a way to make a point of it; a copy aims at a state of pure transparency, like an idealized performer. But a photograph of a work of art may very well be an artwork in its own right, if it presents content in a way that shows something about the content presented.

The Lichtenstein painting has many properties the Loran diagram lacks, but it is difficult to suppose the difference between them can simply be found there. It is, for instance, much larger than its counterpart. But then the counterpart is much smaller than it. It is painted on canvas. But its counterpart is printed on paper. And so on. There is nothing about any of this which shows that one of each pair of inverse properties must make something an artwork; we can imagine cases in which the opposite works as readily. But I have tried to identify a property of an essentially different sort, a property to the appreciation of which I intend to devote the remainder of this book. The Lichtenstein self-consciously exploits the format of the diagram to make a point, and of course it itself is not a diagram. To the degree that we can speak at all of diagrammatic styles, Lichtenstein's *Portrait of Madame Cezanne* has none of these: its style consists in the fact that it uses a diagram, whatever the latter's style (if it can be said to have a style); the style in question is consistent with other works of Lichtenstein which happen not to use diagrams at all. Here, Lichtenstein uses the diagrammatic idiom *rhetorically*. Loran does not use the idiom of diagrams; he simply uses diagrams (which happen, since they are diagrams, to be in that idiom). Whatever Lichtenstein is doing, he is not diagramming. The activity of diagramming has criteria of success and failure and infelicity. In the case of Loran's work, indeed, the diagram can be false to the degree that further empirical work can show that it has the eye movements all wrong. His is a contribution to the psychology of art, not art, which has criteria of an altogether different sort that have to be worked out case by case as we open up the structures of individual works.

From case to case. But it would be evasion of philosophical responsibility not to press past this concession and see what general principles may be involved. The principle cannot yield formulas for art appreciation, which requires us to work through each artwork in its own terms. It at best will specify the sorts of terms the analysis of the artwork will have to contain. So I shall offer a thesis.

The thesis is that works of art, in categorical contrast with mere representations, use the means of representation in a way that is not exhaustively specified when one has exhaustively specified what is being represented. This is a use that transcends semantic considerations (considerations of *Sinn* and *Bedeutung*). Whatever Lichtenstein's work finally represents, it *expresses* something about that content. It manages to do this in part because of the connotations diagrams themselves have in our culture, belonging to the domain of economics, statistics, mechanical engineering, descriptive geometry, and *modes d'emplois*. By virtue of these connotations, the diagram is virtually a metaphor for whatever it shows. And it is this double role of representation and expression which has to be worked out in the final analysis of the work. Diagrams as diagrams typically express nothing about whatever it is they show. It is not that they are inexpressive, but that for such representations there is no place for the concept of expression. So it is not as if we use *zero* for the expression variable; there is no expression variable in the imagined equation to assign even zero to.

Expression, I admit, is too ill-defined a concept for us to pretend that we have probed deeply by its means into the metaphysical structure of the artwork. It must also be noted that no more than the concept of expression are the concepts of style, rhetoric, or metaphor altogether well-understood concepts. I have brought them in casually, but the fact that each comes naturally to hand, at the same crucial point in the analysis, suggests that they may have a common structure. And this, if true, means that we might be able to find out a great deal about each by taking them all together, rather than seeking to study metaphor or expression on its own.

[...]

7   Metaphor, Expression, and Style

[...] we might now return to our juxtuposed exemplars of the previous chapter. Once more, it will be instructive to somewhat refract the different structures of Loran's diagram of Cezanne's portrait of his wife and Lichtenstein's takeover of that diagram as an exercise in logical crystallography. The same painting, that very portrait, is the subject of the two representations. In the one case the diagram maps the eye's trajectory, more or less. In the other, as we saw, the intention is wholly different. We may interpret it as a metaphor in this sense: it

is, as it were, the *Portrait of Madame Cezanne* as a diagram. It is
a transfiguration of the portrait, in which the portrait – like Napoleon
– retains its identity through a substitution which is meant to illuminate it under novel attributes: to see that portrait as a diagram is to
see that artist as seeing the world as a schematized structure. In order
for the viewer to collaborate in the transfiguration, he must of course
know the portrait, know the diagram of Loran, and accept certain
connotations of the concept of the diagram, and then he must infuse
that portrait with those connotations. So the artwork is constituted as
a transfigurative representation rather than a representation *tout
court*, and I think this is true of artworks, when representations,
in general, whether this is achieved self-consciously, as in the arch
work I have been discussing, or naively, when the artist simply happens to vest his subject with surprising yet penetrating attributes. To
understand the artwork is to grasp the metaphor that is, I think,
always there. Thus, to vary the example, consider Gainsborough's
painting of St. James's Mall. It is indeed a picture of Regency ladies
promenading. But the women are also transfigured into flowers and
the *allée* into a stream they float along, and the painting is more than
a document of leisure and fashion, becoming a metaphor on time and
beauty. But every artwork is an example of the theory if it is correct:
Rembrandt as prophet, Parmigianino as convex mirror image, Dio-
cletian as Hercules, Christ as Lamb. But the greatest metaphors of art
I believe to be those in which the spectator identifies himself with the
attributes of the represented character: and sees his or her life in terms
of the life depicted: it is oneself as Anna Karenina, or Isabelle Archer,
or Elizabeth Bennett, or O: oneself sipping limetea; in the Marabar
Caves; in the waters off East Egg; in the Red Chamber...where the
artwork becomes a metaphor for life and life is transfigured. The
structure of such transfigurations may indeed be like the structures
of making believe – of pretending for whatever pleasure that brings
and not for the purposes of deceit. But in such pretending one must
always know that one is not what one is pretending to be, and
pretending, like a game, ceases when done. But artistic metaphors
are different to the extent that they are in some way true: to see
oneself as Anna is in some way to *be* Anna, and to see one's life as
her life, so as to be changed by experience of being her. So the thought
that art is a mirror (a convex mirror!) has after all some substance,
for, as we saw at the beginning of our inquiry, mirrors tell us what we
would not know about ourselves without them, and are instruments
of self-revelation. One has learned something about oneself if one
can see oneself as Anna, knowing of course that one is not a Fine
Woman or necessarily a woman at all, let alone a Russian and a

nineteenth-century person. You cannot altogether separate from your identity your beliefs about what that identity is: to believe yourself to be Anna is to be Anna for the time you believe it, to see your life as a sexual trap and yourself as a victim of duty and passion. Art, if a metaphor at times on life, entails that the not unfamiliar experience of being taken out of oneself by art – the familiar artistic illusion – is virtually the enactment of a metaphoric transformation with oneself as subject: you are what the work ultimately is about, a commonplace person transfigured into an amazing woman.

These are exalted reflections to be sure. But, to be sure again, one must at some point touch upon whatever it is that makes art itself an exalted activity in terms of the almost universal respect in which it is held. Making beautiful things is of course an exalted activity, as beauty is an exalted quality: but aesthetics, as we have so often seen, hardly touches the heart of art and certainly not of great art, which is certainly not the art that happens to be most beautiful. And so much of our discussion has been based upon such minimal exemplars, on squares of bare canvas and rude boxes and single lines, that it is intoxicating, if but for a moment, to ponder the masterpieces. But for the moment we must descend from heights on which it is difficult not to sound portentous, and point out one or two more obvious features and implications of artworks construed in terms of rhetoric.

The first is that if the structure of artworks is, or is very close to the structure of metaphors, then no paraphrase or summary of an artwork can engage the participatory mind in at all the ways that it can; and no critical account of the internal metaphor of the work can substitute for the work inasmuch as a description of a metaphor simply does not have the power of the metaphor it describes, just as a description of a cry of anguish does not activate the same responses as the cry of anguish itself. It is always a danger, in connection with an artwork one admires, to put into words what the painting means, for it is always available to anyone to say "is that all?" meaning that they can see very little recommendatory in *that*. To try then to respond to this deflationary response by adding more to one's description leaves it always a possibility to rerespond with the same question. And this is because what more there always is is not merely a quantitative overcharge one may hope with more words to redeem; it is rather the power of the work which is implicated in the metaphor, and power is something that must be *felt*. Metaphors do not simply have rather wider connotations than can be specified – perhaps one can in this sense "unpack" the metaphor into the full array of its connotative elements. But once more the power the metaphor has is simply not carried by its connotative equivalent which, as a list of attributes, is of a different logical sort altogether than the metaphor. Criticism then, which consists in interpreting metaphor in this extended sense, cannot be intended as a substitute for the work. Its function rather is to equip the reader or viewer with the information needed to respond to the work's power which, after all, can be lost as concepts change or be inaccessible because of the outward difficulties of the work, which the received cultural equipment is insufficient to accommodate. It is not just, as is so often said, that metaphors go stale; they go dead in a way that sometimes requires scholarly resurrection. And it is the great value of such disciplines as the history of art and of literature to make such works approachable again.

There is, then, a measure of truth to the claim that we ought to "pay attention to the work itself," that there is and can be no substitute for direct experience. It is a suggestion that has its analogue in certain very familiar empiricist theories, and it may be countered, on a shallow reading, that the analogy in some degree undermines something hoped to be distinctive of artworks. For there is no possible substitute for the direct experience of simple such qualities as red if one is to understand such predicates as "red," and no description, however protracted, can be equivalent to such primitive experiences. No doubt one could propose, on the basis of this analogy, that there is something as unique and irreducible about artworks as there is about the primitive qualities celebrated by empiricism, that in its own way the unique quality of *The Night Watch* is as much part of the basic stuff of the universe as is the simple quality of red. And so one would have an explanation of the uniqueness of art! This is an attractive theory, but not a finally persuasive one. It is not because, once more, the structure of artworks is like the structure of metaphors and *artistic* experience is internally related to this structure. Because of this it is a cognitive response and involves an act of understanding of a complexity wholly different from those basic encounters between simple properties and us: learning the meaning by acquaintance with its denotation may enable us to apply the name "The Night Watch" as the parallel encounter with red enables us to apply "red." But responding to that or any painting is considerably more than being able to identify it. Exactly this complexity of responsive understanding must, in many cases explicitly, be abetted by the mediation of criticism. But as the impugning of secondary works is part of what those have in mind who direct us to "the work itself," it is they who are open to the analogy from primitive experience – and characteristically they do treat artistic experience as a kind of aesthetic blur or blow whose only verbal correlative is an expletive – overlooking the complexity of structure the possibility of receiving the work involves

as well as the intricate interrelationship between the language we use
to describe the work and the experience of the work itself.

v→   There is a further point. I have inveighed against the isolation of
artworks from the historical and generally causal matrices from
which they derive their identities and structures. The "work itself"
thus presupposes so many causal connections with its artistic environment that an ahistorical theory of art can have no philosophical
defense. But this is more strongly than ever supported by the references of rhetorical force just brought forward. The rhetoric of the
work presupposes accessibility to the concepts out of which enthy-
memes, rhetorical questions, and the tropes themselves are completed, and without this the power of the work and hence the work
cannot be felt. But beyond this, I think it an analytical truth that
rhetoric itself is an intentional activity, and that beings only of a
certain sort are capable of it. If true this implies an important relationship between work and artist. That is, there is an implicit reference to the fact that someone is trying to move one rhetorically to the
extent that one responds (perhaps mistakenly) to the work. "Intentional" does not entail "consciously," of course, and there may be
room for a theory that refers art to the unconscious of the artist
without this in any way changing the conceptual relationships between art and its intentions: metaphors have to be *made*. So the
psychology, which I shall not further pursue, is certain to be exceed-
ingly intricate.

Commentary on Danto

In his opening chapter 'Interpretation and Identification' Danto uses two
main thought experiments, one based around Breughel's painting *The Fall
of Icarus*, the other around the invented example of the artists J and K. The
Breughel painting shows a scene in which there is a pair of legs splashing in
the water amid ordinary life activities going on, such as people ploughing and
fishing and a ship sailing by. Only the title of the painting gives us the clue to
link the legs, which are otherwise a strange little local feature, with the Greek
legend of Icarus, who flew too close to the sun on artificial wings and
plummeted to his death. Danto also mentions a particular reading of the
painting given in W. H. Auden's poem 'Musée des Beaux Arts'. Auden's
interpretation involves the meaning of suffering and its place within an
undisturbed ordinary life.

Danto's discussion of the Breughel painting gets properly underway around
a→ in the text and proceeds in a discursive fashion, constantly throwing up
new suggestions and finding comparisons with other art works, until f→ .

This makes for entertaining reading, but we should be alert to a more analytical kind of question.

What points are illustrated by Danto's discussion of the Breughel painting?

First let us locate the more general conclusions that Danto wants to establish. On this see $\boxed{i}\mapsto$, $\boxed{j}\mapsto$, and $\boxed{k}\mapsto$. Danto argues that a work of art exists only when some object is interpreted. Its existence is its being interpreted (as he says at $\boxed{k}\mapsto$ in a parody of Bishop Berkeley's Latin phrase concerning ideas existing only when perceived). That is a fundamental difference between an art work and a 'mere real thing': a real Brillo box or a real urinal simply exists without requiring any interpretation. A work of art occurs when there is an interpretation that places the object in some relation to the artworld. And if there is a new interpretation there is a new art work. What kind of interpretation is in play here we shall need to enquire later. At the minimum, however, an interpretation assigns to the work a content or subject, and its assigning this content can be justified by appeal to the elements of the work (see $\boxed{e}\mapsto$).

This may sound in tune with Barthes' idea of removing limits from texts, and of a text's unity lying not in its origin but its destination. It looks as if for Danto the artworld embodies a potentially endless production of new works as we re-interpret the canvasses, texts and other objects presented to us. But is this the right impression?

How does Danto envisage the relationship between artist and audience?

He makes an explicit statement on this, almost in passing, at $\boxed{c}\mapsto$: 'responding to a painting complements the making of one, and spectator stands to artist as reader to writer in a kind of spontaneous collaboration'.

That Danto in no sense envisages a 'death of the author' is borne out by the way he discusses the different imaginary interpretations of the Breughel painting. See, for example, the paragraph starting at $\boxed{b}\mapsto$. What would support the various interpretations of the legs visible in the painting are different theories about 'what Breughel had in mind'. Danto pays much attention to alternative titles the painting could have had, considering titles to be an important directive from the artist as to what interpretations may be in play. They are not mere names or labels; and even 'Untitled' functions as a direction for interpretation (see $\boxed{d}\mapsto$). Danto also discusses styles in which a painting may be seen as standing: in particular Mannerism, with its tendency to invert the scale of the subject and its surroundings.

The implication of these discussions is that there can be mistaken interpretations. Being apprised of the title of a work and the style in which the artist was working enables us to have some information about what was 'in his mind' – the artist's intentions – and enables us to know how to interpret it. This fits with the collaborative conception mentioned above: the viewer must impose interpretations upon what he or she sees, but these interpretations will be arbitrary if not grounded in a theory of what the artist intends. Such a theory must be justified by knowledge of the artworld (such as that there is a Mannerist style which Breughel was in a position to use) and by the structuring and intelligibility of the elements of the painting that the theory allows.

At $\boxed{f}\mapsto$ Danto shifts to a new thought experiment, this time involving a pair of initially indistinguishable paintings that he has invented, by artists whom he calls J and K.

> What more is shown by the example of the paintings by J and K than has been shown already? How does this example show that the transformation of a work by an interpretation can go 'deeper' (see $\boxed{f}\mapsto$)?

The passage at $\boxed{h}\mapsto$ will assist us to answer. In the Breughel example we could at least identify representational elements of the picture (the legs, the ploughman, the ship) and ask about how to interpret their relationship. In the case of the minimal paintings by J and K we cannot even do this. Although the two paintings are indistinguishable in ordinary 'neutral' perception, we cannot even answer say how many elements (planes, lines, edges) each contains – at least, we cannot do so independently of the interpretation of what each artist intended to do in his picture.

Danto refers to 'purists' who believe a painting should 'speak for itself' and who refuse even to look at a work's title. If he is right, this stance should seem a questionable one. In the case of the imagined paintings by J and K, the two works would speak little without knowledge of their different background intentions, and the purist would be unable to detect which of the two he or she was looking at without benefit of the titles, the context for which the paintings were made, and even some minimal knowledge of Newton's laws.

However, this discussion raises further questions.

> Can two perceptually indistinguishable works differ from one another aesthetically?

At $\boxed{g}\mapsto$ Danto imagines just this. But now we may come up against an intuition, or commonly held assumption. Can aesthetic properties change without any corresponding change in the perceptual properties of a thing? A presupposition sometimes made is that the aesthetic properties of a thing *supervene on* its perceptual properties (or material properties). This would mean that there cannot be an aesthetic difference between A and B, if there is no perceptual (or material) difference between A and B; or that any A and B with identical perceptual (or material) properties cannot differ aesthetically from one another. If this is true, then we ought to be able to judge a thing's aesthetic properties in ignorance of its causal history, i.e. when it was made, if it was made, what sort of person made it, with what beliefs and intentions, and so on.

If we think of an aesthetic property as something like beauty or pleasingness of form or colour, then we might be inclined to accept this supervenience claim. Wittgenstein once wrote a note which says 'Suppose someone were to say: "Imagine this butterfly exactly as it is, but ugly instead of beautiful"?!' The import is presumably that some material change would be required for the butterfly to change in respect of its beauty. And if there were a distinct but indistinguishable butterfly, would it not have to be beautiful too?

But Danto imagines that the two art works by J and K differ aesthetically: one is weak, the other by implication powerful. One fails as a work of art, the other succeeds. So here, even though we could not imagine *this* painting – the one by J with Newton's third law as its subject-matter – exactly as it is, but powerful instead of weak, we can nevertheless imagine another painting which pure perception could not distinguish from this one, but which differed aesthetically from it.

What sort of interpretation constitutes an art work for Danto?

Here we shall need to take into account the extracts from later parts of Danto's book. Danto piles on the examples: in these extracts we (chiefly) have a Roy Lichtenstein painting and an indistinguishable art-historical diagram by the critic Loran (see $\boxed{l} \mapsto$ to $\boxed{n} \mapsto$) and a non-fiction art-story that is indistinguishable from, but distinct from, a newspaper report ($\boxed{p} \mapsto$ to $\boxed{q} \mapsto$). Danto's ruminative, comparative style of presentation makes summary difficult, but, interspersed among the examples, the passages to be found at $\boxed{m} \mapsto$, $\boxed{r} \mapsto$, $\boxed{s} \mapsto$, $\boxed{t} \mapsto$, and $\boxed{u} \mapsto$ introduce some of the most important concepts he wishes to use.

The Lichtenstein and M examples are supposedly cases where one thing is an art work and there is an indistinguishable thing with the same representational content that is not an art work. For Danto an art work must be *about* something, have a content or subject. The present examples suggest that an art work takes a content and expresses something rhetorically, not just about the content, but about the way the content is presented (see especially $\boxed{r} \mapsto$). Art, then, is distinguished by the fact that we can interpret it as making a rhetorical point which has a certain self-referentiality to it. To grasp something as art is to grasp it as presenting an object or content in a certain way, and as presenting some comment or attitude towards the way it is presented.

To revert to the much-discussed work by Duchamp, we have to know that the object presented is a urinal, and know that what is presented to us is a urinal under the thought 'urinal-as-work-of-art'. We have to be able to interpret the rhetorical point made by presenting that object at that point in the history of the artworld. Only interpreted in some such way could it *be* a work of art. It is thus that a work engages an audience in interpretation, which is a filling in of the metaphor under which the subject presented can be understood. For Danto, this process of interpreting the metaphor that, in its art-historical context, an object can be seen as presenting, is the process that constitutes something's being an art work.

It should be apparent that Danto must oppose both the internalist kind of criticism that seeks to elucidate solely 'the work itself' and any version of the 'death of the author' thesis that seeks to dispense with any interpretation of the artist's intentions.

> **Why must the artist's intentions play a role in interpretation of art works for Danto?**

The paragraph at ⊡→ shows why this must be the case. If interpreting a work of art involves discovering rhetorically expressed attitudes to its subject-matter and the way its subject-matter is presented, then, since rhetoric is a matter of intention (Danto calls this an analytical truth), interpretation of art can never dispense with consideration of the relationship of the work to the artist.

We may end with a critical question:

> **Does Danto's account of the way interpretations constitute art account for everything that we regard as art?**

Danto's mode of persuasion uses carefully constructed examples of indistin-guishable counterparts. But need it be the case that *everything* that is art gets to be art in the way his examples do? Danto's context is very much the New York experimental artworld seen from the later twentieth century. Duchamp's readymades, Warhol's *Brillo Boxes*, and Lichtenstein's reworkings of non-artistic representational media pose the explicit question whether they are art and what art in general might be – they prompt a theory about what makes these things art and other indistinguishable things not. Danto's subtle reflec-tions produce a convincing answer for these cases: they are art because they are self-reflexive pieces about what can be art and because they make some rhetorical move when read against the background of art history and theor-izing.

But does everything we categorize and admire as art have the same kind of status? If we started by considering single canonical works rather than weird duplicates, would the same questions about what makes art art arise? And would there be the need for the same kind of answer? Finally, would we be likely to have the concepts of *art* and *work of art*, if these concepts applied only or mostly to things of the kind which demand Danto's kind of explan-ation?

6

Depiction in Art

Introduction to the Issues

Here we return to an issue addressed by Plato in my first chapter: how is something a representation of something else? How does a marked surface, available to visual perception, depict things of certain kinds? Although the once popular definition of art in terms of representation has long been out of favour, a great deal of visual art is essentially concerned with representing things, people, events, and so on, and any philosophy of art ought to give some account of how it does so. The phenomenon is familiar to most of us from early childhood; but the task of analysing what it takes for X to be a picture of Y has received considerable attention in recent years from thinkers working basically in the tradition of analytical philosophy, and has proved to be a peculiarly difficult task. I shall take 'depiction' and 'pictorial representation' to be interchangeable terms.

Though representation occurs in various art forms, it seems the most vital issue in the visual arts. The extracts in this chapter restrict themselves to the one central task of trying to understand how it is that something can be a *pictorial* representation, a task that proves hard enough. It is likely that pictorial representation is something divorced from linguistic representation, irreducible to it, and requiring an analysis of its own. But our two authors differ on how far removed from linguistic representation picturing is. Goodman rebuts the intuitively popular idea that representation is a matter of resemblance between a picture and the thing it represents. He wants to say that a picture operates analogously to language in that it is a conventional symbol that denotes the thing that it represents. Wollheim agrees with the rejection of the resemblance theory, but rejects Goodman's view as well. For

Wollheim, a picture's relation to its subject matter is unique and not at all like the way a word or sentence represents. Wollheim's central notion is 'seeing-in'. It is a psychological fact that when we look at certain objects and surfaces, we can see in them something that is not there to be literally seen – such as a face in the clouds or a large animal in the contour of a distant tree. In Wollheim's account pictorial representations arise through an intentional exploiting of this psychological capacity for seeing-in.

Introduction to Goodman

Nelson Goodman (1906–98) was one of the most distinguished American philosophers of the twentieth century, contributing work of lasting import-ance in epistemology and metaphysics as well as aesthetics. He was active as a museum curator and art collector as well as in academic philosophy where, among other appointments, he was for some time Professor of Philosophy at Harvard University. His book *Languages of Art* (1968) gives him a firm place in the recent history of the philosophy of art. It is a forthright attempt to demystify the arts, removing the notion of aesthetic value from centre-stage, and treating the various art forms as systems of symbols that make reference to the world. Language stands for things by describing them, pictures by representing them, and all the arts function as referring symbols that provide different structurings or give us different takes on the world.

The passages we include here are from the opening chapter of *Languages of Art*. Goodman's aim here is to break abruptly with some traditional but, as he would say, sloppy thinking about the nature of pictorial representation. We may think that for a picture to be of a woman, or of Queen Elizabeth I, is for it to be very much *like* her, or like women or a woman of a particular type – that to be a picture of something is to resemble that something, or things of that kind. The notion of resemblance needs to be questioned further: perhaps it means the sharing of properties by two things, or perhaps the sharing of some subset of properties that have to do with appearance. At the extreme – influenced by popular conceptions such as 'lifelikeness' – it may be thought that resemblance shades into illusion. If a picture shares enough properties with its subject, or is similar enough to it in appearance, we may think that it could be taken for the real subject. If by that we were to mean that people generally believe they are seeing a woman when they confront a picture of a woman, then we would not have a credible theory. Few theorists can be found who would accept that when seeing a picture and recognizing it to be of a woman or of Elizabeth I we are under an illusion.

Goodman goes further than this, and argues forcefully that the whole notion of resemblance between a picture and a subject is a mistaken start-ing-point if we want to understand representation. Instead, representation is a relation of denotation between a picture and a thing: the picture stands for, is a symbol for, the thing. Just as linguistic description is a conventional denotational relation between words and things, so artistic representation is a conventional denotational relation between pictures and things.

Before reading the extracts from Goodman, and as a preparation for following much recent debate about pictorial representation, it may help to consider an important distinction between two ways in which something may be said to be a 'picture of' something. We might call these 'relational' and 'non-relational' pictorial representation. Both of our authors give explicit attention to this distinction, though they exploit it to different ends.

A portrait of J. S. Mill represents J. S. Mill by being related to a definite existent object, the man himself. A painting of the tower of Babel represents something, but not by standing in any obvious relation to any real object in the world. A painting of a horse might just be a sheer invention, not related to any particular horse. There are horse portraits, but there is a quite distinct kind of painting which is *of a horse*, but where there would be no answer to the question 'Which horse?' Finally, a painting of a unicorn or a centaur has to be a sheer invention, since there are no originals to portray here, and so no object for the painting to be related to in the way in which Mill's portrait relates to Mill. So we can depict at least the following: real particular things, fictional particular things, things of a real kind (but in relation to no particular real thing), and things of fictional kinds. This complicates the analysis of depiction, but not hopelessly so, provided that one keeps in mind the various distinctions. Goodman, as we shall see, takes relational depiction as his paradigm. Representation by a picture occurs, for him, strictly when there is something to which the picture stands in a denoting relation.

Nelson Goodman, *Languages of Art* (extracts)

I Reality Remade

*Art is not a copy of the real world. One of the damn things is enough.**

1 Denotation

Whether a picture ought to be a representation or not is a question much less crucial than might appear from current bitter battles among artists, critics, and propagandists. Nevertheless, the nature of

---

* Reported as occurring in an essay on Virginia Woolf. I have been unable to locate the source.

representation wants early study in any philosophical examination of the ways symbols function in and out of the arts. That representation is frequent in some arts, such as painting, and infrequent in others, such as music, threatens trouble for a unified aesthetics; and confusion over how pictorial representation as a mode of signification is allied to and distinguished from verbal description on the one hand and, say, facial expression on the other is fatal to any general theory of symbols.

[a] → The most naive view of representation might perhaps be put somewhat like this: "*A* represents *B* if and only if *A* appreciably resembles *B*", or "*A* represents *B* to the extent that *A* resembles *B*". Vestiges of this view, with assorted refinements, persist in most writing on representation. Yet more error could hardly be compressed into so short a formula.

[b] → Some of the faults are obvious enough. An object resembles itself to the maximum degree but rarely represents itself; resemblance, unlike representation, is reflexive. Again, unlike representation, resemblance is symmetric: *B* is as much like *A* as *A* is like *B*, but while a painting may represent the Duke of Wellington, the Duke doesn't represent the painting. Furthermore, in many cases neither one of a pair of very like objects represents the other: none of the automobiles off an assembly line is a picture of any of the rest; and a man is not normally a representation of another man, even his twin brother. Plainly, resemblance in any degree is no sufficient condition for representation.[1]

[c] → Just what correction to make in the formula is not so obvious. We may attempt less, and prefix the condition "If *A* is a picture,...". Of course, if we then construe "picture" as "representation", we resign a large part of the question: namely, what constitutes a representation. But even if we construe "picture" broadly enough to cover all paintings, the formula is wide of the mark in other ways. A Constable painting of Marlborough Castle is more like any other picture than it is like the Castle, yet it represents the Castle and not another picture – not even the closest copy. To add the requirement that *B* must not be a picture would be desperate and futile; for a picture may represent another, and indeed each of the once popular paintings of art galleries represents many others.

---

[1] What I am considering here is pictorial representation, or depiction, and the comparable representation that may occur in other arts. Natural objects may represent in the same way: witness the man in the moon and the sheep-dog in the clouds. Some writers use "representation" as the general term for all varieties of what I call symbolization or reference, and use "symbolic" for the verbal and other nonpictorial signs I call nonrepresentational. "Represent" and its derivatives have many other uses, and while I shall mention some of these later, others do not concern us here at all. Among the latter, for example, are the uses according to which an ambassador represents a nation and makes representations to a foreign government.

d→   The plain fact is that a picture, to represent an object,[2] must be a symbol for it, stand for it, refer to it; and that no degree of resemblance is sufficient to establish the requisite relationship of reference. Nor is resemblance *necessary* for reference; almost anything may stand for almost anything else. A picture that represents – like a passage that describes – an object refers to and, more particularly, *denotes*[3] it. Denotation is the core of representation and is independent of resemblance.

If the relation between a picture and what it represents is thus assimilated to the relation between a predicate and what it applies to, we must examine the characteristics of representation as a special kind of denotation. What does pictorial denotation have in common with, and how does it differ from, verbal or diagrammatic denotation? One not implausible answer is that resemblance, while no sufficient condition for representation, is just the feature that distinguishes representation from denotation of other kinds. Is it perhaps the case that if A denotes B, then A represents B just to the extent that A resembles B? I think even this watered-down and innocuous-looking version of our initial formula betrays a grave misconception of the nature of representation.

2   *Imitation*

"To make a faithful picture, come as close as possible to copying the object just as it is." This simple-minded injunction baffles me; for the object before me is a man, a swarm of atoms, a complex of cells, a fiddler, a friend, a fool, and much more. If none of these constitute the object as it is, what else might? If all are ways the object is, then none is *the* way the object is.[4] I cannot copy all these at once; and the more nearly I succeeded, the less would the result be a realistic picture.

---

[2] I use "object" indifferently for anything a picture represents, whether an apple or a battle. A quirk of language makes a represented object a subject.

[3] Not until the next chapter will denotation be distinguished from other varieties of reference.

[4] In "The Way the World Is", *Review of Metaphysics*, vol. 14 (1960), pp. 48–56, I have argued that the world is as many ways as it can be truly described, seen, pictured, etc., and that there is no such thing as *the* way the world is. Ryle takes a somewhat similar position (*Dilemmas* [Cambridge: Cambridge University Press, 1954], pp. 75–7) in comparing the relation between a table as a perceived solid object and the table as a swarm of atoms with the relation between a college library according to the catalogue and according to the accountant. Some have proposed that the way the world is could be arrived at by conjoining all the several ways. This overlooks the fact that conjunction itself is peculiar to certain systems; for example, we cannot conjoin a paragraph and a picture. And any attempted combination of all the ways would be itself only one – and a peculiarly indigestible one – of the ways the world is. But what is *the world* that is in so many ways? To speak of ways the world is, or ways of describing or picturing the world, is to speak of world-descriptions or world-pictures, and does not imply there is a unique thing – or indeed anything – that is described or pictured. Of course, none of this implies, either, that nothing is described or pictured. See further section 5 and note 19 below.

e→   What I am to copy then, it seems, is one such aspect, one of the ways the object is or looks. But not, of course, any one of these at random – not, for example, the Duke of Wellington as he looks to a drunk through a raindrop. Rather, we may suppose, the way the object looks to the normal eye, at proper range, from a favorable angle, in good light, without instrumentation, unprejudiced by affections or animosities or interests, and unembellished by thought or interpretation. In short, the object is to be copied as seen under aseptic conditions by the free and innocent eye.

f→   The catch here, as Ernst Gombrich insists, is that there is no innocent eye.[5] The eye comes always ancient to its work, obsessed by its own past and by old and new insinuations of the ear, nose, tongue, fingers, heart, and brain. It functions not as an instrument self-powered and alone, but as a dutiful member of a complex and capricious organism. Not only how but what it sees is regulated by need and prejudice.[6] It selects, rejects, organizes, discriminates, associates, classifies, analyzes, constructs. It does not so much mirror as take and make; and what it takes and makes it sees not bare, as items without attributes, but as things, as food, as people, as enemies, as stars, as weapons. Nothing is seen nakedly or naked.

     The myths of the innocent eye and of the absolute given are unholy accomplices. Both derive from and foster the idea of knowing as a processing of raw material received from the senses, and of this raw material as being discoverable either through purification rites or by methodical disinterpretation. But reception and interpretation are not

g→ separable operations; they are thoroughly interdependent. The Kantian dictum echoes here: the innocent eye is blind and the virgin mind empty. Moreover, what has been received and what has been done to it cannot be distinguished within the finished product. Content cannot be extracted by peeling off layers of comment.[7]

---

[5]   In *Art and Illusion* (New York: Pantheon Books, 1960), pp. 297–8 and elsewhere. On the general matter of the relativity of vision, see also such works as R. L. Gregory, *Eye and Brain* (New York: McGraw-Hill, 1966), and Marshall H. Segall, Donald Campbell, and Melville J. Herskovits, *The Influence of Culture on Visual Perception* (Indianapolis and New York: The Bobbs-Merrill Co., 1966).

[6]   For samples of psychological investigation of this point, see Jerome S. Bruner's "On Perceptual Readiness", *Psychological Review*, vol. 64 (1957), pp. 123–52, and other articles there cited; also William P. Brown, "Conceptions of Perceptual Defense", *British Journal of Psychology, Monograph Supplement* xxxv (Cambridge: Cambridge University Press, 1961).

[7]   On the emptiness of the notion of epistemological primacy and the futility of the search for the absolute given, see my *Structure of Appearance*, 2nd edn (Indianapolis and New York: The Bobbs-Merrill Co., 1966 – hereinafter referred to as *SA*), pp. 132–45, and "Sense and Certainty", *Philosophical Review*, vol. 61 (1952), pp. 160–7.

All the same, an artist may often do well to strive for innocence of eye. The effort sometimes rescues him from the tired patterns of everyday seeing, and results in fresh insight. The opposite effort, to give fullest rein to a personal reading, can be equally tonic – and for the same reason. But the most neutral eye and the most biased are merely sophisticated in different ways. The most ascetic vision and the most prodigal, like the sober portrait and the vitriolic caricature, differ not in how *much* but only in *how* they interpret.

The copy theory of representation, then, is stopped at the start by inability to specify what is to be copied. Not an object the way it is, nor all the ways it is, nor the way it looks to the mindless eye. Moreover, something is wrong with the very notion of copying any of the ways an object is, any aspect of it. For an aspect is not just the object-from-a-given-distance-and-angle-and-in-a-given-light; it is the object as we look upon or conceive it, a version or construal of the object. In representing an object, we do not copy such a construal or interpretation – we *achieve* it.[8]

[...]

5   Fictions

So far, I have been considering only the representation of a particular person or group or thing or scene; but a picture, like a predicate, may denote severally the members of a given class. A picture accompanying a definition in a dictionary is often such a representation, not denoting uniquely some one eagle, say, or collectively the class of eagles, but distributively eagles in general.

Other representations have neither unique nor multiple denotation. What, for example, do pictures of Pickwick or of a unicorn represent? They do not represent anything; they are representations with null denotation. Yet how can we say that a picture represents Pickwick, or a unicorn, and also say that it does not represent anything? Since there is no Pickwick and no unicorn, what a picture of Pickwick and a picture of a unicorn represent is the same. Yet surely to be a picture of Pickwick and to be a picture of a unicorn are not at all the same.

The simple fact is that much as most pieces of furniture are readily sorted out as desks, chairs, tables, etc., so most pictures are readily sorted out as pictures of Pickwick, of Pegasus, of a unicorn, etc.,

---

8   And this is no less true when the instrument we use is a camera rather than a pen or brush. The choice and handling of the instrument participate in the construal. A photographer's work, like a painter's, can evince a personal style.

without reference to anything represented. What tends to mislead us is that such locutions as "picture of" and "represents" have the appearance of mannerly two-place predicates and can sometimes be so interpreted. But "picture of Pickwick" and "represents a unicorn" are better considered unbreakable one-place predicates, or class-terms, like "desk" and "table". We cannot reach inside any of these and quantify over parts of them. From the fact that P is a picture of or represents a unicorn we cannot infer that there is something that P is a picture of or represents. Furthermore, a picture of Pickwick is a picture of a man, even though there is no man it represents. Saying that a picture represents a so-and-so is thus highly ambiguous as between saying what the picture denotes and saying what kind of picture it is. Some confusion can be avoided if in the latter case we speak rather of a "Pickwick-representing-picture" or a "unicorn-representing-picture" or a "man-representing-picture" or, for short, of a "Pickwick-picture" or "unicorn-picture" or "man-picture". Obviously a picture cannot, barring equivocation, both represent Pickwick and represent nothing. But a picture may be of a certain kind – be a Pickwick-picture or a man-picture – without representing anything.[9]

The difference between a man-picture and a picture of a man has a close parallel in the difference between a man-description (or man-term) and a description of (or term for) a man. "Pickwick", "the Duke of Wellington", "the man who conquered Napoleon", "a man", "a fat man", "the man with three heads", are all man-descriptions, but not all describe a man. Some denote a particular man, some denote each

---

[9] The substance of this and the following two paragraphs is contained in my paper, "On Likeness of Meaning", *Analysis*, vol. 1 (1949), pp. 1–7, and discussed further in the sequel, "On Some Differences about Meaning", *Analysis*, vol. 13 (1953), pp. 90–6. See also the parallel treatment of the problem of statements "about fictive entities" in "About", *Mind*, vol. 70 (1961), esp. pp. 18–22. In a series of papers from 1939 on (many of them reworked and republished in *From a Logical Point of View* [Cambridge, Mass.: Harvard University Press, 1953]), W. V. Quine had sharpened the distinction between syncategorematic and other expressions, and had shown that careful observance of this distinction could dispel many philosophical problems.

I use the device of hyphenation (e.g., in "man-picture") as an aid in technical discourse only, not as a reform of everyday usage, where the context normally prevents confusion and where the impetus to fallacious existential inference is less compulsive, if not less consequential, than in philosophy. In what follows, "man-picture" will always be an abbreviation for the longer and more usual "picture representing a man", taken as an unbreakable one-place predicate that need not apply to all or only to pictures that represent an actual man. The same general principle will govern use of all compounds of the form "—picture". Thus, for example, I shall not use "Churchill-picture" as an abbreviation for "picture painted by Churchill" or for "picture belonging to Churchill". Note, furthermore, that a square-picture is not necessarily a square picture but a square-representing-picture.

of many men, and some denote nothing.[10] And although "Pickwick" and "the three-headed man" and "Pegasus" all have the same null extension, the second differs from the first in being, for example, a many-headed-man-description, while the last differs from the other two in being a winged-horse-description.

The way pictures and descriptions are thus classified into kinds, like most habitual ways of classifying, is far from sharp or stable, and resists codification. Borderlines shift and blur, new categories are always coming into prominence, and the canons of the classification are less clear than the practice. But this is only to say that we may have some trouble in telling whether certain pictures (in common parlance) "represent a unicorn", or in setting forth rules for deciding in every case whether a picture is a man-picture. Exact and general conditions under which something is a so-and-so-picture or a so-and-so-description would indeed be hard to formulate. We can cite examples: Van Gogh's *Postman* is a man-picture; and in English, "a man" is a man-description. And we may note, for instance, that to be a so-and-so-picture is to be a so-and-so-picture as a whole, so that a picture containing or contained in a man-picture need not itself be a man-picture. But to attempt much more is to become engulfed in a notorious philosophical morass; and the frustrating, if fascinating, problems involved are no part of our present task. All that directly matters here, I repeat, is that pictures are indeed sorted with varying degrees of ease into man-pictures, unicorn-pictures, Pickwick-pictures, winged-horse-pictures, etc., just as pieces of furniture are sorted into desks, tables, chairs, etc. And this fact is unaffected by the difficulty, in either case, of framing definitions for the several classes or eliciting a general principle of classification.

The possible objection that we must first understand what a man or a unicorn is in order to know how to apply "man-picture" or "unicorn-picture" seems to me quite perverted. We can learn to apply "corncob pipe" or "staghorn" without first understanding, or knowing how to apply, "corn" or "cob" or "corncob" or "pipe" or "stag" or "horn" as separate terms. And we can learn, on the basis of samples, to apply "unicorn-picture" not only without ever having seen any unicorns but without ever having seen or heard the word "unicorn" before. Indeed, largely by learning what are unicorn-pictures and unicorn-descriptions do we come to understand the word "unicorn";

<hr />

[10] Strictly, we should speak here of utterances and inscriptions; for different instances of the same term may differ in denotation. Indeed, classifying replicas together to constitute terms is only one, and a far from simple, way of classifying utterances and inscriptions into kinds. See further *SA*, pp. 359–63.

and our ability to recognize a staghorn may help us to recognize a stag when we see one. We may begin to understand a term by learning how to apply either the term itself or some larger term containing it. Acquiring any of these skills may aid in acquiring, but does not imply possessing, any of the others. Understanding a term is not a precondition, and may often be a result, of learning how to apply the term and its compounds.[11]

Earlier I said that denotation is a necessary condition for representation, and then encountered representations without denotation. But the explanation is now clear. A picture must denote a man to represent him, but need not denote anything to be a man-representation. Incidentally, the copy theory of representation takes a further beating here; for where a representation does not represent anything there can be no question of resemblance to what it represents.

Use of such examples as Pickwick-pictures and unicorn-pictures may suggest that representations with null denotation are comparatively rare. Quite the contrary; the world of pictures teems with anonymous fictional persons, places, and things. The man in Rembrandt's *Landscape with a Huntsman* is presumably no actual person; he is just the man in Rembrandt's etching. In other words, the etching represents no man but is simply a man-picture, and more particularly a the-man-in-Rembrandt's-*Landscape-with-a-Huntsman*-picture. And even if an actual man be depicted here, his identity matters as little as the artist's blood-type. Furthermore, the information needed to determine what if anything is denoted by a picture is not always accessible. We may, for example, be unable to tell whether a given representation is multiple, like an eagle-picture in the dictionary, or fictive, like a Pickwick-picture. But where we cannot determine whether a picture denotes anything or not, we can only proceed as if it did not – that is, confine ourselves to considering what kind of picture it is. Thus cases of indeterminate denotation are treated in the same way as cases of null denotation.

But not only where the denotation is null or indeterminate does the classification of a picture need to be considered. For the denotation of

---

[11] To know how to apply all compounds of a term would entail knowing how to apply at least some compounds of all other terms in the language. We normally say we understand a term when we know reasonably well how to apply it and enough of its more usual compounds. If for a given "—— picture" compound we are in doubt about how to apply it in a rather high percentage of cases, this is also true of the correlative "represents as a ——" predicate. Of course, understanding a term is not exclusively a matter of knowing how to apply it and its compounds; such other factors enter as knowing what inferences can be drawn from and to statements containing the term.

a picture no more determines its kind than the kind of picture determines the denotation. Not every man-picture represents a man, and
conversely not every picture that represents a man is a man-picture.
And in the difference between being and not being a man-picture lies
the difference, among pictures that represent a man, between those
that do and those that do not represent him as a man.
[...]

7   Invention

If representing is a matter of classifying objects rather than of imitating them, of characterizing rather than of copying, it is not a matter of
passive reporting. The object does not sit as a docile model with its
attributes neatly separated and thrust out for us to admire and portray. It is one of countless objects, and may be grouped with any
selection of them; and for every such grouping there is an attribute of
the object. To admit all classifications on equal footing amounts to
making no classification at all. Classification involves preferment;
and application of a label (pictorial, verbal, etc.) as often *effects* as
it records a classification. The "natural" kinds are simply those we are
in the habit of picking out for and by labeling. Moreover, the object
itself is not ready-made but results from a way of taking the world.
The making of a picture commonly participates in making what is to
be pictured. The object and its aspects depend upon organization; and
labels of all sorts are tools of organization.

Representation and description thus involve and are often involved
in organization. A label associates together such objects as it applies
to, and is associated with the other labels of a kind or kinds. Less
directly, it associates its referents with these other labels and with
their referents, and so on. Not all these associations have equal force;
their strength varies with their directness, with the specificity of the
classifications in question, and with the firmness of foothold these
classifications and labelings have secured. But in all these ways a
representation or description, by virtue of how it classifies and is
classified, may make or mark connections, analyze objects, and organize the world.

Representation or description is apt, effective, illuminating, subtle,
intriguing, to the extent that the artist or writer grasps fresh and
significant relationships and devises means for making them manifest.
Discourse or depiction that marks off familiar units and sorts them into
standard sets under well-worn labels may sometimes be serviceable
even if humdrum. The marking off of new elements or classes, or of
familiar ones by labels of new kinds or by new combinations of old

labels, may provide new insight. Gombrich stresses Constable's metaphor: "Painting is a science ... of which pictures are but the experiments."[12] In representation, the artist must make use of old habits when he wants to elicit novel objects and connections. If his picture is recognized as almost but not quite referring to the commonplace furniture of the everyday world, or if it calls for and yet resists assignment to a usual kind of picture, it may bring out neglected likenesses and differences, force unaccustomed associations, and in some measure remake our world. And if the point of the picture is not only successfully made but is also well-taken, if the realignments it directly and indirectly effects are interesting and important, the picture – like a crucial experiment – makes a genuine contribution to knowledge. To a complaint that his portrait of Gertrude Stein did not look like her, Picasso is said to have answered, "No matter; it will."

In sum, effective representation and description require invention. They are creative. They inform each other; and they form, relate, and distinguish objects. That nature imitates art is too timid a dictum. Nature is a product of art and discourse.

8 Realism

This leaves unanswered the minor question what constitutes realism of representation. Surely not, in view of the foregoing, any sort of resemblance to reality. Yet we do in fact compare representations with respect to their realism or naturalism or fidelity. If resemblance is not the criterion, what is?

One popular answer is that the test of fidelity is deception, that a picture is realistic just to the extent that it is a successful illusion, leading the viewer to suppose that it is, or has the characteristics of, what it represents. The proposed measure of realism, in other words, is the probability of confusing the representation with the represented. This is some improvement over the copy theory; for what counts here is not how closely the picture duplicates an object but how far the picture and object, under conditions of observation appropriate to each, give rise to the same responses and expectations. Furthermore, the theory is not immediately confounded by the fact that fictive representations differ in degree of realism; for even though there are no centaurs, a realistic picture might deceive me into taking it for a centaur.

---

[12] From Constable's fourth lecture at the Royal Institution in 1836; see C. R. Leslie, *Memoirs of the Life of John Constable*, ed. Jonathan Mayne (London: Phaidon Press, 1951), p. 323.

Yet there are difficulties. What deceives depends upon what is observed, and what is observed varies with interests and habits. If the probability of confusion is 1, we no longer have representation – we have identity. Moreover, the probability seldom rises noticeably above zero for even the most guileful *trompe-l'œil* painting seen under ordinary gallery conditions. For seeing a picture as a picture precludes mistaking it for anything else; and the appropriate conditions of observation (e.g., framed, against a uniform background, etc.) are calculated to defeat deception. Deception enlists such mischief as a suggestive setting, or a peephole that occludes frame and background. And deception under such nonstandard conditions is no test of realism; for with enough staging, even the most unrealistic picture can deceive. Deception counts less as a measure of realism than as evidence of magicianship, and is a highly atypical mishap. In looking at the most realistic picture, I seldom suppose that I can literally reach into the distance, slice the tomato, or beat the drum. Rather, I recognize the images as signs for the objects and characteristics represented – signs that work instantly and unequivocally without being confused with what they denote. Of course, sometimes where deception does occur – say by a painted window in a mural – we may indeed call the picture realistic; but such cases provide no basis for the usual ordering of pictures in general as more or less realistic.

Thoughts along these lines have led to the suggestion that the most realistic picture is the one that provides the greatest amount of pertinent information. But this hypothesis can be quickly and completely refuted. Consider a realistic picture, painted in ordinary perspective and normal colour, and a second picture just like the first except that the perspective is reversed and each colour is replaced by its complementary. The second picture, appropriately interpreted, yields exactly the same information as the first. And any number of other drastic but information-preserving transformations are possible. Obviously, realistic and unrealistic pictures may be equally informative; informational yield is no test of realism.

So far, we have not needed to distinguish between fidelity and realism. The criteria considered earlier have been as unsatisfactory for the one as for the other. But we can no longer equate them. The two pictures just described are equally correct, equally faithful to what they represent, provide the same and hence equally true information; yet they are not equally realistic or literal. For a picture to be faithful is simply for the object represented to have the properties that the picture in effect ascribes to it. But such fidelity or correctness or truth is not a sufficient condition for literalism or realism.

The alert absolutist will argue that for the second picture but not the first we need a key. Rather, the difference is that for the first the key is ready at hand. For proper reading of the second picture, we have to discover rules of interpretation and apply them deliberately. Reading of the first is by virtually automatic habit; practice has rendered the symbols so transparent that we are not aware of any effort, of any alternatives, or of making any interpretation at all.[13] Just here, I think, lies the touchstone of realism: not in quantity of information but in how easily it issues. And this depends upon how stereotyped the mode of representation is, upon how commonplace the labels and their uses have become.

Realism is relative, determined by the system of representation standard for a given culture or person at a given time. Newer or older or alien systems are accounted artificial or unskilled. For a Fifth-Dynasty Egyptian the straightforward way of representing something is not the same as for an eighteenth-century Japanese; and neither way is the same as for an early twentieth-century Englishman. Each would to some extent have to learn how to read a picture in either of the other styles. This relativity is obscured by our tendency to omit specifying a frame of reference when it is our own. "Realism" thus often comes to be used as the name for a particular style or system of representation. Just as on this planet we usually think of objects as fixed if they are at a constant position in relation to the earth, so in this period and place we usually think of paintings as literal or realistic if they are in a traditional[14] European style of representation. But such egocentric ellipsis must not tempt us to infer that these objects (or any others) are absolutely fixed, or that such pictures (or any others) are absolutely realistic.

Shifts in standard can occur rather rapidly. The very effectiveness that may attend judicious departure from a traditional system of representation sometimes inclines us at least temporarily to install the newer mode as standard. We then speak of an artist's having achieved a new degree of realism, or having found new means for the realistic rendering of (say) light or motion. What happens here is something like the "discovery" that not the earth but the sun is "really fixed". Advantages of a new frame of reference, partly because of

---

[13] Cf. Descartes, *Meditations on the First Philosophy*, trans. E. S. Haldane and G. R. T. Ross (New York: Dover Publications, 1955), vol. 1, p. 155; also Berkeley, "Essay Towards a New Theory of Vision", in *Works on Vision*, ed. C. M. Turbayne (New York: The Bobbs-Merrill Co., 1963), p. 42.

[14] Or conventional; but "conventional" is a dangerously ambiguous term: witness the contrast between "very conventional" (as "very ordinary") and "highly conventional" or "highly conventionalized" (as "very artificial").

their novelty, encourage its enthronement on some occasions in place of the customary frame. Nevertheless, whether an object is "really fixed" or a picture is realistic depends at any time entirely upon what frame or mode is then standard. Realism is a matter not of any constant or absolute relationship between a picture and its object but of a relationship between the system of representation employed in the picture and the standard system. Most of the time, of course, the traditional system is taken as standard; and the literal or realistic or naturalistic system of representation is simply the customary one.

Realistic representation, in brief, depends not upon imitation or illusion or information but upon inculcation. Almost any picture may represent almost anything; that is, given picture and object there is usually a system of representation, a plan of correlation, under which the picture represents the object.[15] How correct the picture is under that system depends upon how accurate is the information about the object that is obtained by reading the picture according to that system. But how literal or realistic the picture is depends upon how standard the system is. If representation is a matter of choice and correctness a matter of information, realism is a matter of habit.

Our addiction, in the face of overwhelming counter-evidence, to thinking of resemblance as the measure of realism is easily understood in these terms. Representational customs, which govern realism, also tend to generate resemblance. That a picture looks like nature often means only that it looks the way nature is usually painted. Again, what will deceive me into supposing that an object of a given kind is before me depends upon what I have noticed about such objects, and this in turn is affected by the way I am used to seeing them depicted. Resemblance and deceptiveness, far from being constant and independent sources and criteria of representational practice are in some degree products of it.[16]

---

[15] Indeed, there are usually many such systems. A picture that under one (unfamiliar) system is a correct but highly unrealistic representation of an object may under another (the standard) system be a realistic but very incorrect representation of the same object. Only if accurate information is yielded under the standard system will the picture represent the object both correctly and literally.

[16] Neither here nor elsewhere have I argued that there is no constant relation of resemblance; judgments of similarity in selected and familiar respects are, even though rough and fallible, as objective and categorical as any that are made in describing the world. But judgments of complex overall resemblance are another matter. In the first place, they depend upon the aspects or factors in terms of which the objects in question are compared; and this depends heavily on conceptual and perceptual habit. In the second place, even with these factors determined, similarities along the several axes are not immediately commensurate, and the degree of total resemblance will depend upon how the several factors are weighted. Normally, for example, nearness in geographical location has little to do with our judgment of resemblance among

Commentary on Goodman

In the passages included here Goodman argues: (1) that resemblance is neither necessary nor sufficient for representation; (2) that a conventional relation of denotation between picture and thing is what constitutes representation.

Arguments against resemblance

In Goodman's view, for a picture to represent a thing, resemblance between the picture and the thing is neither sufficient nor necessary. But he believes that this is not commonly recognized. 'The most naïve view' of representation holds just what he denies, and it is hard to shake off its influence (see $\boxed{\text{a}}\mapsto$). Hence Goodman needs some arguments.

> What are Goodman's reasons for holding that resemblance is not sufficient for representation?

This is the easier side of the question, and needs only minimal argument. Think of the resemblance between twins or between cars from an assembly line (Goodman's examples in the paragraph marked $\boxed{\text{b}}\mapsto$), where no representation occurs. But Goodman tightens his case by pointing out that the logic of the two relations '...resembles...' and '...represents...' are quite different, resemblance being a reflexive and symmetric relation, representation not. So even if there are many cases where A both represents and resembles B, the two relations could not be equivalent.

Goodman next (from $\boxed{\text{c}}\mapsto$) anticipates what is likely to be an objection: cars do not represent similar cars and people do not represent their twins, but that is because they are not *pictures*.

> Why does Goodman reject the formula 'If A is a picture, A represents B if and only if A appreciably resembles B'? Are his reasons convincing?

The reason given in the paragraph beginning at $\boxed{\text{c}}\mapsto$ is that a painting most resembles other paintings, and does not resemble a castle, a human being, or whatever to any appreciable degree. To take this line we have to be thinking of resemblance as merely the having of properties in common. A painting is flat,

---

buildings but much to do with our judgment of resemblance among building lots. The assessment of total resemblance is subject to influences galore, and our representational customs are not least among these. In sum, I have sought to show that insofar as resemblance is a constant and objective relation, resemblance between a picture and what it represents does not coincide with realism: and that insofar as resemblance does coincide with realism, the criteria of resemblance vary with changes in representational practice.

rectangular, inanimate, cold to the touch, weighs a certain number of kilos, and so on. A living human being does not have many of these properties, a castle happens to have a few of them, but has a vast list of other properties that do not match those of the painting.

The reader may wonder whether Goodman moves too quickly here. Could there not be other senses in which a painting resembles a castle? Something perhaps to do with aspects of its appearance, or aspects of the experiences that would be had by observers of both? Goodman in fact returns to some such suggestions below in his section 2 (entitled 'Imitation') and, as we shall see, rejects them.

The more difficult claim to sustain is probably that a picture need not resemble what it represents.

> What are Goodman's reasons for holding that resemblance is not necessary for representation?

Goodman asserts this in the paragraph marked $\boxed{d} \mapsto$, but without argument: he merely juxtaposes this assertion with his own view that 'a picture, to represent an object, must be a symbol for it, stand for it, refer to it'. But Goodman does not leave these assertions unsupported. From this point on he uses mainly two kinds of argument: (1) expounding the notions of reference and denotation in order to show them as sufficient to account for representation, thereby showing that resemblance is not necessary; and (2) pursuing the notion of resemblance further to show that it is incoherent. Let us deal with strategy (2) here, leaving (1) for the next section of the commentary.

Goodman argues against a kind of resemblance theory, best stated at $\boxed{e} \mapsto$ in the text: if a picture is a representation of something, then it copies an aspect of the way the thing looks. As part of his case against this view, Goodman argues for a conclusion stated at $\boxed{f} \mapsto$ as 'there is no innocent eye'.

> What does it mean to say there is no innocent eye? How does establishing this bear on Goodman's attack on the theory that equates representation with copying an aspect of the way a thing looks?

The so-called innocent eye would be a way of perceiving an object that is shorn of all particular interest, bias, and active interpretation on the part of the perceiver. Goodman rejects this because all perception involves interpretation and interest of some kind: the idea that in perception there is some 'raw material' that could be preserved by subtracting the perceiving subject's contribution to experience, is, he suggests (as many recent thinkers have), a myth. (It is interesting that Goodman should invoke Kant here ($\boxed{g} \mapsto$). Kant held that in ordinary perception of the objective world no experience was free of the active contributions of the interpreting subject. Yet he is often read as holding that aesthetic experience is an exception to this rule.)

If there is no innocent eye, then there is no coherent way of specifying the aspects of a thing that a picture must resemble in order to represent it. To reach this conclusion, Goodman needs two other claims: (1) that we could not in a picture copy an object 'the way it is', and (2) that we could not copy 'all the ways it is'. This – summed up in compressed fashion at $\boxed{h}\rightarrow$ – is Goodman's case for saying that the resemblance view of representation falls into incoherence. We cannot say in what way a picture resembles an object, or even specify what object it is trying to resemble.

Arguments for denotation

Having stated that denotation is the core of representation, Goodman has to make this plausible. He explicitly assimilates pictorial representation to linguistic description. Just as a word stands for a thing, without resembling it, and simply by the convention of some particular language, so a picture stands for a thing, without resembling it, by the convention of some particular representational system. There are two aspects of this that may bear some further scrutiny: conventionality and the notion of 'standing for'.

First, conventionality. Philosophers usually take a convention to be a matter of common agreement in practice (not necessarily explicit agreement) about how to achieve an end, where other parallel means of achieving the end would be perfectly possible. A convention is a right way of doing something just because it is the agreed way of doing something. Which words stand for which things in a particular language is a matter of convention, as are the rules of games, which side of the road to drive on, and so on.

> Goodman claims that what represents what pictorially is wholly a matter of convention. Is this a sustainable view?

Goodman's apparently most extreme statement on this matter comes late in the first chapter in his discussion of realism in pictures. At $\boxed{o}\rightarrow$ he says 'Almost any picture may represent almost anything.'

Reflecting on the history of art we may gather some support for Goodman's view. There are numerous ways of representing things, such as the human body: think of the human figure in ancient Egyptian art forms, in Christian medieval painting, in Japanese prints, in Cubism, and so on. What is represented and how it is represented depends upon the style used, with its conventions that often have to be learned to grasp the picture properly. The Egyptians were not representing a flat kind of person with head twisted to the side, nor medieval artists people of vastly differing size, nor Cubists fragmented people.

For Goodman naturalism is relative to the conventional mode of represent-ing in which a picture is taken to be situated. An objection would be that some systems of representation are in themselves more naturalistic than others. But Goodman has a reply: systems of representation seem more naturalistic to us because we are more familiar with them (see $\boxed{p}\!\!\to$ on 'habit' and 'standard-ness', and the reference to 'inculcation' just before $\boxed{o}\!\!\to$). We have learned some conventions so thoroughly that we cannot see past them and imagine other ways of representing. A final point is that the idea of resemblance is *produced* by learned conventions: we think certain landscape paintings rep-resent nature just as it is because we are used to seeing that style of landscape paintings.

Does Goodman really mean that, given the right conventions, a single black dot could represent the battle of Pearl Harbor, or a row of red triangles King Henry VIII? Goodman could rightly reply that we do not in practice have such conventional sign systems, because they are not very useful, interesting, or creative of new ways of structuring reality. But could he reply that in principle such representations would be impossible? At $\boxed{o}\!\!\to$ he says that *almost* any picture could represent *almost* anything. But this leaves it unclear what would be ruled out and why.

Goodman's view becomes easier to understand, however, if we return to the other notion highlighted above, namely 'standing for'. On a map, or in the explanation of a road traffic accident, anything can indeed stand for anything. We could put a dot on a map of the Pacific to stand for – represent – the Battle of Pearl Harbor, for example. So if by representing we just mean standing for as a symbol, then it is relatively harmless to say that anything can represent anything.

> Does this construal of representing as symbolic 'standing for' capture our ordinary notion of a picture?

An important point – and one with potentially drastic consequences – is that Goodman restricts representation explicitly to what we earlier called 'rela-tional' representation, where a picture represents by virtue of its relation to some existing thing, and would not represent if that thing did not exist.

This can be seen by following the discussion through $\boxed{i}\!\!\to$, $\boxed{j}\!\!\to$, $\boxed{k}\!\!\to$, and $\boxed{l}\!\!\to$. Pictures of Mr Pickwick and of unicorns *represent nothing*. We must add (see $\boxed{m}\!\!\to$) that a huge number of paintings also represent nothing: paintings of scenes from Greek mythology, Greek tragedy, Biblical legend (unless involving historical figures), surrealist fantasy scenes, purely imagined landscapes, and so on.

Is that an objection? Not for Goodman, because, as he makes clear at $\boxed{j}\!\!\to$, 'represents' is ambiguous. It either means 'stands in a denoting relation to some existent object' (Goodman's own preferred usage) or it means 'is a picture of a certain kind'. What then is his explanation of pictures that are 'of a certain kind'? He calls them man-pictures, unicorn-pictures, and the like, and says that here there is just the sheer fact that we classify certain pictures together as all man-pictures, and so on. No doubt we could classify them differently. But there is nothing much more to say in answer to the question why one picture is classed as a man-picture, while another is not (see k →).

This seems disappointing, since many people might think as follows: never mind whether this picture of a man actually denotes an existing man, the crucial question is: what makes it a picture of a man, as opposed to a description of a man, or a picture of another kind of thing? This latter question, says Goodman, involves notoriously difficult questions which are 'no part of our present task'. So Goodman has not answered the question 'What makes a marked surface a picture of a man?', only the question 'What makes a picture stand for some particular man as a symbol for him?' It would be unfair to complain that Goodman had moved the goalposts. But he seems to have omitted from his enquiries the most interesting phenomenon concerning depiction. At the risk of pre-empting the discussion in the following extract, we might point out that *all depiction* is depiction of a thing of some kind. We want to know why it is that we interpret a picture as a picture of a horse, quite independently of knowing or caring whether it 'represents' in Goodman's sense, i.e. whether or not there exists some particular horse it denotes.

So far then, we seem to have learned neither what makes a picture of a man a picture *of a man* (other than it in fact being classified by us in a certain way), nor what makes a symbol that denotes a man a *picture* of a man (i.e. what distinguishes this form of denotation from others, e.g. that of language).

Later in his book Goodman provides the latter explanation, after a long discussion of the structural differences between different symbol systems. Pictures are distinct from linguistic and notational systems because they do not have finitely distinguishable characters. In the alphabet, for example, *a* is quite distinct from *b*, from *c*, and so on, and for any mark it must be decidable whether it is *a*, *b*, or another determinate letter, or no letter at all and hence not part of the system. A mark halfway between *p* and *q* is not a letter in the system, for example. But in a pictorial system, there is no such finite stock of symbols, and between any two pictorial marks there can be another different from both that is still part of the 'language' of depiction. Moreover, there can be an infinite scale of objects in the world that would count as correctly denoted within a pictorial system. Goodman also distinguishes pictures from diagrams and graphs, in that in the case of a picture a change in any of its perceptible features potentially makes it a different picture – 'any thickening or thinning of the line, its color, its contrast with the background, its size, even the qualities of the paper', none of which is usually the case with a diagram or graph.

But will this dispel the doubts about Goodman's account? His conventionalism may seem too radical, ignoring the ease or naturalness with which many systems of picturing are learned and assimilated by the mind. Also, to say why we tend to sort pictures out into man-pictures, horse-pictures, and so on, we would require some account of the way the human mind works in perception. Goodman's refusal to enter this territory, sticking to the model of representation as purely denotational, is unsatisfying.

Introduction to Wollheim

Richard Wollheim (1923–2003) was one of the most respected and influential philosophers of his time. He held posts in a number of universities, most notably University College London and the University of California, Berkeley. He made important contributions not only to aesthetics but also the philosophy of mind and psychology, where psychoanalysis and the emotions were his chief interests. In *Art and its Objects* (1968) Wollheim examined the ontology of artworks, asking whether they are physical objects. In the course of his discussion of the visual arts he presented the concept of 'seeing-as' as the key to understanding representation. In a later edition (1980), a supplementary essay argues that the operative concept is rather 'seeing-in'. Wollheim holds it be a primitive fact of human psychology that we can see one thing in another, and he builds a theory of pictorial representation around this psychological capacity and its intentional exploitation by artists.

In 1987 Wollheim published *Painting as an Art*, based on the Andrew W. Mellon lectures he had given at the National Gallery of Art in Washington. Here, as a preliminary to many reflections on the use of representation in the works of particular artists and their relation to the spectators' ways of perceiving, Wollheim returns to his conception of 'seeing-in' and gives a deeper and more systematic account of it. The passage presented here is an extract from that discussion.

There are a couple of points that may be worth considering in advance of reading the extract. Firstly, although Wollheim opposes Goodman's account of representation, he is equally opposed to any analysis of representation in terms of resemblance. At the end of our extract he lists theories that he opposes. Goodman's is there (under the more general heading of 'Semiotic' theory), but so is the 'Resemblance' view. So whatever 'seeing-in' is in Wollheim's theory, it is not the seeing or noticing of resemblances. If we are prone to link his view with resemblance, it may be because we think that the horse we see in a picture resembles real horses, or that the face we see in a portrait resembles the sitter. That is fair enough, but for Wollheim the much more fundamental question is: How does the horse or the face come to be 'in' the picture in the first place? And that, he contends, is both the foundation of all depiction and something that cannot be explained by way of resemblance.

A second point is that this piece re-introduces the notion of the artist's intentions. Not everything that I can see in a picture or other kind of marked surface is a representation. Wollheim needs in addition the notion of what we are intended to see in a picture. For him, artists intentionally exploit the pre-existing primitive tendency that is at the centre of his theory.

Richard Wollheim,
Painting as an Art (extract)

[...]

1. I begin with 'seeing-in'.[1]

a→   Seeing-in is a distinct kind of perception, and it is triggered off by the presence within the field of vision of a differentiated surface. Not all differentiated surfaces will have this effect, but I doubt that anything significant can be said about exactly what a surface must be like for it to have this effect. When the surface is right, then

b→   an experience with a certain phenomenology will occur, and it is this phenomenology that is distinctive about seeing-in. Theorists of representation consistently overlook or reduce this phenomenology with the result that they garble representation. The distinctive phenomenological feature I call 'twofoldness',[2] because, when

---

[1] For seeing-in, see my *Art and its Objects* (2nd edition, New York, 1980, and Cambridge, England, 1983), Supplementary Essay V, 'Seeing-as, Seeing-in, and Pictorial Representation', and my 'Imagination and Pictorial Understanding', *Proceedings of the Artistotelian Society*, supplementary vol. LX (1986), pp. 45–60. In the first of these two essays I give my reasons for preferring the concept of seeing-in to that of seeing-as, which derives from Ludwig Wittgenstein, trans. G. E. M. Anscombe, *Philosophical Investigations* (Oxford, 1953), Part II, section XI, and which I had used in the first edition of *Art and its Objects* (New York, 1968, and London, 1970). For the concept of seeing-in, I am indebted to Richard Damann. See also Christopher Peacocke, 'Depiction', *Philosophical Review*, vol. XCVI, no. 3 (July 1987), pp. 383–410, for an attempt at a more extended analysis of seeing-in than I am inclined to think possible.

[2] For twofoldness, see my 'Reflections on *Art and Illusion*', *Arts Yearbook*, no.4, (1961) and my *On Drawing an Object*, both reprinted, the former in a much extended form, in my *On Art and the Mind*. However in both these writings I had conceived of twofoldness as a matter of two distinct experiences occurring simultaneously. I owe the abandonment of this view to Malcolm Budd and Michael Podro. For the relevant considerations, see Michael Podro, review of my *Art and its Objects*, *Burlington Magazine*, vol.CXXIV, no. 947 (February 1982), pp. 100–2, 'Fiction and Reality in Painting', *Poetik und Hermeneutik*, vol. X (1983), pp. 225–37, and 'Depiction and the Golden Calf', in *Philosophy and the Visual Arts: Seeing and Abstracting*, ed. Andrew Harrison (The Hague, 1987).

E. H. Gombrich, *Art and Illusion* (New York and London, 1959) denies the possibility of twofoldness, either in the sense of two simultaneous experiences or (though he does not explicitly consider this possibility) in the sense of two aspects of one experience, and he does so partly by appeal to intuitive considerations, partly by assimilating what I call the recognitional/configurational distinction, or what he calls the nature/canvas dichotomy, to the distinction between the duck and the rabbit aspects of the duck–rabbit figure. For he then claims that,

c→ seeing-in occurs, two things happen: I am visually aware of the surface I look at, and I discern something standing out in front of, or (in certain cases) receding behind, something else. So, for instance, I follow the famous advice of Leonardo da Vinci to an aspirant painter and I look at a stained wall,[3] or I let my eyes wander over a frosty pane of glass, and at one and the same time I am visually aware of the wall, or of the glass, and I recognize a naked boy, or dancers in mysterious gauze dresses, in front of (in each case) a darker ground. In virtue of this experience I can be said to see the boy in the wall, the dancers in the frosty glass.

d→ The two things that happen when I look at, for instance, the stained wall are, it must be stressed, two aspects of a single experience that I have, and the two aspects are distinguishable but also inseparable. They are two aspects of a single experience, they are not two experiences. They are neither two separate simultaneous experiences, which I somehow hold in the mind at once, nor two separate alternating experiences, between which I oscillate – though it is true that each aspect of the single experience is capable of being described as analogous to a separate experience. It can be described as though it were a case of simply looking at a wall or a case of seeing a boy face-to-face. But it is error to think that this is what it is. And we get not so much into error as into confusion if, without equating either aspect of the

just as we cannot simultaneously see the duck and the rabbit aspects of the duck–rabbit figure, so we cannot simultaneously see nature and canvas. It is true that we cannot simultaneously see the duck and the rabbit aspects of the duck–rabbit figure. To do so would require, in my terminology, an experience with two recognitional aspects, which nothing – and certainly nothing in my account of twofoldness – leads me to anticipate. But the assimilation of the two sets of experiences, on which Gombrich rests his case, seems without justification unless it is assumed from the outset that twofoldness is impossible. For what do the two pairs of experiences have in common – if we do not make the assumption that in both cases the experiences are incompatible? Indeed there is one obvious discrepancy between the two pairs. In the duck–rabbit case the two experiences are homogeneous: in both cases I see something in the world. But in the nature/canvas case the two experiences are at least *prima facie* heterogeneous: in one case I see something in the world, in the other case I see something in the picture. Until this heterogeneity is explained away, the assimilation on which Gombrich partially relies lacks plausibility. Gombrich returns to the impossibility of twofoldness in 'Mirror and Map: Theories of Pictorial Representation', *Philosophical Transactions of the Royal Society of London*, vol. 270 (1975), pp. 119–49, reprinted in his *The Image and the Eye* (Oxford, 1982).
In M. H. Pirenne, *Optics, Paintings, and Photography* (London, 1970), there is an empirical argument which in effect supports my view of the matter, for it claims that twofoldness is required in order to explain the fact that represented objects maintain a constant appearance even though the spectator changes his position in front of the painting. This argument is made use of in Michael Polanyi, 'What is a Painting?', *British Journal of Aesthetics*, vol. 10, no. 3 (July 1970), pp. 225–36.
[3] See *The Notebooks of Leonardo da Vinci*, ed. and trans. Edward McCurdy (London, 1938), p. 231.

complex experience with the simple experience after which it can be described, we ask how experientially like or unlike each aspect is to the analogous experience. We get lost once we start comparing the phenomenology of our perception of the boy when we see him in the wall, or the phenomenology of our perception of the wall when we see the boy in it, with that of our perception of boy or wall seen face-to-face. Such a comparison seems easy enough to take on, but it proves impossible to carry out. The particular complexity that one kind of experience has and the other lacks makes their phenomenology incommensurate. None of this is to deny that there is an important causal traffic between seeing-in and seeing face-to-face. Children learn to recognize many familiar and unfamiliar objects through first seeing them in the pages of books.[4]

The twofoldness of seeing-in does not, of course, preclude one aspect of the complex experience being emphasized at the expense of the other. In seeing a boy in a stained wall I may very well concentrate on the stains, and how they are formed, and the materials and colours they consist of, and how they encrust or obscure the original texture of the wall, and I might in consequence lose all but a shadowy awareness of the boy. Alternatively, I might concentrate on the boy, and on the long ears he seems to be sprouting and the box he is carrying – is it a bomb, or a present for someone? – and thus have only the vaguest sense of how the wall is marked. One aspect of the experience comes to the fore, the other recedes. And sometimes this preference for one aspect of the experience gets carried to the point where the other aspect evaporates. Twofoldness is lost, and then seeing-in succumbs to an altogether different kind of experience. This shift can take place in either direction, so that seeing-in may be succeeded by seeing the wall and its stains face-to-face, or it may give way to visualizing the boy in the mind's eye. But, given that the wall was adequately differentiated so as to permit seeing-in in the first place, it is unlikely that either of these successor experiences will prove stable. Seeing-in will probably reassert itself: such is its pull.

2.   Seeing-in, as I have described it, precedes representation: it is prior to it, logically and historically. Seeing-in is prior to representation logically in that I can see something in surfaces that neither are nor are believed by me to be representations. To the examples we have just looked at, others can readily be added. Clouds: I can, for instance,

---

[4]   I think that it is right to regard the ability to account for this widespread phenomenon as a requirement upon any satisfactory account of representation. Both the semiotic and the make-believe theories of representation have grave difficulties in meeting the requirement. See Christopher Peacocke, *op. cit*.

see headless torsos or great Wagnerian conductors in clouds ranged against the vault of the sky. And seeing-in is prior to representation historically in that surely our remotest ancestors engaged in these exercises long before they thought to decorate their caves with images of the animals they hunted.

But it is not just that seeing-in precedes representation. Representation can be explained in terms of seeing-in, as the following situation reveals: In a community where seeing-in is firmly established, some member of the community – let us call him (prematurely) an artist – sets about marking a surface with the intention of getting others around him to see some definite thing in it: say, a bison. If the artist's intention is successful to the extent that a bison can be seen in the surface as he has marked it, then the community closes ranks in that someone who does indeed see a bison in it is now held to see the surface correctly, and anyone is held to see it incorrectly if he sees, as he might, something else in it, or nothing at all. Now the marked surface represents a bison.

Representation arrives, then, when there is imposed upon the natural capacity of seeing-in something that so far it had been without: a standard of correctness and incorrectness. This standard is set – set for each painting – by the intentions of the artist in so far as they are fulfilled. Holbein's famous portrait, which has come down to us in various versions, is not a portrait of Charles Laughton, though old film buffs can, and I dare say will, see Charles Laughton in it. It is a portrait of Henry VIII, because Henry VIII too can be seen in it and this is the visual experience that Holbein intended. With damp-stains, with frosted panes of glass, with clouds, there is – as the famous interchange between Hamlet and Polonius makes clear – nothing that it is correct to see in them. It is not even correct to see something in them rather than nothing.

What prompts this very last point is that there is a kind of picture that is a half-way house to representation. There are pictures in which it is correct to see something – to see something rather than nothing – but there is nothing – there is no one thing – of which it is true to say that it is correct to see it in the picture. A good example is the Rorschach card. The efficacy of these simulated ink-blots as diagnostic tests depends upon the satisfaction of two conditions: that it is possible to see something in them, but that nothing, no one thing, has a stronger claim to be seen there than anything else.

However, even with full-blown representation, where the standard of correctness stipulates specifically what is to be seen in the picture, it is still possible, enjoyable, and maybe profitable, to take holidays from this standard and select out of the various things we can see in a

painting what we choose to. Proust, for instance, used to do this: he
would go to the Louvre and find in the paintings of the Old Masters
likenesses of his friends or his acquaintances from the Faubourg.
Lucien Daudet tells us that, standing in front of the Ghirlandaio
double portrait, he pretended that the figure with a polyp at the end
of his nose was the old friend of the Comtesse de Greffuhle, the
clubman *pur sang*, the Marquis du Lau, whose features are preserved
in a faded photograph.[5] And readers of *Swann's Way* will recall how
Swann himself had the same fondness for these tricks of perception,
feeling that they somehow enhanced his friends for him. His infatu-
ation with Odette was sealed when he found her features in Botticelli's
representation of Zipporah, daughter of Jethro.[6] But neither in the
person of Swann nor in his own person did Proust claim that these
games transformed the representational content of the paintings he
played them on. He simply, for the pleasure of the moment, or for
some enduring consideration, overruled the intention of the artist.

3. 'The intention of the artist'. In the last lecture explicitly, in this
lecture implicitly, I have held out against both an excessively narrow
and an excessively broad understanding of artist's intention. But now it
might seem as if I have shifted ground, and that, in looking to intention
as providing the criterion of correctness for representation, I have, if
without saying so, moved towards the narrow understanding. For, if
the artist's intention is something that is in the artist's head and that
determines that a bison, say, and not an ox, or Henry VIII and not
Charles Laughton, is to be seen in a given surface, then it looks as
though the candidate that is best qualified for this role is a mere volition
on the artist's part that the spectator should identify what he, the artist,
sets out to represent. What need is there for the thoughts, beliefs,
experiences, emotions, commitments that the broader understanding
of artist's intention brings in train? It might seem that there is no call for
them.

However this would follow only if what I have just been saying was
that, in setting himself to represent something, the artist may mark the
canvas in any way whatsoever just so long as a certain effect is
achieved: that is, that the spectator identifies what the artist wants
the picture to represent. But this is not at all what I have been saying.
Clearly there is more than one way in which a spectator can identify

[5] The story is told in Lucien Daudet, *Autour de Soixante Lettres de Marcel Proust* (Paris, 1928), pp. 18–19.
[6] Marcel Proust, *À la Recherche du Temps Perdu*, vol. I: *Du Côté de Chez Swann* (Paris, 1914), pp. 273–7, trans. C. K. Scott Moncrieff and Terence Kilmartin, as *Remembrance of Things Past*, vol. I: *Swann's Way* (London, 1981), pp. 242–6.

an object or an event in a picture. There is a diversity of clues that he can use. For instance, he might anticipate the artist's intention. However it is only if the spectator identifies an object or an event through seeing it in the picture's surface that his response bears on the picture's representational content. In consequence the representational artist must at least set himself to do this: to mark the canvas in such a way as to ensure that the spectator will not merely identify, he will be able to see, to see in the picture, what the picture is intended to represent. And this requirement has the effect that the artist must at any rate draw on his perceptual beliefs. Perceptual beliefs about the thing to be represented must contribute causally to the making of the representation, and this means that they will be included in the artist's intention.

But, though this has the consequence that the very narrowest interpretation of the artist's intention proves inadequate to account for representation, might it not still be the case – the objection would run – that a fairly narrow interpretation is in order, and that the broad understanding that I have been proposing is inappropriate? Can we not eliminate from the intention of the representational artist further mental phenomena like thoughts, emotions, and commitments?

At this point it is necessary to go back to the title of these lectures and remind ourselves of the distinction that it assumes: painting as an art versus painting practised some other way. For, once painting is practised as an art, then it is certain that the agent will mobilize not only his perceptual beliefs about what he represents but also a range of attitudes towards that thing. Indeed some of the perceptual beliefs that he mobilizes will themselves rest upon such attitudes. The way he represents a face will be bound up with what he feels about its owner: the way he represents a building is now inextricable from how he responds to its dignity or charm.

This last point is sometimes put by saying that the artist – in contrast, say, to the Ur-painter – is concerned to do justice not only to the *what*, but also to the *how*, of representation: he will try to set down how what he represents is likely to strike its viewer. But this is not a good way of putting the point. For, in producing an ever more refined image of how the represented thing looks, the artist is in effect representing an ever more specific kind of thing. There is within the representational task no line worth drawing between the what and the how: each fresh how that is captured generates a new what.

4.   At one time it used to be believed that seeing-in, hence representation, was culturally relative: occurring, that is to say, in some societies

but not in others. But the evidence that some anthropologists assembled to make this point actually shows something far more limited and of no general significance.[7] So, for instance, they presented tribesmen of south-west Africa with drawings of the sort I illustrate, and then they asked them, Could the huntsman, standing where he is, hit the stag? Now in so far as the subjects answered, No, he couldn't, for the hill, or the road, is in between, what these answers reveal is that it takes experience to grasp paintings that depict comparatively complex spatial relations, and, in doing so, depend upon comparatively subtle visual cues. But the fact that the subjects answered the questions at all, or could apply such terms as 'huntsman', 'stag', 'hill', 'road', to the picture, showed, surely beyond a doubt, that they had the capacity for seeing-in, even if to a less developed degree than well-primed Europeans.

But a more sweeping, a more momentous, point is that seeing-in appears to be biologically grounded. It is an innate capacity, though, as with all innate capacities, it requires an environment sufficiently congenial and sufficiently stimulating, in which to mature. A baby a few days old will respond to the drawing of a face: fleetingly, of course, but the same goes for all its responses to the external world.[8] I show you a photograph of my daughter, taken four years ago when she was twelve months old, hailing a represented companion in the Kunsthistorisches Museum in Vienna. This photograph was taken by a total stranger, who only let us know what he was doing after he had done it. It exemplifies one of the least tainted experiments in psychology.

---

[7] These cross-cultural studies are reported in W. Hudson, 'Pictorial Depth Perception in Sub-Cultural Groups in Africa', *Journal of Social Psychology*, vol. 52 (November 1960), pp. 183–208, and 'Cultural Problems in Pictorial Perception', *South African Journal of Science*, vol. 58, no. 7 (July 1962), pp. 189–95. Hudson's methodology has been considerably criticized in, e.g., G. Jahoda and H. McGurk, 'Pictorial Depth Perception in Scottish and Ghanaian Children: A Critique of Some Findings with the Hudson Test', *International Journal of Psychology* vol. 9, no. 4 (1974), pp. 255–67; and Margaret A. Hagen and M. M. Johnson, 'Hudson Pictorial Depth Perception: Cultural Content and Question with a Western Sample', *Journal of Social Psychology*, vol. 101 (February 1977), pp. 3–11. A good survey article of the field is Rebecca K. Jones and Margaret A. Hagen, 'A Perspective on Cross-Cultural Picture Perception', in *The Perception of Pictures*, vol. II, ed. Margaret A. Hagen (New York, 1980). Jones and Hagen distinguish between the perception of pictures of isolated objects and the perception of pictures of spatial relations. For me this can be at best a distinction of convenience, since both kinds of picture fall within the scope of the same perceptual capacity.

J. Hochberg and V. Brooks, 'Pictorial Recognition as an Unlearned Ability: a Study of One Child's Performance', *American Journal of Psychology*, vol. 75 (1962), pp. 624–8, showed that a child of nineteen months, reared with severely restricted access to pictures, could recognize familiar objects in photographs and line drawings, and it concluded that there must be 'an irreducible minimum of native ability for picture recognition'.

[8] I owe this information to Jerome Bruner.

5. The connection between representation and seeing-in was noted by theorists of representation both in antiquity and in the Renaissance.[9] Yet almost to a person these thinkers got the connection the wrong way round: they treated seeing-in as – logically and historically – posterior to representation. For they held that, whenever we see, say, a horse in a cloud, or in a stained wall, or in a shadow, this is because there is a representation of a horse already there – a representation made, of course, by no human hand. These representations, which would be the work of the gods or the result of chance, wait for persons of exceptional sensitivity to discern them, and then they deliver themselves up.

This reversal of explanatory direction got into, and created an interesting problem for, representation when Quattrocento artists wished to represent the activity of seeing-in: seeing-in, that is, directed on to natural phenomena. For in order to represent this activity, they had to represent that which, on their account of the matter, this activity presupposes: they had to display nature as an album of well-contrived but also well-concealed representations. A famous example is provided by Andrea Mantegna, *Martyrdom of St Sebastian* (Kunsthistorisches Museum, Vienna), where the artist, in attempting to represent the kind of cloud in which a horseman can be seen, represents the cloud as though it were an antique cameo of a horseman. Weirder examples are two mythological paintings by Piero di Cosimo: *The Misfortunes of Silenus* (Fogg Art Museum, Harvard University, Cambridge, Mass.) and *The Discovery of Honey* (Worcester Art Museum, Worcester, Mass.). In these paintings wild figures have their images cunningly stamped into the branches and pollarded trunks of the trees.

Of course, even once the traditional account of representation, which reverses the proper explanatory direction, is discarded, it still remains a problem, and it might be thought an insuperable problem, for representational artists to refer in their work to the kind of perception on which, according to my account of the matter, their work depends. It asks for something that is probably inherently beyond their means. Examples of an attempt to solve the problem are provided by two drawings (Clark Institute, Williamstown, Mass.) by Charles Meryon, the great architectural draughtsman and etcher of nineteenth-century Paris, which set out to represent clouds in which women can be seen. The task, as Meryon saw it, was to represent the

---

[9] In this section I am much indebted to H. W. Janson, 'The "Image made by Chance" in Renaissance Thought', in *De artibus opuscula XL: Essays in Honor of Erwin Panofsky*, ed. Millard Meiss (New York, 1961), reprinted in his *16 Studies* (New York, 1973).

clouds but not to represent the women: the women, in other words, are to be seen in the clouds but not in the drawings.

In her book *The Art of Describing*, Svetlana Alpers provides us with an amusing example of the attempt to come to grips with seeing-in.[10] In the year 1628, in a village just outside the city of Haarlem, an old apple tree was cut down. Inside its bark there were said by the pious to be miraculous images of Catholic priests. A devout print was soon published to celebrate this discovery. Then, within the year, in order to rebut these superstitious beliefs, to 'belie rumours', and to furnish the materials for a naturalistic explanation of how these beliefs arose, Pieter Saenredam executed a drawing, after which another print was made, exhibiting the tree in cross-section. To make his point Saenredam was committed to showing that the bark was so formed that priests could be seen in it. But, though they could be seen in it, they could not be seen in it with such force, or such clarity, as to make us conclude that this is what some divine artificer expected us to see: unless, the print hints, we were superstitiously motivated to think so.

6.   That representation is grounded in seeing-in is confirmed by the way seeing-in serves to explain the broad features of representation. For the most general questions about representation become amenable once we start to recognize that representation at once respects and reflects the nature and limits of seeing-in – so long as we also recognize that seeing-in is itself stretched by the experience of looking at representations. I have in mind three general questions. They are, (one) How do we *demarcate representation*?, or, What is, and what is not, a representation?; (two) What can be represented?, or, more particularly, What are the different kinds of thing that can get represented, and what are the *varieties of representation* to which they give rise?; and, (three) What is it for a representational painting to be – and now I use these terms interchangeably to refer to the same elusive property – *realistic, naturalistic, lifelike, true*? This last question is one that we can pursue without attaching any particular value to the property itself.

I shall consider these three general questions in turn.

7.   First, then, how do we demarcate representations?

Pretheoretically, or before a discussion like this starts, we do not have many strong convictions on this issue, and connecting representation and seeing-in has the advantage of allowing us to organize our

10   See Svetlana Alpers, *The Art of Describing* (Chicago, 1983), pp. 80–2.

thinking about representation in such a way as to preserve and foster those intuitions we do have.

j→   In the first place, then, the connection tells us that representation does not have a very sharp boundary. International road signs, logos, stickmen, the signs on public lavatories – are they representations or not? Availing ourselves of the connection I propose, we may now recast the question as, Do we, when we look at such things, see whatever they are of in their surface, or do we just see the things as marks, which we then, in virtue of our knowledge of the system to which they belong, recognize to be signs of what they are of? Another way of putting the question is, Do we, in so far as we treat these things as meaningful, have to be aware of depth as well as to pay attention to the marked surface? And I think that in answer to such questions we are likely to say in some of these cases that we probably do, and in other cases that we probably don't: but neither way round are we likely to say this with much conviction. And this suggests that all such cases are on the borderline of representation. That they are, and furthermore that representation exhibits a broad swathe of borderline cases, coincides, I believe, with our pre-existent intuitions such as they are.

Secondly, the connection allows us to exclude from representationality signs like maps that are not of whatever it is that they are of because we can see this in them. We may or we may not be able to see in them what they are of but, if we can, it is not this fact that secures their meaning. A map of Holland is not of Holland for the reason that the land mass of Holland can be seen in it – even if to a modern traveller a map reminds him of what he can see, looking down upon the earth, at the flying altitude of a plane. No: what makes the map be of Holland is what we might summarily call a convention.

This fact about maps and what they map is confirmed by the way we extract from them such information as they contain. To do so we do not rely on a natural perceptual capacity, such as I hold seeing-in to be. We rely on a skill we learn. It is called, significantly, 'map-reading': 'map-*reading*'.

The difference between representations and maps – the difference between the two things and between the ways in which we relate to the two things – is well brought out if we juxtapose representation and map: better still, if we consider a representation that embeds a representation of a map. Consider, for instance, Jan Vermeer, *Officer and Laughing Girl* (Frick Collection, New York City), which represents a man and a woman and a map of Holland. For that which makes some area of Vermeer's painting be of a woman, and, for that matter, that which makes some other area of the painting be of a map,

is something quite different from that which makes that map be of
Holland. As a consequence, quite different capacities on the part of
the spectator, with quite different histories within his life-history, have
to be mobilized if he is to learn, on the one hand, what the picture can
inform him about the map, and, on the other hand, what the map
could inform him about Holland. If he made the grossly inefficient
decision to look at the Vermeer in order to find out the facts of Dutch
geography, then he would have to mobilize the two capacities serially:
first, seeing-in, to tell him that there is a map on the wall and what it
looks like, then, map-reading, to tell him what the map, given how it
looks, has to say about the land surface of Holland.

Once again, the distinction between representations and maps fits
in with our prior intuitions, even if they do not clamour for it.

Thirdly, the connection between representation and seeing-in allows us to reject the contrast, often drawn but quite unwarranted,
between representational and abstract painting. To appreciate this
point we need to get clear, first, the full scope of seeing-in and,
secondly, the nature of abstract painting as we have it or the demands
that it characteristically makes upon the spectator. I shall take them in
turn.

In one respect the examples I have given of seeing things in natural
phenomena could be misleading. I have quoted seeing a boy in a
stained wall; seeing dancers in a frosted pane of glass; or seeing a
torso or a great Wagnerian conductor in towering clouds. But continuous with this kind of case are cases in which we see an irregular
solid in a sheet of oxidized metal, or a sphere in the bare branches of a
tree, or just space in some roughly prepared wall. The two kinds of
case differ primarily in the kind of concept under which we bring that
which we see in the differentiated surface. In the kind of case I have so
far been considering, we use 'boy', 'dancer', 'torso': we use figurative
concepts. In the new kind of case, we use 'irregular solid', 'sphere',
'space': we use non-figurative or abstract concepts. This being so, a
natural thing to think is that, while both kinds of case are genuine
cases of seeing-in, and as such both pave the way for an art of
representation, they differ in that they pave the way for different
kinds of representational art. One paves the way for a representational art that is figurative, the other for a representational art that is
abstract.

When we now turn to abstract painting as it has in fact emerged in
this century, we can see there that this way of thinking is fully borne
out. Abstract art, as we have it, tends to be an art that is at once
representational and abstract. Most abstract paintings display images:
or, to put it another way, the experience that we are required to have

in front of them is certainly one that involves attention to the marked surface but it is also one that involves an awareness of depth. In imposing the second demand as well as the first, abstract paintings reveal themselves to be representational, and it is at this point irrelevant that we can seldom put into adequate words just what they represent.

Consideration of a painting like the magnificent Hans Hofmann, *Pompeii* (Tate Gallery, London) should clarify the point. For manifestly this painting requires that we see some planes of colour in front of other planes, or that we see something in its surface. And this is true despite the fact that we shall be able to say only in the most general terms what it is that we see in the surface.

I have talked of what most abstract paintings are like. This provokes the question whether there are indeed any abstract paintings that are non-representational or that do not ask for seeing-in. (I have noticed as a strange fact that, once people have had their resistance broken down to the idea that some abstract paintings are representational, they become dogmatic that all abstract paintings are representational: they repudiate the very idea of a non-representational abstract painting.) On this point there is cause for circumspection. It is plausible to think that, for instance, some of the vast machines of Barnett Newmann, such as *Vir Heroicus Sublimis* (Museum of Modern Art, New York City), are non-representational. Arguably correct perception of such a picture, or perception that coheres with the fulfilled intention of the artist, is not characterized by twofoldness.

It is however worth noting that, if there are certain abstract paintings that are non-representational for the reason that they do not call for awareness of depth, there are also paintings that are non-representational for the complementary reason, or because they do not invoke, indeed they repel, attention to the marked surface. *Trompe l'oeil* paintings, like the exquisite series of cabinets executed in gouache by Leroy de Barde (Cabinet des Dessins, Louvre, Paris), are surely in this category. They incite our awareness of depth, but do so in a way designed to baffle our attention to the marks upon the surface.

8.   The second broad question is, What can be represented?, or, on the plausible assumption that what can be represented is sub-divisible in some principled way, What kinds of thing can be represented? What, in other words, are the varieties of representation?

It might seem plausible to think that an answer to the question, What can be represented? is to be found, not in the connection that I have been canvassing between representation and seeing-in, but in the connection, seemingly more fundamental, between representation and seeing. More fundamental: for how can something be seen in a marked surface unless it can be seen – seen, as I have been putting it, face-to-face? So the answer that proposes itself is that what can be represented is whatever can be seen face-to-face. Representation is essentially of the visible.

Later, by the end of the next section, I shall suggest that, for comparatively subtle reasons, this answer is less adequate than it might initially seem, and that, in the matter of scope too, seeing-in, rather than seeing, remains the more reliable guide to representation. However, since the reason why seeing is the less reliable guide is because it is too restrictive in scope, or unduly limits the varieties of representation, it follows that any account of representation that not only bases itself on seeing but then takes an excessively restrictive view of what can be seen compounds it inadequacy. It is in double trouble. Just such an account is to be found in what is perhaps the most remarkable treatise dedicated to – some would say, against – the visual arts: Gotthold Ephraim Lessing's *Laocoon*. In discussing the scope of representation I shall start from the *Laocoon*.[11]

Lessing puts at the centre of his argument the claim that the pictorial arts, being directed to the eye, can be only of what can be entrapped by the eye. However from this acceptable premiss Lessing proceeds to derive unacceptably strong conclusions about what cannot be represented, and it is here that his restrictive view of what can be seen makes itself felt. Lessing concludes, for instance, that a visual work of art cannot represent an action, and that any representation of a cloak must be neutral between representing a cloak that cloaks a figure and representing a cloak with nothing immediately underneath it. These, and other restrictions upon representation, follow directly, Lessing would have us believe, from the self-evident limits of vision: and to drive home the point, he contrasts the limited nature of vision, and the narrow scope of the visual arts, with the free nature of language, and the wider scope of literature.

At this stage, I suggest that we remind ourselves of certain broad truths about what it is possible to see: that is, to see face-to-face. We are recalled to a better sense of the scope of vision when we remember such things as that we can see something or other even if we cannot see every part of it; that we can see one thing rather than another, even if the two look so alike that, in other circumstances, or knowing nothing about either, we might not be able to tell them apart or

---

[11] Gotthold Ephraim Lessing, *Laokoon: oder über die Grenzen der Mahlerey und Poesie* (Berlin, 1766), trans. Sir R. Phillimore, as *Laocoon* (London, 1905).

might mistake one for the other; or that we can see something doing or undergoing something, even if what it does or undergoes cannot be identified except by referring to something we cannot see.

So long as we keep these truths in mind, then, even if we continue to think that what can be represented is co-extensive with what can be seen, we shall be freed from thinking that representation is circumscribed in the way that Lessing thought. We shall be able, for instance, to acknowledge the existence of the following representations: In the first place, Frans Hals, in his group-portrait of *The Company of St George 1616* (Frans Halsmuseum, Haarlem), represented their colonel, even though, since the colonel is seated at table, his lower half is not visible. Indeed in depicting the music-playing angels in *The Adoration of the Mystic Lamb* (Church of St Bavon, Ghent), van Eyck went further and represented an angel blowing the bellows of an organ, even though, since the angel is behind the organ, everything except a tress of the angel's hair and a sliver of drapery is not visible. Secondly, Edouard Manet, *Woman with a Parrot* (Metropolitan Museum of Art, New York City) represents a woman with a live parrot, and Nicolas Poussin, *The Death of Germanicus* (Minneapolis Institute of Arts, Minneapolis) represents a man on his deathbed, even though a live parrot is not necessarily distinguishable from a cunningly stuffed parrot, and a man on his deathbed cannot invariably be discriminated from a man shamming illness. Thirdly, and this takes direct issue with Lessing's own example, a painting of Laocoon can represent Laocoon as about to cry out in agony or as caught in the coils of serpents sent by Pallas Athene to afflict him, even though his crying out lies in the future and Pallas Athene is in a distant land, so that neither is visible.

However, even if, on a juster understanding of visibility, the limits that Lessing set to the visual arts would have to be massively expanded, it remains the case that what can be seen gives us an inadequate criterion of what can be represented. This will emerge more clearly once we move beyond the general requirement upon representation, and start to classify the varieties of representation. It is to this that I now turn.

9.   There are, of course, many many ways of classifying representations by what they represent, as many ways indeed as there are of being interested in the things represented, but the most basic way – basic, because it takes us to the core of how representations relate to reality – gives us a cross-classification. Read one way, the

k⟶ classification divides representations into representations of *objects* and representations of *events*. Read the other way, it divides them into representations of *particular* objects-or-events and representations of objects-or-events *that are merely of some particular kind*.[12] Examples will elucidate this classification.

A painting can represent a young woman: then it would represent an object. Or it can represent a battle: then it would represent an event. If it represents a young woman, then it might; like Ingres's portrait, represent Madame Moitessier (National Gallery of Art, Washington, DC): then it would represent a particular object. Similarly, it might, if it represents a battle, represent, like Uccello's painting, the *Rout of San Romano* (National Gallery, London): then it would represent a particular event. However, in representing a young woman, a picture might, like Manet, *La Prune* (National Gallery of Art, Washington, DC), represent just *a* young woman, or *a* young Frenchwoman, or *a* young Frenchwoman of a particular epoch and class and age and character and occupation and prospects, but still not any young woman in particular: then it would represent something that was merely an object of a particular kind. Similarly, in representing a battle, a picture might represent just a battle, or maybe a cavalry battle, or even a cavalry battle fought between horsemen unevenly matched, some armed with muskets, some with sabres, some with pistols, some with, some without, breastplates, in a terrain that

---

[12] The most extended and most rigorous discussion of this distinction is to be found in Nelson Goodman, *The Languages of Art* (Indianapolis and New York, 1986). Goodman's distinction is made in terms of existential generalization. In other words, for him a picture denotes a particular man (his phrase) just in case it is valid to infer from 'This picture represents a man', 'There exists something that this picture represents'. Otherwise the picture is (his phrase again) a man-representing picture. I prefer to make the distinction in terms of modes of reference as these are employed by pictures. There are two advantages to my method. One is that it allows me to ground the distinction in the nature of pictures rather than in what we say about them. The other is that it enables me to group pictures of Venus and Mr Pickwick together with pictures of Napoleon and Madame Moitessier, which is where I believe they belong, rather than with goddess-, or man-, representing pictures, which is where Goodman locates them. The reason behind this last point is that a picture of Venus employs the same pictorial mode of reference as a picture of Napoleon, though, of course, 'This is a picture of Venus' does not permit of existential generalization. It is arguable that Goodman, if he wanted, could allow for the same grouping of pictures as I favour by relativizing the existential operator ('There exists...') to a universe of discourse. Other metaphysical commitments on Goodman's part would not incline him to this tactic, but that is irrelevant to the point that I am making. For the theoretical underpinning of my method, see Gareth Evans, *Varieties of Reference* (Oxford, 1982).

The best discussion of modes of pictorial reference is to be found in Antonia Phillips, *Picture and Object* (forthcoming, 1988).

made ambush easy, but still no battle in particular: then it would represent something that was merely an event of a particular kind.

A way of bringing out this second distinction between pictures that represent particular objects-or-events versus pictures that represent objects-or-events that are merely of a particular kind would be this: Told of a painting that it represents, say, a young woman, we might ask, Which young woman? Now for some pictures like the Ingres portrait, there *is* an answer to this question even if the actual person we ask turns out not to know it. In such cases the picture represents a particular object. However for other pictures such as the genre picture by Manet, there is no answer to the question, and asking the question shows only that we have misunderstood what we have been told. In such cases, the painting represents merely an object or an event of a particular kind.

But the situation has a twist to it.

☐1→ The exclusive categories are not paintings that represent particular objects-or-events versus paintings that represent objects-or-events of a particular kind. No: the exclusive categories are paintings that represent particular objects-or-events versus paintings that represent objects-or-events that are *merely* of a particular kind. For every representational painting represents something of a particular kind. And this is not an idle fact about it. For if, additionally, the picture represents something particular, then it represents whatever that something is as belonging to that very kind.[13] So Ingres's portrait of Madame Moitessier representing (as it does) a woman, young, French, born in the early nineteenth century, self-assured, expensive, represents its sitter as just such a person.

A principle to which paintings by and large will seek to conform is that they represent things as belonging only to those kinds to which in fact they belong – though, of course, no picture can represent something as belonging to every kind of which it is actually a member. We might call the principle to which no painting can be expected to subscribe, *The whole truth*, and that to which most paintings aim to subscribe, *Nothing but the truth*, and there are various motives over and above sheer ignorance or incompetence that could from time to time lead a painter to diverge from it too: for instance, flattery. However a more or less systematic departure from *Nothing but the truth* is to be found in a category of painting which makes a virtue of representing things as they aren't: caricatures. We can see this in Philippon's excessively well-known caricature of Louis Philippe, representing him as a pear, which he wasn't, and in an ingenious

---

[13]   For representing-as, see Nelson Goodman, *op. cit.*, Chapter 1.

Victorian portrait of *Sir Edwin Landseer* (National Portrait Gallery, London) representing him twice over – once as himself, and once as one of the lions which he executed for Trafalgar Square.

And now I must emphasize that the distinction between pictures of particular things and pictures of things merely of a particular kind is a distinction that applies in virtue of the intentions, the fulfilled intentions, of the artist. It has to do with how the artist desired the picture to be taken, and how well he succeeded in making the picture adequate to this desire. The distinction in no way depends upon what we happen to know about who or what the picture is of. So, for instance, a Renaissance portrait of some man, or a Fayum portrait of some princess, whose identity has long been lost and will never be recovered, is now and ever will be what it originally was: it is, like Ingres's portrait of Madame Moitessier, a picture of a particular person, and the fact that probably no one will ever know who does not alter this fact.

In a lecture that set itself a more narrowly theoretical or philosophical aim, much more would be heard of this cross-classification: just because it takes us to the core of how representation relates to the world. In this lecture, it is intended to serve only one purpose, which is to confirm and to expand the dependence of representation upon seeing-in – upon seeing-in rather than seeing face-to-face. For what I see in a surface is subject to precisely the same cross-classification as what a painting represents: objects versus events, and particular objects-or-events versus objects-or-events that are merely of a particular kind. And, even if the first part of this classification also applies to what I see face-to-face, it is significant that the second part doesn't. If I claim to see a young woman face-to-face, I cannot, when asked, Which young woman?, beg off and say that the question doesn't apply and that to ask it only betrays a misunderstanding of what I have said. Of course I can say that I don't know the answer: but not that there isn't one. It is this fact that argues most conclusively for the view that what can be represented is just what can be seen in a marked surface rather than what can be seen face-to-face.

 10.   Thirdly, there is that elusive but noteworthy property in terms of which we can sort representations and which we may call, interchangeably I have suggested, naturalism, realism, lifelikeness, truth to nature. I say 'interchangeably' rather than 'synonymously', because I doubt if they are synonyms. It seems to me that we use a variety of words, which do not mean exactly the same, to pick out a property with which we are familiar, and of which each word catches some aspect. It is the property itself that interests us, and the property is

identified partly by reference to a certain effect that is brought about in the spectator, and partly by reference to the way in which the picture brings about this effect. The effect is one that we have all experienced in front of works like Rogier van der Weyden, *Portrait of a Lady* and George Romney, *Sir Archibald Campbell* (both National Gallery of Art, Washington, DC). The effect is however not capturable in words, and therefore the property is best approached, I suggest, through the way in which the effect is brought about. It is on this subject that I shall say something. For the property itself I shall use throughout the term 'naturalism'.

Once again my claim is that, in order to appreciate a crucial aspect of representation – this time, how the naturalistic effect is achieved – the connection between representation and seeing-in provides the essential materials. Specifically we need to invoke the phenomenology of seeing-in: twofoldness.

What in effect most accounts of naturalism do, and how they go wrong, is that they concentrate on just one of the two aspects of seeing-in, and then try to explain the naturalistic effect solely by reference to it. More specifically, they concentrate on our discerning something in the marked surface, or what I shall call the *recognitional aspect*, and they then proceed to identify the naturalistic effect with the facility, or with the speed, or with the irresistibility, with which what the picture represents breaks in upon us. The other aspect of seeing-in, which is our awareness of the marked surface itself, or the *configurational aspect*, is ignored as though it were irrelevant to the issue.

I believe that all accounts reached in this way are fundamentally misguided.[14] Any such account covers only a limited number of cases, and it covers them only coincidentally. To get an adequate account of naturalism, or one which covers all cases and explains them, we have to reintroduce the configurational aspect, for the naturalistic effect comes about through a reciprocity, a particular kind of reciprocity, between the two aspects of the visual experience that we have in front of those pictures which we therefore think of as naturalistic. It is not

---

[14] Two accounts of naturalism are offered in E. H. Gombrich, *op. cit.*, of which one is in terms of illusion, the other in terms of quantity of information. Nelson Goodman, *op. cit.*, offers an account in terms of the familiarity, or degree of entrenchment, of the symbol system employed: this account deems it a virtue that it relativizes naturalism, or makes it 'a matter of habit'. All three accounts manifestly appeal to only one aspect of the seeing-in experience – that is, the recognitional aspect – and in this respect they are typical. A fourth account is to be found in Patrick Maynard, 'Depiction, Vision and Convention', *American Philosophical Quarterly*, vol. 9, no. 3 (July 1972) pp. 243–50, where naturalism is explained in terms of vividness. Maynard's account is the only one I know that anticipates the point that I emphasize: that both aspects of the seeing-in experience are properly recruited by naturalism.

any kind of reciprocity: it is, I emphasize, a particular kind of reciprocity. There is no formula for this reciprocity, which is what we should expect, and this is why the naturalistic effect has to be rediscovered for each age: more specifically, for each change in subject-matter, and for each change in technique. The very imprecision of the word 'reciprocity' is a good thing if it allows us to keep the improvisatory character of naturalism to the fore.

n→   It is only an account like this, concocted out of richer materials than are generally used for this purpose, that can accommodate, indeed that can predict, the wide variety in appearance exhibited by paintings all of which are equally naturalistic. This wide variety of look is well exemplified in the paintings by van der Weyden and Romney, which is why I have chosen them: and the same contrast of appearance within naturalism could be illustrated from painters as far apart as, say, Pieter de Hooch and Grünewald; or Monet and Fantin-Latour; or Bronzino and Picasso. All these painters, different though they otherwise are, are capable of the naturalistic effect.

The point that I must now clarify is that, in thinking of naturalism as lying in some kind of reciprocity or match between the two aspects of seeing-in, we must be careful not to equate awareness of the marked surface with attention to the brushwork. Attention to the brushwork is just one form that awareness of the marked surface can take, and it is not a form that, for historical reasons, it could have taken before 1500 or so, when the unit mark or stroke came to be thematized. But, long before the stroke became a required object of aesthetic scrutiny, there were plenty of other features of the marked surface that claimed attention: contour, modulation, punch mark, aerial perspective, fineness of detail, as well as, for that matter, smoothness of surface or invisibility of the brushwork.

11.   So much for the broad questions that can be raised about representation, and for the contribution that the view of representation that I have been urging, or the connection with seeing-in, can make to their resolution. And now I want to bring my view into sharper focus by contrasting it with its principal competitors. They are:

o→   (one)   the *Illusion view*, which holds that a picture represents whatever it does in virtue of giving the spectator the false perceptual belief that he is in the presence of what it represents;[15]

---

[15]   For the Illusion view, see, e.g., S. K. Langer, *Feeling and Form* (London, 1953); E. H. Gombrich, *Art and Illusion*; and Clement Greenberg, *Art and Culture* (Boston, 1961). *Art and Illusion* also contains other views of the nature of representation.

(two)   the *Resemblance view*, which holds that a picture represents whatever it does in virtue of being like what it represents – or, a variant, in virtue of producing an experience which is like the experience of looking at what it represents;[16]

(three)   the *Make-believe view*, which holds that a picture represents whatever it does in virtue of our correctly making-believe that we see face-to-face what it represents;[17]

[16] For the Resemblance view, see, e.g., Plato, *The Republic*, Book X; Monroe Beardsley, *Aesthetics* (New York, 1958); Ruby Meager, 'Seeing Paintings', *Proceedings of the Aristotelian Society*, Supplementary vol. 40 (1966), pp. 63–84; and Jerry Fodor, *The Language of Thought* (New York, 1975), Chapter 4. For a variant of this view, which replaces resemblance between the representation and the thing represented with resemblance between the experience that the representation causes and the experience that the thing represented causes, see Roger Scruton, *Art and Imagination* (London, 1974).

The Resemblance view can acquire an undeserved plausibility because of the way we often seem to settle what a picture represents by standing in front of it and saying 'It looks like....' What the picture represents is then thought to be given by whatever description, inserted into the gap, makes the sentence true. But the support that this consideration appears to lend to the Resemblance view is spurious because the 'it' in the quoted sentence is so used as to pick out not the picture itself, either in whole or in part, as the Resemblance view would have to claim, but the object or the event in the picture. So, for instance, we conclude that a picture represents Sydney Freedberg because the man in the picture – not some fragment of the marked surface – looks like Sydney Freedberg. However not only is this not the resemblance in terms of which the Resemblance view claims to explain representation, but 'the man in the picture' means 'the man that the picture represents'. And this has the consequence that the quoted sentence, so far from being able to explain representation, presupposes it.

[17] For the Make-believe view, see Kendall Walton, 'Pictures and Make-Believe', *Philosophical Review*, vol. LXXXII, no. 3 (July 1973), pp. 283–319, 'Are Representations Symbols?', *The Monist*, vol. 58, no. 2 (April 1974), pp. 285–93, 'Points of View in Narrative and Depictive Representation', *Noûs*, vol. X, no. 1 (March 1976), pp. 49–61, and 'Transparent Pictures: On the Nature of Photographic Realism', *Critical Inquiry*, vol. 11, no. 2 (December 1984), pp. 246–77.

The distinctive feature of Walton's view is that a picture represents an object or event when we are led, on the basis of its appearance, to make believe that we see that object or event. The requirement that the picture must have this effect on the basis of its appearance differentiates Walton's from a semiotic view, but, since Walton's view holds that there is a conventional link between the appearance of the picture and what we are led to make-believedly see, and therefore does not require that we bring a special kind of perceptual capacity to bear on the appearance of the picture, there is a considerable divergence between the Make-believe view and my view. One way in which this divergence manifests itself is that Walton thinks, and I do not, that the two sentences, 'I see peasants' and 'There are peasants there', uttered in front of a picture of haymakers, require a similar kind of analysis, which amounts to thinking of both of them as exercises in make-believe. While I am ready to think that something like this analysis is required for the second or existential sentence, I regard the first sentence as expressing a genuine perceptual judgment: it reports, elliptically, the fact that I see peasants in the picture in front of me.

(four)   the *Information view*, which holds that a picture represents
          whatever it does in virtue of giving us the same information
          as we should receive if we saw face-to-face what it repre-
          sents;[18]

p ⊢→ (five)   the *Semiotic view*, which holds that a picture represents
          whatever it does in virtue of belonging to a symbol system
          which, in the course of laying down rules or conventions
          linking marked surfaces or parts of marked surfaces with
          external things and relations, specifically links it or some
          part of it with what it represents.[19]

Each one of these views can be faulted on points peculiar to it. So it is
a grave objection to the Semiotic theory that it cannot account for the
evident fact of transfer. By the term 'transfer' I mean, for instance,
that, if I can recognize a picture of a cat, and I know what a dog looks
like, then I can be expected to recognize a picture of a dog. But on the
Semiotic view this ought to be baffling. It should be as baffling as if,
knowing that the French word *chat* means a cat, and knowing what
dogs look like, I should, on hearing it, be able to understand what the
word *chien* means.

But the basic divide within views of representation is between those
views which ground what a painting represents in the kind of visual
experience that the representation will cause in a suitably informed
and sensitive spectator and those views which do not. Those views
which do not ground representation in visual experience disqualify

[18]   For the Information view, see J. J. Gibson, 'The Information Available in Pictures', *Leo-
nardo*, vol. 4, no. 1 (Winter 1971), pp. 27–35; and John M. Kennedy, *A Psychology of Picture
Perception* (San Francisco, 1974). The theory is criticized in Nelson Goodman, 'Professor
Gibson's New Perspective', *Leonardo*, vol. 4, no. 4 (Autumn 1971), pp. 359–60; and in
T. G. Roupas, 'Information and Pictorial Representation', in *The Arts and Cognition*, eds.
David Perkins and Barbara Leondar (Baltimore, 1977). Some support is given to the Information view in E. H. Gombrich, *op. cit.*
[19]   The Semiotic view is a rather special case. For within mainstream semiotics, which descends
from C. S. Peirce, a distinction is made between, on the one hand, signs that are conventional in
their application and hence arbitrary in the way they match sign and signified and, on the other
hand, those where there is a natural link between sign and signified: the latter are called 'iconic',
and pictures are generally taken to be the supreme example of iconic signs. With semioticians
who take this line I have no particular dispute, and it would be hard to have one since they are
not associated with any specific positive account of pictorial meaning. It is with radical
semioticians who hold that all signs, including pictures, are conventional that I have my
disagreement. The boldest and also the most sophisticated version of such a view is to be
found in Nelson Goodman, *The Languages of Art*. For more informal versions of the radical
semiotic view see Gyorgy Kepes, *Language of Vision* (Chicago, 1944); Louis Marin, *Études
sémiologiques: Écriture, peinture* (Paris, 1971); Umberto Eco, *A Theory of Semiotics*
(Bloomington, 1976); and Rosalind E. Krauss, *The Originality of the Avant-Garde and other
Modernist Myths* (Cambridge, Mass., 1985).

$\boxed{q}\mapsto$ themselves on the spot. Those which do are, my view apart, the Resemblance view and the Illusion view, but both these views misconceive the crucial experience. The Illusion view identifies it with the sort of experience that a spectator is likely to mistake for seeing the represented thing face-to-face, and the Resemblance view identifies it with the sort of experience in which the spectator compares, in some unspecified respect, what is in front of him with something that is absent. The Resemblance view gives the visual experience a gratuitous complexity, whereas the Illusion view denies it the special complexity that it has: that is, twofoldness.

Commentary on Wollheim

At the end of this extract, from $\boxed{p}\mapsto$ onwards, we find an objection to Goodman's view of representation, here referred to as the 'semiotic view'. The objection is that normally, if I am familiar with cats and dogs in ordinary life, and if I can recognize a picture as a picture of a cat, then I am without further ado in a position to recognize pictures of dogs. Wollheim calls this common phenomenon 'transfer', and alleges that Goodman's view must find it utterly mysterious. If it is simply conventional what stands for what in any given symbol system, then in some system what we ordinarily take to be a cat-picture could represent a cat, while what we ordinarily take to be a dog-picture could represent anything at all. If representational systems are like languages, we should no more be able to recognize dogs in pictures on the basis of recognizing pictures of cats, than someone could understand sentences containing the word 'dog' upon knowing what 'cat' denotes in English. However, let us now turn to Wollheim's account of representation in its own right.

In certain respects Wollheim's approach is the opposite of Goodman's. His is a perceptual account: it takes as basic some facts about the way human beings perceive certain marked surfaces. It also exploits in a way that runs counter to Goodman the distinction I earlier called that between 'relational' and 'non-relational' depiction. A passage at $\boxed{k}\mapsto$ deals with essentially the same distinction, calling it more accurately the distinction between 'representations of *particular* objects-or-events' and 'representations of objects-or-events *that are merely of some particular kind*'.

Why is the addition of 'merely' important in this latter formulation?

Wollheim comments on this at $\boxed{l}\mapsto$: even a painting such as a portrait that represents some particular object (i.e. denotes it, as Goodman would say) – even such a painting represents something of a particular kind. The portrait of

Madame Moitessier by Ingres represents a particular existing woman, so it does not represent *merely* something or someone of some particular kind. But it does represent something of someone of a particular kind, nevertheless.

Why is this point worth labouring? If Wollheim is right, then the more general phenomenon in depiction is representing something of a particular kind. This suggests a reversal of Goodman's priorities: if we can understand what it is to represent something of a particular kind, then we shall have an account that covers *both* cases where there is some particular object denoted *and* purely fictional cases which represent *merely* something of a particular kind. This might then provide us with a general account of depiction.

What is Wollheim's account of a picture's representing something of a particular kind?

His clearest statement is perhaps at $\boxed{f} \mapsto$: 'Representation arrives [...] when there is imposed upon the natural capacity for seeing-in [...] a standard of correctness and incorrectness. This standard is set – set for each painting – by the intentions of the artist in so far as they are fulfilled.' Let us deal in turn with the two components of the account: the natural capacity for seeing-in and the intentions that set a standard of correctness.

What is seeing-in?

For Wollheim's basic account of seeing-in as such, a phenomenon that both historically and analytically precedes art and even the making of pictures, we need to read from the beginning of the extract up until around $\boxed{e} \mapsto$. Wollheim gives some evocative examples of this phenomenon, which undoubtedly exists and which plausibly plays a role in our interpreting of pictures: the figure of a boy seen in mere patches on a wall, the human torso seen in clouds in the sky, and so on. But what is there to be said about seeing-in, other than that it is (see $\boxed{a} \mapsto$) 'a distinct kind of perception'? Wollheim gives effectively only one answer, which he states at $\boxed{b} \mapsto$ and then pursues at length: seeing-in is distinguished by a particular phenomenology, a particular way that it strikes the subject having the experience. The phenomenology is that of 'twofold-ness'.

What is twofoldness? Must all representational seeing be characterized by this feature?

For Wollheim, there are two things experienced in seeing-in. One is the marked (or differentiated) surface, the wall with stains, paper with pencil lines, canvas with coloured paint marks; the other is the thing (object or event) seen in the marks, something 'standing out in front of, or (in certain cases) receding behind, something else' ($\boxed{c}\to$). Wollheim's prime thesis is that a unique double awareness of both these things is what characterizes seeing-in, and hence all representational seeing, of which seeing-in is the core.

Some questions may be raised about this account. First, can we make clearer what twofoldness is, or feels like? Apparently not, given Wollheim's comments in the paragraph beginning at $\boxed{d}\to$. We cannot analyse seeing-in into two separate experiences, we cannot ask 'How like seeing a boy is seeing a boy in the stained wall?' or 'How like seeing the ordinary surface of the wall is seeing a boy in it?' Seeing-in is unique and is just different from ordinary seeing (or what Wollheim calls seeing 'face to face'). That, to a number of commentators, has seemed to offer something of mystery instead of an explanation. Why is it natural to describe one aspect of the twofold experience as seeing a *boy* in the surface, if there can be no comparison at all between that aspect and really seeing a boy?

Another problem concerns the generality of twofoldness: does all seeing of pictorial representations have this phenomenology? Wollheim's is the experience of someone appreciating works of art, which are not only paintings, but painted in particular styles predominantly in the period from 1500 to the present day. It is plausible to suppose that someone not having the twofold awareness Wollheim describes would miss a great deal of what is to be appreciated in such paintings. But that is different from saying that one could not simply see what is depicted in paintings without experiencing twofoldness. Walking casually through a gallery, one could still recognize the subject-matter of most of the paintings without any particular attention to the painted surfaces. Also, are there not art-pictures which seek to conceal or make elusive the actual surface?

Finally, if seeing-in is supposed to be a general phenomenon that makes all pictorial representation possible, is it really true that to see any picture one must have an awareness of twofoldness? At $\boxed{j}\to$ Wollheim considers a range of non-art examples commonly throught of as pictures. Are they representations or not, these road signs, logos, stickmen? Wollheim's criterion is whether we experience them with twofoldness or not. But there would be a case for saying that these are representations to which the phenomenology of twofoldness applies only questionably, if at all. Wollheim's aim is to illuminate a particularly rewarding experience possible before great art works. More questionable is his claim that central features of this experience are general features of the seeing of all pictorial representations.

This brings us to further queries about seeing-in.

Does Wollheim have good grounds for his claims that seeing-in is not culturally relative and that it is biologically grounded? Can he accommodate the conventionality of styles of representation?

In the text at ⟦g⟧↦ and ⟦h⟧↦ Wollheim alludes to two visual illustrations that he used when delivering his lectures. One is a line drawing showing a human figure aiming his spear at a deer. Those familiar with perspective drawing would interpret other objects in the middle of the picture as receding into the background rather than blocking the path of the spear. Evidently not all cultures readily interpret the drawings the same way. The other illustration is a charming photograph of Wollheim's daughter pointing at a child in a painting. The evidence for the claim that seeing-in is biologically grounded is that babies recognize and respond to drawings of faces when very young, too young to have been taught this ability. But a problem suggests itself: do babies experience the phenomenology of twofoldness?

Wollheim, in common with most writers in this area, rejects any analysis of representation in terms of illusion (see ⟦o⟧↦ and ⟦q⟧↦). The 'Illusion view' denies representational seeing 'the special complexity that it has: that is, twofoldness'. But how confident can we be that babies, when they recognize drawn faces, are not under a sort of illusion? Perhaps the distinction between recognizing a face in a surface and thinking that there is a slightly odd immobile, simplified face in front of one does not clearly apply to infant perception. If twofoldness does not obviously occur in babies' seeing, and if what they are doing is seeing-in, Wollheim should not say that twofoldness is the essential characteristic of seeing-in. If twofoldness must be present for seeing-in, and hence for representational seeing, to occur, then it is unclear that seeing-in applies to babies, and hence some of the evidence for the innate, biological status of seeing-in goes missing.

On the issue of cultural relativity Wollheim points out that even though not everyone in the world can interpret every picture correctly straight off, they are nevertheless able to see something in it. So he would argue that the general capacity for seeing-in is invariant, while what can be seen-in which marks is subject to cultural difference. Another possibility can be raised, which is that not all cultures that have visual art forms would necessarily exploit the natural capacity to the same extent, and some might scarcely exploit it at all – just as, we might think, human beings have a natural capacity to hear sounds as in harmony, but many developed musical systems make little or no use of harmony.

But Wollheim can deal with all these kinds of relativity because of his account of the conditions for correct interpretation of representations. The question of what can be seen-in a painting clearly cannot be the sole factor that decides what the painting represents. The point is made effectively by Wollheim's example of seeing the actor Charles Laughton in a portait done hundreds of years before Laughton lived. In less familiar styles of painting, we might find it easy to see a woman where what was intended was that we see a man or a lizard where we were meant to see a dragon, and so on. What a painting represents is what it is correct to see in it, and what makes it correct to see one thing rather than another in a painting is what the artist intended to be seen in it.

Do artists' intentions set the sole standard for correctness of interpretation
of a representation?

Wollheim makes some qualificatory points in relation to this question. In
particular he says at [f]→ that the standard of correctness is set 'by the
intentions of the artist *in so far as they are fulfilled*' (my emphasis). For
example, if I produce a tangle of lines on paper, in which can be seen a
severely damaged spider's web, the fact that I sincerely intended an apple
tree to be seen in the marked surface is not sufficient for it to be correct to see
an apple tree. Young children's drawings are a good example here. 'It's a
house', they explain. They are thinking of a house and intend the lines to be
interpreted as a house, but they do not succeed in representing a house.

At [i]→ Wollheim offers further support for his 'seeing-in' account on the
grounds that it makes amenable three of the most basic questions concerning
representation. Two of these we have already touched on: how do we demarcate representation, and what can be represented? The third is: 'What is it for
a representational painting to be [...] realistic, naturalistic, lifelike, true?'

How well does Wollheim's theory explain naturalism in painting?

This question is addressed at [m]→ – though how adequately remains in doubt.
Wollheim chiefly seems to repeat the twofoldness thesis, more or less asserting
that the effect of naturalism is always achieved by a reciprocity between the
two aspects of seeing-in. There is little argument in the passage for this claim.
He claims at [n]→ that only the twofoldness account can accommodate the
wide variety of paintings that count as naturalistic. But it might be replied that
Goodman's view accounts for this variety much more crisply, i.e. that so many
styles qualify as naturalistic because naturalism is a matter of having learned
and become habituated to any number of conventions.

Wollheim's theory is evocative and shows great insight into paintings, but is
not finally satisfying because the central notion of seeing-in leaves too many
unanswered questions. The contrast of Goodman and Wollheim presents one
of the main polarities in the debate about representation: that between the
conventional and the natural, the learned sign-system versus the basic perceptual capacity. More recent theorists have wanted to return to some notion of
resemblance, though not the simple form of resemblance between marked
surface and subject-matter that Goodman and Wollheim agree in rejecting.
Perhaps, for example, the resemblance is between what the observer of the
painting experiences and what he or she would experience in a two-dimen-
sional portion of the visual field when seeing an object of a certain type. Some
of the items in the Further Reading pursue this line of thought.

Further Reading

Here I list works refered to in the Commentaries and suggested items of further reading on the various topics raised.

Chapter 1   Art, Value, and Philosophy

Danto, A. C., *The Philosophical Disenfranchisement of Art* (New York: Columbia University Press, 1986).

Ferrari, G. R. F., 'Plato and Poetry', in G. A. Kennedy (ed.), *The Cambridge History of Literary Criticism*, vol. i: *Classical Criticism* (Cambridge: Cambridge University Press, 1989), pp. 92–148.

Janaway, C., *Images of Excellence: Plato's Critique of the Arts* (Oxford: Clarendon Press, 1995).

Kemal, S., Gaskell, I. and Conway, D. (eds), *Nietzsche, Philosophy and the Arts* (Cambridge: Cambridge University Press, 1998).

Moravcsik, J. and Temko, P. (eds), *Plato on Beauty, Wisdom and the Arts* (Lanham, MD: Rowman & Littlefield, 1982).

Silk, M. S., and Stern, J. P., *Nietzsche on Tragedy* (Cambridge: Cambridge University Press, 1981).

Young, J., *Nietzsche's Philosophy of Art* (Cambridge: Cambridge University Press, 1992).

Chapter 2   Aesthetics, Art, and Nature

Beardsley, M. C., 'An Aesthetic Definition of Art', in H. Curtler (ed.), *What is Art?* (New York: Haven, 1983), pp. 15–29.

Budd, M., *The Aesthetic Appreciation of Nature* (Oxford: Clarendon Press, 2002).
Carlson, A., *Aesthetics and the Environment* (London: Routledge, 2000).
Dickie, G., 'The Myth of Aesthetic Attitude', *American Philosophical Quarterly* 1 (1964), pp. 56–65.
Tolhurst, W., 'Toward an Aesthetic Account of the Nature of Art', *Journal of Aesthetics and Art Criticism* 42 (1984), pp. 261–9.
Walton, K., 'Categories of Art', *Philosophical Review* 79 (1970), pp. 334–67.

Chapter 3 Aesthetic Judgements

Budd, M., *Values of Art* (London: Penguin Books, 1995), chapter 1.
Guyer, P., *Kant and the Experience of Freedom: Essays on Aesthetics and Morality* (Cambridge: Cambridge University Press, 1993).
Guyer, P. (ed.), *Kant's Critique of the Power of Judgement: Critical Essays* (Lanham, MD: Rowman & Littlefield, 2003).
McCloskey, M., *Kant's Aesthetic* (Basingstoke: Macmillan, 1987).
Mothersill, M., *Beauty Restored* (Oxford: Clarendon Press, 1984), chapters 7 and 8.
Savile, A., *Kantian Aesthetics Pursued* (Edinburgh: Edinburgh University Press, 1993).
Townsend, D., *Hume's Aesthetic Theory* (London: Routledge, 2001).

Chapter 4 The Nature of Art

Bell, C., 'Significant Form' (1913), in J. Mospers (ed.), *Introductory Readings in Aesthetics* (New York: The Free Press, 1969).
Carroll, N., *Philosophy of Art: A Contemporary Introduction* (London: Routledge, 1999).
Davies, S., *Definitions of Art* (Ithaca, NY: Cornell University Press, 1991).
Krausz, M. (ed.), *Critical Essays on the Philosophy of R. G. Collingwood* (Oxford: Oxford University Press, 1972).
Levinson, J., 'Defining Art Historically', *British Journal of Aesthetics* 19 (1979), pp. 232–50.
Ridley, A., *R. G. Collingwood: A Philosophy of Art* (London: Phoenix, 1998).
Tolstoy, L., *What is Art?*, trans. A. Mande (Oxford: Oxford University Press, 1896).
Wollheim, R., 'The Institutional Theory of Art', in *Art and its Objects*, 2nd edn (Cambridge: Cambridge University Press, 1980), pp. 157–66.

Chapter 5 Authors and Works

Carroll, N., 'Essence, Expression, and History: Arthur Danto's Philosophy of Art', in M. Rollins (ed.), *Danto and his Critics* (Oxford: Blackwell, 1993), pp. 79–106.
Carroll, N., 'Interpretation and Intention: The Debate between Hypothetical and Actual Intentionalism', in *Beyond Aesthetics*, pp. 197–213.

Foucault, M., 'What is an Author?', in James D. Faubion, *Aesthetics, Method, and Epistemology* (London: Allen Lane, 1994), pp. 205–22; reprinted in W. Irwin (ed.), *The Death and Resurrection of the Author* (Cambridge: Cambridge University Press, 2001).

Hirsch, E. D., *Validity in Interpretation* (New Haven, CT: Yale University Press, 1967).

Irwin, W. (ed.), *The Death and Resurrection of the Author* (Greenwood, IL, 2002).

Lamarque, P., 'The Death of the Author: an Analytical Autopsy', *British Journal of Aesthetics* 30 (1990), pp. 319–31; reprinted in W. Irwin (ed.), *The Death and Resurrection of the Author*.

Wimsatt, W. K., and Beardsley, M. C., 'The Intentional Fallacy', in D. Newton-De Molina (ed.), *On Literary Intention* (Edinburgh: Edinburgh University Press, 1976).

Wollheim, R., 'Criticism as Retrieval', in *Art and Objects*, 2nd edition (Cambridge: Cambridge University Press, 1980), pp. 185–205.

Wollheim, R., 'Danto's Gallery of Indiscernibles', in M. Rollins (ed.), *Danto and his Critics* (Oxford: Blackwell, 1993), pp. 28–38.

Chapter 6   Depiction in Art

Budd, M., 'How Pictures Look', in Dudley Knowles and John Skorupski (eds), *Virtue and Taste* (Oxford: Blackwell, 1993), pp. 154–75.

Gerwen, R., van (ed.), *Richard Wollheim on the Art of Painting: Art as Expression and Representation* (Cambridge: Cambridge University Press, 2001).

Hopkins, R., *Picture, Image and Experience* (Cambridge: Cambridge University Press, 1998).

Lopes, D., *Understanding Pictures* (Oxford: Clarendon Press, 1996).

Peacocke, C., 'Depiction', *Philosophical Review* 96 (1987), pp. 383–410.

Schier, F., *Deeper into Pictures: An Essay on Pictorial Representation* (Cambridge: Cambridge University Press, 1986).

Walton, K., *Mimesis as Make-Believe: On the Foundations of the Representational Arts* (Cambridge, MA: Harvard University Press, 1990).

Wollheim, R., 'Nelson Goodman's *Languages of Art*', in *On Art and the Mind: Essays and Lectures* (Cambridge, MA: Harvard University Press, 1974).

Index

Reading Philosophy

Reading Philosophy is a series of textbooks offering interactive commentaries on selected readings, and covering the major sub-disciplines of the field. Each volume contains a number of topical chapters each containing primary readings, accompanied by an introduction to the topic, introductions to the readings as well as the commentary. Edited by leading scholars, the aim of the books is to encourage the practice of philosophy in the process of engagement with philosophical texts.

Reading Philosophy
Samuel Guttenplan, Jennifer Hornsby and Christopher Janaway

Reading Philosophy of Language
Jennifer Hornsby and Guy Longworth

Reading Aesthetics and Philosophy of Art
Christopher Janaway

Reading Epistemology
Sven Bernecker

Reading Aesthetics and Philosophy of Art